Heritage Languages in America

Preserving a National Resource

Joy Kreeft Peyton
Donald A. Ranard
Scott McGinnis
Editors

 Delta Systems Co., Inc.   CAL   ERIC

Printed in the United States of America

10 9 8 7 6 5 4 3 2 1

Language in Education: Theory and Practice 96

Copyediting: Donald A. Ranard
Editorial assistance: Amy Fitch and Sonia Kundert
Production: Sonia Kundert
Cover: SAGARTdesign

ISBN 1-887744-68-1

The writing and production of this volume were supported by the U.S. Department of Education, Office of Educational Research and Improvement, National Library of Education, under contract No. ED-99-CO-0008. The opinions expressed in this report do not necessarily reflect the positions or policies of the U.S. Department of Education.

Library of Congress Cataloging-in-Publication Data

Heritage languages in America : preserving a national resource / Joy Kreeft Peyton, Scott McGinnis, Donald A. Ranard, eds.
    p. cm.
    Based on papers presented at the First National Conference on Heritage Languages in America, held Oct. 1999, in Long Beach, Calif.
    Includes bibliographical references.
    ISBN 1-887744-68-1 (pbk.)
    1. Linguistic minorities—United States—Congresses. 2. Language and languages—Study and teaching—United States—Congresses. 3. Language policy—United States—Congresses. 4. Language planning—United States—Congresses.   I. Peyton, Joy Kreeft. II. McGinnis, Scott. III. Ranard, Donald A. (Donald Adam), date . IV. National Conference on Heritage Languages in America (1st : 1999 : Long Beach, Calif.)
  P119.315 .H47 2001
  408'.6'930973—dc21
                                    2001047529

**Winning conference poster by Kha Bao,
a student at Westminster High School, Westminster, California**

Heritage Languages in America

Preserving a National Resource

Contents

Acknowledgments

The First National Conference on Heritage Languages in America brought together almost 300 representatives from highly diverse constituencies, including almost two dozen state and national government and private organizations, and 30 different heritage languages.* While each of these made a significant contribution to the work conducted at the Long Beach conference, a number of individuals, organizations, and institutions were invaluable:

The Conference Sponsors

The President's Office, the Odyssey Program, and the College of Liberal Arts at California State University, Long Beach, CA; the Center for Applied Linguistics, Washington, DC; John Wiley & Sons, New York, NY; and the National Foreign Language Center at the University of Maryland, Washington DC and College Park, MD.

The Contest and Raffle Sponsors

Best Buy, Harcourt Brace, K Mart, Multilingual Matters, Sport Chalet, Star Jump, and Target.

The Exhibitors

Center for Applied Linguistics, Delta Systems, Harcourt Brace, John Wiley and Sons, and Multilingual Matters.

The Plenary Speakers

Lily Wong Fillmore (University of California, Berkeley), Joshua A. Fishman (Yeshiva and Stanford Universities), the

---

*The following languages were represented at the conference: Amerindian (Tiipay, Yuchi), Arabic, Bengali, Chinese, Filipino/Tagalog, French, German, Greek, Haitian Creole, Hawai'ian, Hebrew, Hindi, Ilokano, Italian, Japanese, Khmer, Korean, Lao, Mien, Polish, Romanian, Russian, Spanish, Swahili, Thai, Urdu, Vietnamese, and Yiddish.

Honorable Cruz Reynoso (University of California, Los Angeles), and Guadalupe Valdés (Stanford University).

The Professional Opportunities Panelists

Harold Cannon (California State University, Long Beach), Margarita Cannon (Velasco & Associates), Terrence Geoghegan (attorney at law), Margaret Gulotta (Federal Bureau of Investigation), Julio Morán (The Chicano News Media Association), and Alexander Rainof (California State University, Long Beach).

The Session Facilitators

Regla Armengol (Center for Applied Linguistics), Richard D. Brecht (National Foreign Language Center), Russell N. Campbell (University of California, Los Angeles), Donna Christian (Center for Applied Linguistics), Carol Compton (University of Wisconsin), Joshua Fishman (Yeshiva and Stanford Universities), Surendra Gambhir (University of Pennsylvania), Vijay Gambhir (University of Pennsylvania), Nancy Green (Long Beach Unified School District), Catherine W. Ingold (National Foreign Language Center), Hiroko C. Kataoka (The Japan Foundation and Language Center in Los Angeles and California State University, Long Beach), Joy Kreeft Peyton (Center for Applied Linguistics), Cecilia Pino (New Mexico State University), Alexander Rainof (California State University, Long Beach), Ana Roca (Florida International University), Fabián Samaniego (University of California, Davis), Guadalupe Valdés (Stanford University), Shuhan C. Wang (State of Delaware Department of Education), and Terrence Wiley (California Polytechnic University, Pomona; now Arizona State University).

The Invited Participants

Harata Te Aika (Waikato University, New Zealand), James E. Alatis (Georgetown University), Carlos Cerecedo (California Court Interpreters Association), Ming Lee Chung (University of

California, Los Angeles), Sharon Toomey Clark (California State University, San Bernadino), Gella Fishman (Secular Yiddish Schools of America, Special Collections, Stanford University), Elizabeth Hartung-Cole (Long Beach Unified School District), Lorie Inman (Long Beach Unified School District), Michel Laurier (University of Montreal, Canada), Alexander Rainof (California State University, Long Beach), Alice Rainof (El Marino Language School, Culver City, CA), Montserrant Reguant (University of California, Los Angeles), Lynn Sandstedt (American Association of Teachers of Spanish and Portuguese), Antonia Schleicher (University of Wisconsin), Khatoune Temisjian (University of Montreal, Canada), Shu-Shu Tsai (Southern California Council of Chinese Schools), Janne Underriner (University of Oregon), Darith Ung (Long Beach Unified School District), Mirta Vidal (National Association of Judiciary Interpreters and Translators), Richard Wetherby (California Court Interpreters Association), Joseph Wong (Judicial Council of California), and Viken Yacoubian (Rose and Alex Pilibos Armenian School, Los Angeles, CA).

The Session Recorders

Isabel Bustamante (California Polytechnic University, Pomona), Evelyn Canabal (University of Maryland, College Park), Diana Hartunian (Loyola Marymount University), Lorenzo Ineno (California State University, Long Beach), Patricia McGregor (New Mexico State University), Griselda Sasayama (California State University, Long Beach), Harold Schefski (California State University, Long Beach), Ana María Schwartz (University of Maryland, Baltimore County), and Carmen Suárez (California State University, Long Beach).

The Poster Session Presenters

The Poster Session presenters are named and their presentations abstracted in chapter 13 of this volume.

The Contest Winning Essay Writers and Artists

Kha Bao (Westminster High School, Westminster, CA), whose artwork is the frontispiece of this book, Beverly Chen (Mira Costa High School, Manhattan Beach, CA), Anabella N. Pascucci (West High School, Torrance, CA) and Christopher Romo (Minnie Grant Elementary School, Long Beach, CA).

The Local Conference Organizers at California State University, Long Beach

Dee Abrahamse (Dean of the College of Liberal Arts); María Carreira, Claire Martin, and Cindy McCarty (Department of Romance, German, and Russian Languages and Literatures); and Maryann Annunziata (Head of Development for the College of Liberal Arts).

The Heritage Languages Initiative Advisory Committee

Richard D. Brecht (National Foreign Language Center), Russell N. Campbell (University of California, Los Angeles), Donna Christian (Center for Applied Linguistics), Joshua Fishman (Yeshiva and Stanford Universities), Susan Gonzo (University of Illinois, Urbana–Champaign), Catherine W. Ingold (National Foreign Language Center), Mary McGroarty (Northern Arizona University), and Guadalupe Valdés (Stanford University).

We are also grateful to the scholars who improved the quality of this book with their helpful suggestions on early drafts, Donna Christian and G. Richard Tucker; and for the excellent editing, design, and production skills of Amy Fitch, Sonia Kundert, Jeanne Rennie, and Vincent Sagart.

To these and a large number of unnamed individuals who provided support for the conference and the publication of this book, we offer our deepest thanks.

Joy Kreeft Peyton, Center for Applied Linguistics
Donald A. Ranard, Center for Applied Linguistics
Scott McGinnis, National Foreign Language Center

Introduction

1
Charting a New Course: Heritage Language Education in the United States

Joy Kreeft Peyton, Center for Applied Linguistics
Donald A. Ranard, Center for Applied Linguistics
Scott McGinnis, National Foreign Language Center

For those of us committed to the goal of preserving our nation's rich linguistic heritage, the times are at once troubling and hopeful. At the same time that a well-organized and highly publicized English-only movement has rolled back bilingual education in California and Arizona, grassroots efforts are quietly underway in ethnic communities, schools, and colleges to preserve what language educators call *heritage languages*—the non-English languages spoken by newcomers and indigenous peoples. Community-based language schools teaching Arabic, Chinese, Khmer, Korean, Russian, and Spanish—to name just a few of the dozens of languages being taught—are sprouting up in cities and suburbs across America (Compton, Fishman, this volume). K–12 and higher education language programs are seeing a growing number of heritage language learners; in some school and college language departments, the number of heritage language learners exceeds the number of foreign language learners—that is, learners with no family connection to the language (Gambhir, this volume).

There are new, if little-noticed, signs of life among America's endangered indigenous languages as well. Hawai'ian now shares official language status with English in Hawaii and is a medium of instruction in some public schools there (Wilson, 1998). On the U.S. mainland, several Native American groups have done what only a few years ago would have seemed impossible: They have halted the shift in their communities toward English monolingualism (McCarty, Watahomigie, & Yamamoto, 1999; McCarty & Zepeda, 1998). Few Native Americans dispute the need to learn English, but more and more are seeing the value of knowing their native languages as well. One measure of this interest is the growing number of Amerindian languages offered at junior colleges (Fishman, this volume).

What is especially heartening about this development is its grassroots nature. The heritage language movement has grown out of a deeply felt desire on the part of immigrants and indigenous peoples to preserve their languages and cultures (Compton, Gambhir, Kono, this volume). This is a hopeful sign, since, as Fishman (1991; see also Fishman, Wiley, this volume) argues, language maintenance depends in large part on the communities where the languages are spoken. The work of policymakers and educators will have little impact unless it is matched by a community's commitment to make the language a vital part of daily life.

Efforts to preserve America's immigrant and indigenous languages are not new. They are, in fact, as old as the country itself, as Fishman (this volume) tells us. But efforts today differ in at least three important ways from efforts in the past. For the most part, past efforts took place either with heavy community involvement in public schools or, more commonly, outside of the public school system, either in private religious schools or in community centers run by community members (Leibowitz, 1971; Toth, 1990). Today, while community-based schools continue to play an important role in heritage language education, the formal educational systems—public and private K–12 schools and institutions of higher education—are increasingly involved.

Second, these efforts are taking place at a time when we know vastly more than we once did about how languages are

4

learned and how they should be taught. Thus, today's educators have access to a wealth of knowledge that simply did not exist in the past.

A third difference between past and present efforts is in the timeliness of the language preservation issue and, perhaps for the first time in our history, the possibility of public support for it. While bilingual education remains a highly charged issue, there is a growing recognition in schools and in government that speakers of languages other than English represent an untapped resource for a country that suffers from a critical shortage of citizens able to function in languages other than English.

Written for educators, community leaders, researchers, grantmakers, and policymakers, this book has two basic purposes. Its first purpose is to explain why those who are involved in the heritage language movement believe that it is important for the United States to preserve its non-English languages. Its second purpose is to discuss the issues that the burgeoning field of heritage language education faces as it grapples with new challenges posed by a new population of learners. Exploring the subject from a variety of perspectives, this book seeks answers to several basic questions: Who are heritage language learners? How are they different from first and second language learners? What special strengths and needs do they bring to the classroom? What do community-based, K–12, and college and university educators need to do to improve the quality of heritage language teaching and learning?

The focus of this book is on the practical challenges that educators face as they attempt to develop effective heritage language programs in schools, colleges, and community-based programs. The larger social and historical forces are not ignored, however. Before turning to the educational issues, let us briefly consider some of the social forces that have made heritage language education an important and timely topic.

Why Interest in Heritage Languages Now?

Behind the heritage language movement is a profound demographic shift: We are becoming more culturally and linguistically diverse than we have been for a long time. Indeed, we may be approaching the time when everyone is a member of a minority, rendering the label *minority* virtually meaningless. In Los Angeles, our most culturally diverse city, this moment has already arrived. To be a White native-English speaker in Los Angeles today is to be a member of one of many minority groups (U.S. Census Bureau, 2001c).

The number of people in the United States who speak a language other than English increases daily, as a result of both birth patterns and immigration. In 2000, the foreign-born population in this country reached over 30 million, slightly over 10% of the U.S. resident population (U.S. Census Bureau, 2001a), the highest proportion of foreign-born residents in the United States since the early 1900s when the percentage reached 15% (Brimelow, 1996). This represents a huge influx of recent immigrants: Between 1990 and 2000, 13.3 million people, roughly 44% of all foreign-born residents, arrived in this country (U.S. Census Bureau, 2001a). As a result, the percentage of students with a language other than English in their home background has also risen dramatically in recent years. In 2000, nearly 18% of U.S. residents age 5 and older spoke a language other than English at home (U.S. Census Bureau, 2001a).

Not only has the number of people speaking languages other than English increased, but the number of languages they are speaking is on the rise as well. At the turn of the 19th century, the last heyday of immigration, European and Eastern European immigrants predominated; now they make up only 15% of the foreign-born population (U.S. Census Bureau, 2001a, 2001b). Today, more than 50% of the foreign born are Latin Americans, speaking Spanish, Portuguese, French, and various indigenous languages. Another 25% are Asians, speaking a diversity of East, Southeast, and South Asian languages, among them Chinese, Hindi, Khmer, Korean, Lao, Tagalog, Urdu, and Vietnamese. Newcomers from Africa and Oceania, speaking Amharic, Arabic, Fijian, Hausa, Yoruba, Swahili—among other languages—contribute to the cultural and linguistic mix (U.S. Census Bureau, 2001a, 2001b). According to Brecht and Ingold (1998), more than 150 languages are used in the United States today.

Immigrants, and the languages and cultures that they bring with them, are changing America's political, economic, and cultural life. In 1998, California elected an Hispanic lieutenant governor, the first Hispanic statewide official in California in more than a century. Washington state's governor is a second-generation Chinese American, and the mayor of one of its cities is an immigrant from Korea, testimony to the growing political influence of Asian Americans. Across the United States, entrepreneurial activity by immigrants is bringing new life to old, and often depressed, sections of cities and suburbs ("The Immigrants," 1992). Immigrant culture no longer occupies the cultural margins of American life (Carreira & Armengol, this volume). Spanish-named pop singers have topped the English language charts, and America's highest paid baseball player is a Dominican American. Asian American actors and filmmakers have entered the mainstream of American movies, challenging old ethnic stereotypes.

Newspapers in immigrant languages have always been a part of immigrant life. They continue today, in more languages than ever, but now immigrant languages are on the airwaves as well. More than 550 radio stations broadcast in Spanish; in Los Angeles, two of the most popular stations broadcast in that language (Carreira & Armengol, this volume). Today's immigrants can now watch television in their own languages: Satellite technology brings more than 50 foreign languages from around the world into American homes. The number of web pages for immigrants and ethnic minorities has soared in the last few years; the need among newcomers to exchange information has transformed the Internet into a kind of cyberspace mutual assistance association (Bixler, 2001).

Immigrants are not only changing the face of America; they are challenging the ways that the country thinks about the immigrant experience. The term *melting pot* gained currency in the early 1900s to describe what was seen as a seamless process of transformation that automatically turned foreigners into "Americans" (Petersen, Novak, & Gleason, 1980). In fact, the adjustment that immigrants groups have made to their new country is much more complex than most Americans realize (see, for example, Kloss, 1977/1998; Wiley, 1996). It is a common belief that immigrants in the past quickly, even eagerly, gave up their old languages and ways, while today they cling to them and resist learning English. In reality, many immigrant groups in the past struggled mightily to hold onto their languages and traditions. Many even returned to their own countries after some time in the United States (Wyman, 1993, cited in Wiley, 1996). Very few families managed to resist the pressure to assimilate for more than a generation or two, however, and there is no evidence to indicate that the process of assimilation for today's immigrants has changed fundamentally. If anything the process of assimilation seems to be speeding up (Wiley, this volume). For the great majority of immigrants, today as in the past, there is little vestige of the native language after three generations (Veltman, 1988; Wiley, 1996).

While the forces of assimilation remain strong, the notion behind it—that newcomers should give up their languages and cultures in the process of becoming Americans—has been challenged by recent groups of immigrants. Since the 1960s, a new ethnic consciousness has argued that holding onto native languages and cultures, while learning English and adjusting to the new culture, is not only good for immigrant groups but is good for the nation as well, contributing to America's rich cultural and linguistic heritage (Thernstrom, 1980). One does not have to give up one's own language to learn another (e.g., Cummins, 1979). One can be fully bilingual, and the result would be good for the individual, the family, and the country (Simon, 1988).

The recent resurgence of interest in heritage languages and cultures has not in any way dampened the enthusiasm among immigrants for learning English, though support for English-only legislation has turned precisely on the fear that immigrants today resist learning the language. Surveys indicate that immigrants continue to want to learn English. In fact, the demand for English classes in many areas often exceeds the supply (Office of Vocational and Adult Education, 2000).

Heritage Languages: A Solution to a National Problem?

In recent years it has become clear that heritage languages are worth preserving for another reason: They can help solve a growing national problem—America's need for citizens who are proficient in languages other than English (Brecht & Rivers, 2000).

America's poor proficiency in foreign languages is well known (Simon, 1988). What is not widely known is how critical the national need for foreign language proficiency has become. Because English is now spoken and studied in every corner of the world, there might seem to be less, not more, need for English speakers to learn other languages. Other changes in the world, however, have made foreign language proficiency a matter of critical importance for the United States. Three of these changes—globalization, democratization, and the emergence of the United States as the world's sole superpower—have been discussed in detail by Brecht and Rivers (2000) in their recent analysis of language and U.S. national security.

Globalization means that more and more Americans must learn to function in new and unfamiliar parts of the world. Only 40 years ago, international trade constituted a small fraction of the national gross domestic product of the United States; today, it is a driving force in the economy. Globalization has led to new free-trade agreements in which "[l]anguage is a major consideration" so that "even a seemingly obvious issue such as the languages used in product labeling must be negotiated and prescribed" (Brecht & Rivers, 2000, p. 10). The globalized economy has also changed the ways that humans interact, increasing the need for good communication skills: In the modern service economy, "the sale of services entails . . . communication on a continuous basis" (p. 10). Increasingly, these interactions are not restricted to "English-speaking gatekeepers" (p. 10) but also involve ordinary citizens who do not speak English. Moreover, they are taking place not only in culturally familiar countries, but also in " 'truly foreign' cultures . . . where some Americans are less comfortable linguistically and culturally" (p. 10).

Democratization, the second change, has contributed to our need for foreign language proficiency because it has led to the creation of new states with new identities—and new linguistic demands. In the Caspian Sea Basin, for example, the dissolution of the Soviet Union has lessened the importance of Russian as the regional lingua franca and increased the importance of local languages. Recently, CEOs of U.S. oil companies in Kazakhstan reported that they needed to train their onsite managers in Kazakh because they had run out of Russian-speaking workers in the oil fields (Brecht & Rivers, 2000).

The third change is America's emergence as the world's sole superpower. At the same time that the world is becoming linguistically more complex, the United States is assuming unprecedented global roles and responsibilities. The U.S. military, for example, operates in more countries than ever before. Since 1991, U.S. troops have been stationed in more than 110 nations where more than 140 languages are spoken (Brecht & Rivers, 2000, p. 80).

Not only has the number of languages that the U.S. military must learn changed, but the kinds of tasks it must perform in those languages has changed as well. Today the U.S. military performs "diverse, non-traditional missions that include peacekeeping, humanitarian aid, nation-building, and training" (Brecht & Rivers, 2000, p. 79), and with these new missions come new language tasks:

> In the past, linguists assigned to Army units were expected to perform in the "interpretive mode," providing translation of written and broadcast texts, as well as aiding in the interrogation of prisoners. Now, the burden has shifted dramatically to include "interactive" and "presentational" functions. Military linguists must interact with their allied military counterparts as well as civilians, performing communication-based tasks for missions as far-ranging as humanitarian aid, countering terrorism, and supporting democratic elections. Not only do these tasks involve a much broader range of skills, but also the linguist must command the lexicon and pragmatic strategies of many more domains than the traditional military one. (p. 80)

Other sectors of the government are also facing growing demands for foreign language proficiency: The missions of more than 60 U.S. federal agencies depend in part on proficiency in more than 100 languages (Brecht & Rivers, 2000, p. xi). Departments and agencies facing critical shortages in foreign language proficiency include the Department of Defense, the Department of State, the Central Intelligence Agency, the Federal Bureau of Investigation, the National Security Agency, the Library of Congress, the National Institutes of Health, the Secret Service, the Social Security Administration, and the U.S. Postal Service.

Where will the government find the foreign language proficiency it needs? Where will the military? Where will business? One solution to the problem, of course, is to improve foreign language instruction in the U.S. educational system, and there are some signs that after years of neglect our schools are finally beginning to pay attention to foreign languages (Rhodes & Branaman, 1999).[1] Despite these promising developments, very few of our high school and college students graduate with more than a basic proficiency in a foreign language. The reason is the limited amount of time that American students spend in foreign language study in school and college. A few hours of foreign language study a week even over a period of several years will produce basic proficiency at best. What is needed—and rarely provided—is continuous instruction throughout a student's education, from elementary school through college, preferably with periods of intensive study.

Another solution is to look to those individuals who already have some knowledge of another language—heritage language speakers. While English-speaking students struggle to achieve basic proficiency in another language, many heritage language speakers arrive in our schools with "a level of . . . proficiency [in another language] and depth of cultural understanding that would be difficult to replicate in even the most advanced second language learner" (Carreira & Armengol, this volume, p. 109). A national policy that viewed these languages as resources to be preserved and developed, rather than as obstacles to be overcome, could contribute significantly, and in a relatively short time, to America's proficiency in foreign languages.

---

[1] In their survey of early foreign language education programs, Rhodes and Branaman (1999) found that nearly one third of elementary schools were offering foreign language instruction, up from 22% in the 1980s. In addition, national standards for K–12 foreign language education have been created to help guide instruction, assessment, and teacher preparation.

The Task at Hand

The task before us is not without challenge and complexity. Although at first consideration teaching a language to someone who already has a background in that language might seem relatively simple and straightforward, on closer scrutiny the task turns out to be complex. Heritage language speakers vary widely in background characteristics, language proficiencies, and attitudes toward their home cultures and languages. Moreover, we do not yet have a foundation of knowledge and experience on which to build. Although there have been heritage language speakers and learners in this country since before the nation was formed, for the most part they have been ignored by our school systems. As a result, while we know a great deal about teaching foreign languages to English speakers and English to speakers of other languages, we are just beginning to understand how to teach languages other than English to students who already have a home background in them. One thing we do know: The instructional needs of heritage language learners are distinct from those of foreign language learners. We need to develop materials, instructional strategies, and assessment procedures and instruments for this new population of learners. We need to develop them not only for the commonly taught languages, but also for those that are rarely taught and are required for national and international commerce, defense, and diplomacy.[2] There is also a critical need for teacher recruitment, preservice teacher education, and inservice teacher development.

---

[2] These include languages spoken in the Caspian Basin—Armenian, Georgian, Kazakh, Tajik, and Uzbek; languages spoken in areas of U.S. military activity, such as Somalia, the Persian Gulf, and the Balkans; and languages spoken in areas of global market activity, such as China, Japan, and Korea (Brecht & Rivers, 2000).

The Heritage Languages Initiative

To respond to these needs, in 1998, the National Foreign Language Center (NFLC) and the Center for Applied Linguistics (CAL) launched the Heritage Languages Initiative (Brecht & Ingold, 1998). The goals of the initiative are to strengthen the ability of the United States to participate effectively in an increasingly interdependent world, produce a broad cadre of citizens able to function professionally in both English and other languages, and build an education system that is responsive to the national language needs and the heritage language communities in this country. These goals are being accomplished through the following activities:

• Initiating and supporting dialogue among policymakers, language practitioners, and language researchers on both the need to address heritage language development and the most effective strategies for doing so
• Designing and implementing heritage language development programs in K–12 school systems, heritage language community centers, and college and university settings, and fostering articulation within and among those settings
• Supporting the maintenance of existing programs and the development of new ones
• Encouraging and supporting dialogue between formal education systems and heritage community educational schools and programs leading to collaboration, resource sharing, and articulation
• Encouraging and supporting research, both theoretical and applied, on heritage language development and on related public policy issues

These activities will enable us to develop a durable infrastructure that will include representatives from different constituent groups: heritage language schools, pre-K–12 heritage language programs, colleges and universities, and what Brecht and Rivers (2000) call "heritage language consumers"—various government, nongovernment, and business groups that require proficiency in languages other than English.

The first national effort of the Heritage Languages Initiative was the National Conference on Heritage Languages in America. Held in October 1999 in Long Beach, California, this conference was coordinated by the faculty of California State University, Long Beach, in collaboration with the National Foreign Language Center and the Center for Applied Linguistics. (See Acknowledgments for a list of the conference coordinators, sponsors, plenary speakers, and other participants.)

Participants at the conference took the first steps toward forming the constituent groups listed above and articulating the work needed in each of the areas described. The work of the Heritage Languages Initiative continues through a listserv (heritage-list@majordomo.umd.edu), a web site (www.cal.org/heritage), and regularly held national and research-based conferences. For example, the first Heritage Language Research Priorities Conference was held at UCLA, September 21–23, 2000, to identify broad areas of research in heritage language education and within these areas to define key researchable questions that might be political, sociological, psychological, and linguistic in nature (University of California, Los Angeles, 2001). The second national conference is planned for 2002.

This Book

This book grew out of the 1999 conference in Long Beach. In it, leaders in the field of heritage language education synthesize what we know about heritage language learners and their educational needs, describe areas in which we need to develop new knowledge and strategies, and set forth the challenges that we face as we move forward to develop a society that is productively multilingual. The book explores these issues in five sections: Defining the Field, Shaping the Field, Educational Issues, Research and Practice, and A Call to Action. A brief summary of these sections follows.

Defining the Field

As in most new fields, the emerging field of heritage language education is not without debate and disagreement. As we see from Terrence Wiley's chapter on defining the term *heritage language*, the debate begins with this fundamental question: What do we mean by *heritage language* and *heritage language speakers*? The group obviously includes the foreign born, but does it also include Native Americans? Does it include speakers of African American Vernacular English (AAVE)? Does it include individuals who were born in the United States but whose foreign-born ancestors spoke non-English languages (for example, African Americans with an African language in their remote past but who do not speak that language at all)? These are among the questions that Wiley explores.

The answers to these questions have important implications for the development of language programs, language policies, and research agendas. For those who are primarily interested in the revitalization and preservation of heritage languages, it is the personal connection to the language that matters, not proficiency in the language. For those involved in teaching heritage languages, however, proficiency in the language is a defining characteristic, since a learner with a personal connection to the language but no proficiency in it is, in terms of educational needs, not fundamentally different from a foreign language learner.

In this book, our primary interest is in the issues and challenges that educators face in implementing heritage language education programs. Therefore, while we recognize that many kinds of learners find their way into programs using the label *heritage language*, our concern focuses on those learners who—to use Guadalupe Valdés's definition—have been "raised in a home where a non-English language is spoken, . . . speak or at least understand the language, and [are] to some degree bilingual in that language and in English" (p. 38). This proficiency, which may include dialects that vary from the standard variety of the language taught in the classroom, is generally accompanied by a firsthand knowledge of the culture(s) in which the language is used. Unlike traditional foreign language students, heritage language learners are able to build on their proficiency and knowledge.

Language proficiency varies widely from individual to individual, and as Valdés makes clear, complications arise when we consider the different levels of heritage language proficiency possible, in listening and speaking as well as in reading and writing. A learner's level of proficiency depends on a number of factors, including generational patterns of language and cultural transmission, the age of the learner at the time of language instruction, and the motivation of the learner to learn and develop proficiency in the language. These and other variations need to be taken into account when we design programs, group learners, select teachers, and develop instructional strategies.

Shaping the Field

Heritage language education efforts are shaped by a host of historical, political, and economic factors. This section looks at three: the past experiences of heritage language communities in the United States, the impact of government policies on heritage language preservation, and professional opportunities available to those with heritage language proficiency.

In his account of the historical experiences of heritage language communities in the United States, Joshua Fishman distinguishes three groups of non-English languages: indigenous languages spoken by Amerindians; colonial languages (such as Dutch, French, and German) established in the United States before it became a nation; and the immigrant languages

17

brought to our shores by millions of men, women, and children from every region of the world over the past 2 centuries. Contrary to popular myth, many of these groups have struggled to hold onto their languages, and while some have succeeded for a generation or two, virtually all have eventually succumbed to the powerful forces of assimilation and English monolingualism. Nevertheless, Fishman finds some cause for optimism in recent language revitalization and preservation efforts by Amerindian and immigrant groups.

In his discussion of U.S. government policy toward heritage languages, Terry Wiley describes "a laissez-faire position of tolerance" (p. 100) that in the past has occasionally veered toward suppression, and in recent years has edged toward a measure of support for some heritage languages. Given this ambivalence toward non-English languages, we can expect government support to wax and wane. "[H]istory suggests," Wiley writes, "that the best strategy is to use government policies to promote heritage languages during favorable times and to rely on community-based efforts over the long term" (p. 106).

One reason for the rising interest in heritage languages is the rapid growth of professional opportunities, in this country and abroad, for those with bilingual proficiency in a heritage language and English. According to María Carreira and Regla Armengol, "Nearly every sector of our increasingly global economy and culturally diverse workforce needs multilingual, cross-culturally aware workers" (p. 110). Carreira and Armengol examine those sectors where the needs and opportunities are greatest: government, business, media and communication, the performing arts, healthcare, and education. The needs are not only in the languages with large numbers of speakers, such as Spanish and Chinese, but also in the less commonly spoken languages, such as Urdu and Iraqi Arabic (Brecht & Rivers, 2000). While the need for these languages is not widespread, where it exists—such as at the National Security Agency—it is critical.

Clearly, school systems need to be aware of the growing professional opportunities for heritage language speakers. The existence of these opportunities could be a first step in convincing schools and colleges to develop heritage language programs and to link curriculum to real-world needs.

Educational Issues

This section explores critical issues facing educators in the different settings in which heritage language education takes place—community-based schools, K–12 educational programs, and college and university programs.

Much of heritage language education takes place in community-based schools; some are operated independently of local schools, others in collaboration with them. Carol Compton provides an overview of community-based heritage language education. Heritage community schools and classes serve a wide range of individuals, from preschoolers to seniors, and are held in a variety of locations, including community centers, churches, temples, and local public and private schools. Heritage language education in these contexts is often carried out as an extracurricular activity, after school, on weekends, and during school breaks. Learners study the heritage language for a variety of reasons. Some study the language because their parents require them to; others study for reasons of career advancement or personal fulfillment. Community members may be strongly motivated to develop and provide excellent language programs, but the challenges they face can be daunting. The challenges begin with a lack of public awareness about heritage language education and the need for it. Once in place, programs face a host of ongoing issues and challenges: a lack of funding, little or no articulation with other educational institutions, a shortage of trained staff, and a lack of appropriate instructional and assessment materials and processes.

While foreign language education has always been part of elementary and secondary education in this country, school systems have paid little attention to students who already have some proficiency in languages other than English. In their chapter on K–12 heritage language education, Shuhan Wang and Nancy Green discuss the complex issues that teachers of heritage language speakers must sort out. These include how to work with a diverse student population, even within a specific language group, and how to treat nonstandard and (often) stigmatized varieties of the language spoken by students. To explore these and other issues, the authors use Cooper's (1989) language planning matrix: "What *actors* attempt to influence what *behaviors,* of which *people*, for what *ends,* under what *conditions,* by what *means*, through what *decision-making process*, with what *effect*?" (p. 98).

Their chapter concludes with a discussion of the practical problems that K–12 heritage language educators face. These include the identification and development of materials, curricula, and placement and progress assessments appropriate to this population of learners; systems for awarding credit for language study outside the K–12 system; logically sequenced, articulated courses that move students from heritage community to K–12 to college and university programs; and the professional development and credentialing of both native speakers of English and heritage language speakers as language education professionals.

Wang and Green address at some length one difficult issue facing heritage language educators—the issue of identity. Some learners have absorbed negative attitudes held by the mainstream society toward non-English languages and thus may try to distance themselves from their home language and culture. Wang and Green advise that educators approach this issue with sensitivity and tact.

Sometimes it is when students reach college and university that they first feel a need to renew connections to the language and culture of home. Finding a program that takes into account their backgrounds and levels of proficiency is often difficult, however, as Nariyo Kono and Scott McGinnis explain in their chapter on heritage languages in higher education. The low status of some heritage languages and language varieties, coupled with widespread ambivalence about standard and nonstandard language varieties, can cause higher education institutions to maintain traditional language offerings, even though heritage language learners often differ in fundamental ways from the traditional foreign language learner. For example, many heritage language learners are "dealing with deeply felt issues of identity" (p. 201), and their advanced levels of proficiency, particularly in the less commonly taught languages, can put them at odds with college courses that typically focus on the beginning levels. Kono and McGinnis call for a new model of heritage language instruction that recognizes that "heritage languages are legitimate and worthy areas of study in higher education" (p. 204) and builds on the skills and knowledge that learners bring to the classroom.

The challenges that heritage language educators face are compounded when the languages taught are *truly less commonly taught languages* (TLCTLs), the focus of Surendra Gambhir's chapter. TLCTLs, a subset of less commonly taught languages (LCTLs), refer to languages, such as Hindi and Swahili, that are rarely taught in U.S. schools and colleges. Increasingly, TLCTL learners at the college level are heritage learners, and a few innovative programs have responded to this shift by developing a separate accelerated track for them. Finding qualified staff and appropriate instructional materials, however, are challenges that even the best programs face: "When numbers of learners are small, it is difficult to convince school administrators to hire qualified faculty. It is also difficult to expect publishers to invest money in publishing books that will have a limited market" (p. 228). Gambhir applauds the efforts by community-based heritage language programs to teach

TLCTLs, but "such efforts," he writes, "are only part of the solution and should not replace the obligations that educational administrators have to their students and the nation has to its citizens" (p. 228).

Teachers need special preparation to work effectively with the heritage language population. Teacher preparation begins with the understanding that heritage language learners are different from the traditional foreign language learner, Ana María Schwartz writes. Among other differences, heritage language learners tend to bring better oral and less developed literacy skills to the classroom. To help teachers better understand their students, Schwartz suggests that teachers construct student profiles using a questionnaire that examines learners' language proficiency, motivation, academic preparation, connection to the home culture, and socioeconomic backgrounds. Schwartz also encourages teachers to examine their own beliefs and assumptions, especially regarding the often stigmatized language varieties that students bring to the classroom. In addition, teachers need to gain an understanding of the processes of language acquisition and bilingualism, develop a repertoire of appropriate instructional strategies, and learn how to adapt materials and assessment procedures to the needs of their learners.

Research and Practice

The field of heritage language education is new, and, as can be seen from the chapter on research needs by Russell Campbell and Donna Christian, the questions are many: Who are the students? Where are the programs located? What languages are taught? How do parents and other community members support the programs? What approaches to heritage language education are most effective? These are among the many questions that our field needs to answer in order to build a foundation of knowledge that can inform practice.

To build that foundation of knowledge, and to devise effective instructional strategies, educators must first understand what others in the field are doing. Based on presentations from the Long Beach conference, "Heritage Language Education: Summaries of Research and Practice" gives the reader a broad overview of what practitioners and researchers in a variety of educational contexts now know about heritage language learners and their needs.

A Call to Action

While previous sections focus on the educational issues that concern researchers and practitioners, our two final authors, Ana Roca and James Alatis, ask us to think about heritage language education in the larger social context. If we want to create the multilingual nation that this book envisions, we will need to change how Americans think about languages other than English. Roca urges "the entire language profession" to work together to promote "positive and informed views on foreign language, heritage language, and bilingual proficiency in the United States" (p. 310). She calls on the profession as a whole to launch a national public relations campaign that "says yes to languages" (p. 311) and calls on all of us—school administrators, teachers, policymakers, and parents—to do what we can in our work, in our communities, and in our families to promote multilingualism.

In his chapter, James Alatis takes a humorous look at our profession's tendencies toward "fissiparity" and "omphaloskepsis"—institutional separation and self-absorption. Behind the humor, however, is a serious point: Now, at a time when America needs global citizens—men and women who can function in a variety of languages and cultures—we must work together as language educators to promote the core values that we all share. "Since heritage language education cuts across many fields and disciplines, perhaps it might turn out to be not just another separate field with its separate agenda but instead a reunifying force for the language profession as a whole" (p. 324), Alatis concludes hopefully.

We conclude on our own hopeful note. This book has been written for the wide range of individuals concerned about heritage language education—teachers and administrators in K–12 and community language programs, community leaders who are considering establishing such programs, college and university language and teacher-preparation faculty, researchers working on heritage language issues, and policy and grant makers interested in helping to address the language needs that we face. The book reflects a variety of views and perspectives; it also reflects some of the inevitable uncertainties one finds in a new field. We hope that the book not only sparks dialogue and debate, but also encourages further collaboration among educators and policymakers at the national, state, and local levels. Such collaborative efforts will benefit not only heritage language communities but the nation as a whole.

References

Bixler, M. (2001, January 29). Immigrants assimilate with (Web) clicks' help. *The Atlanta Journal-Constitution.* Retrieved February 2, 2001, from http://www.accessatlanta.com/partners/ajc/epaper/editions/monday/local_news_a35741f763ef91c01030.html

Brecht, R.D., & Ingold, C.W. (1998). *Tapping a national resource: Heritage languages in the United States. ERIC Digest.* Washington, DC: ERIC Clearinghouse on Languages and Linguistics. Retrieved from http://www.cal.org/ericcll/digest/brecht01.html

Brecht, R.D., & Rivers, W.P. (2000). *Language and national security in the 21st century: The role of Title VI/Fulbright-Hays in supporting national language capacity.* Dubuque, IA: Kendall/Hunt.

Brimelow, P. (1996). *Alien nation: Common sense about America's immigration disaster.* New York: HarperPerennial.

Cummins, J. (1979). Linguistic interdependence and the educational development of bilingual children. *Review of Educational Research, 49,* 222-251.

Fishman, J. (1991). *Reversing language shift.* Clevedon, UK: Multilingual Matters.

The immigrants: How they're helping to revitalize the U.S. economy. (1992, July 13). *Business Week,* pp. 115-120, 121.

Kloss, H. (1998). *The American Bilingual Tradition.* McHenry, IL, and Washington, DC: Delta Systems and Center for Applied Linguistics. (Original work published 1977)

Leibowitz, A.H. (1971). *Educational policy and political acceptance: The imposition of English as the language of instruction in American schools.* Washington, DC: Center for Applied Linguistics, ERIC Clearinghouse on Languages and Linguistics. ERIC Document Reproduction Service No. ED 047 321

McCarty, T.L., Watahomigie, L.J., & Yamamoto, A.Y. (Eds.). (1999). Reversing language shift in indigenous America: Collaborations and views from the fields [Special issue]. *Practicing Anthropology, 21*(2).

McCarty, T.L., & Zepeda, O. (Eds). (1998). Indigenous language use and change in the Americas [Special issue]. *International Journal of the Sociology of Language, 132.*

Office of Vocational and Adult Education. (March, 2000). *Adult education for limited English proficient adults.* Retrieved from http://www.ed.gov/offices/OVAE/AdultEd/InfoBoard/fact-3.html

Petersen, W., Novak, M., & Gleason, P. (1980). *Concepts of ethnicity.* London: The Belknap Press of Harvard University Press.

Rhodes, N.C., & Branaman, L.E. (1999). *Foreign language instruction in the United States: A national survey of elementary and secondary schools.* McHenry, IL, and Washington, DC: Delta Systems and the Center for Applied Linguistics.

Simon, P. (1988). *The tongue-tied American.* New York: Continuum.

Thernstrom, S.A. (Ed.). (1980). *Harvard encyclopedia of American ethnic groups.* Cambridge, MA: Harvard University Press.

Toth, C.R. (1990). *German-English bilingual schools in America: The Cincinnati tradition in historical context.* New York: Peter Lang.

University of California, Los Angeles. (2001). *Heritage language research priorities conference report.* Los Angeles, CA: Author. Retrieved from http://www.cal.org/heritage

U.S. Census Bureau. (2001a). *Census 2000 supplementary survey: Profile of selected social characteristics.* Retrieved from http://factfinder.census.gov/home/en/c2ss.html

U.S. Census Bureau. (2001b). *The foreign born population in the United States*. Retrieved from http://www.census.gov/prod/2000pubs/p20-534.pdf

U.S. Census Bureau. (2001c). *State and county Quick Facts: Los Angeles County, California*. Retrieved from http://quickfacts.census.gov/qfd/states/06/06037.html

Veltman, C. (1988). *The future of the Spanish language in the United States*. New York & Washington, DC: Hispanic Policy Development Project.

Wiley, T.G. (1996). *Literacy and language diversity in the United States*. McHenry, IL, and Washington, DC: Delta Systems and Center for Applied Linguistics.

Wilson, W.H. (1998). I ka ō lelo Hawaiʻi ke ola, 'Life is found in the Hawaiian language.' *International Journal of the Sociology of Language, 132*, 123-137.

Wyman, M. (1993). *Round-trip to America: The immigrants return to Europe, 1880-1930*. Ithaca, NY: Cornell University Press.

Defining the Field

2
On Defining Heritage Languages and Their Speakers

Terrence G. Wiley
Arizona State University

In the United States, the terms *heritage language*, *heritage language speaker*, and *heritage language learner* are gaining currency, and instructional program initiatives using these labels are helping to promote language learning and, in some cases, to reverse language shift (see Fishman, 1991). Nevertheless, as with any attempt to apply a single label to a complex situation, defining heritage language is problematic. Moreover, perceptions of language educators and linguists do not always coincide with those of various language communities to be served or with those of the public at large. This chapter touches on some of the problems associated with the use of the term. It concludes by offering a definition that may serve those of us who are working with a population of learners whose needs we are only beginning to understand.

In the United States, *heritage language* is being used to refer to immigrant languages, indigenous languages, and colonial languages (see Fishman, this volume). Thus, as Baker and Jones (1998) have observed, both Navajo people and Spanish-speaking Latinos in the United States are heritage language speakers. Before the term gained currency in the United States, it was largely confined to educational contexts in Canada, where, as Baker and Jones (1998) note,

> it has been less favored (as there are pejorative connotations) with "international language" being preferred. The danger of the term "heritage language" is that, rela-

tive to powerful majority languages, it points more to the past and less to the future, to traditions rather than to the contemporary. The danger is that the heritage language becomes associated with ancient cultures, past traditions and more "primitive times." This is also true of the terms "ethnic" (used in the US) and "ancestral." These terms may fail to give the impression of a modern, international language that is of value in a technological society. (p. 509)

Moreover, the elasticity of the term *heritage language learner* raises a number of questions related to the politics of identity. For example, who can be considered a legitimate heritage language learner? Should "outsiders" to the heritage language be encouraged to learn it? Which is more important in determining "outsider" or "insider" status: language proficiency or ethnicity? In the case of Spanish in the United States, Valdés (1997) observes that the language has served to bring the Spanish-speaking community together, to delineate borders, and to provide a means for entry into the work domain where bilingual skills are needed. Thus, when Spanish-speaking children have been brought together with children of the dominant English-speaking majority in dual language programs to learn Spanish and English, some in the Spanish-speaking community have worried about giving their language "away casually to the children of the powerful" (p. 393).

Additional questions can be raised: What about African Americans in the United States who want to learn an African language because it is part of their very remote heritage, even though neither they nor their immediate ancestors have ever spoken it? Should they be considered heritage language learners? If the language were Swahili, which is used as a lingua franca in parts of Africa but is no one's "mother tongue," should it be considered a heritage language? (Scott McGinnis, personal communication, July 17, 1999).

These questions cannot be answered entirely by language planners. Members of the language groups concerned also need to be involved. The discussion above focuses on a definition of heritage language from the perspective of the language learner. In the following sections, I describe three additional perspectives that can be brought to bear on a definition—the educational program, the community, and the language itself. Viewing heritage language speakers and heritage language education from these various perspectives, we are better able to understand the sociolinguistic contexts of language speakers and language use, and thus we are better able to identify and address their different needs.

Definition by Type of Educational Program: A Program Perspective

In describing educational programs, labels other than heritage language have often been used. As Wong and Green (this volume) point out, programs that teach languages other than English have traditionally aligned themselves with foreign language and bilingual education. While heritage language speakers have often been students in these programs, they have only recently been recognized as individuals with needs that are different from those of other students. As a result of this recognition, separate programs and separate classes within programs have been developed for learners who have been labeled *native speakers*, *fluent speakers*, and *heritage speakers*. Where such separations are not possible, teachers have attempted to adjust their instruction so that it is responsive to the needs of both heritage and nonheritage language speakers within the same class.

Definition by Community Needs: A Community Perspective

Although *community language education* and *community-based language learning* are not terms used commonly in the

United States, they are used elsewhere (for example, in Canada) to describe the vital role that communities can play in language education. Although not widely recognized in the United States, a great deal of heritage language education takes place outside the formal school system, in afterschool and weekend programs. Fishman (this volume) argues that these programs are vital to preserving the languages of this country.

Corson (1999), writing about community-based programs for learners of indigenous languages, notes,

> Community-based education begins with people and their immediate reality. Above all, it allows them to become meaningfully involved in shaping their own futures through the school and other agencies in their community. In fact, meaningful school reform often depends on this kind of participation, in which people renegotiate and reconstruct the ways in which a school relates to its community's interests. (p. 10)

To ensure that heritage language programs do not merely become symbolic gestures, imposed by outsiders to the community, it is important to define heritage language programs from a community perspective.

Definition by Sociolinguistic Situation: A Language Use Perspective

In educational program planning, it is useful to consider various relationships between language varieties that can have an impact on language learning. Horvath and Vaughn (1991) identify the following four types of relationships, which need not be viewed as mutually exclusive. (See pp. 9-10 of Horvath & Vaughn for elaboration of this schema and for classification of 58 specific languages within it.)

Sociolectal: Social or informal varieties of the language may vary considerably from the written standard form (for example, standard and colloquial Spanish). Language learners may know the informal varieties but may not have mastered the formal standard used in school.

Standard plus regional dialects: Regional varieties of a language are used colloquially or informally along with a standard variety (e.g., regional varieties of Spanish). The standard taught in school may vary considerably from the regional varieties that the heritage language students use at home. Within the heritage community, attitudes toward different dialects may vary considerably. Both characteristics of language varieties and attitudes toward those varieties need to be understood by those teaching those languages and dialects.

Diglossia: Varieties of a language are used to fulfill different social functions in the community (e.g., oral and written varieties of Arabic). Educators need to understand the different varieties and the functions they serve in the community. In other words, they need to have some sense of who uses what variety under what circumstances.

Bilingual/Multilingual: Two or more languages are used in a community to fulfill major linguistic functions. For example, in a Chinese community, Taiwanese may be used for some purposes, Mandarin for others, and English for others; in some situations the three may be used together, with code switching taking place. However, not all members of the heritage language community may be fluent in both or all of the languages used to fulfill all of the functions. Educators need to gain some understanding of the different roles that the different languages play in the community and different attitudes toward them.

By looking at heritage language communities in terms of these four perspectives, we will have a better idea of who the learners are and what they need. Horvath and Vaughn are careful to point out that the judgments of linguists and even of educators about language use and about perceptions of different language varieties are not always shared by members of the language community to be served. Therefore, language program planners need to work closely with these communities.

The Importance of Definitions

I conclude this chapter by raising one final issue related to the term *heritage language*, which, to some extent, reflects an attempt to apply nonstigmatizing nomenclature to speakers and learners of languages other than English. It is used, however, to refer both to those who have some proficiency in a community or ancestral language (Valdés, 2000; this volume) and to those who merely desire to learn one, including those who speak only English but who want to learn an additional language of a parent, grandparent, ancestor, or other members of their community (Fishman, this volume). This confusion glosses over important knowledge that language professionals need to consider when planning and implementing programs.

In a similar fashion, individuals previously labeled *limited English proficient* have been elevated to the status of *English language learners*. Unfortunately, this term blurs significant differences between nonnative and native English speakers, both of whom are learning English. In addition, both terms render invisible the native language backgrounds of those who speak languages other than English.

There has also been considerable aversion in the United States to use of the expressions *minority language* and *language minority*. Alternative nomenclature, such as *linguistic diversity* and *linguistically diverse students* has been used to avoid the stigma that some feel is ascribed by the term minority.

This fuss over nomenclature could be dismissed as an exercise in mere political correctness. However, the use of labels is often not without political or even legal importance. As Skuttnab-Kangas (2000) contends,

> [while] definitions of both minority and different types
> of minorities (indigenous, national, regional, territorial,

immigrant, etc.) are notoriously difficult. . . . From a human rights point of view, especially in relation to legal implications in education, those groups who reject the label (ethnic/linguistic/national) 'minority' are doing themselves a disfavour and, sometimes unknowingly, rejecting rights which they need and want to have. (p. 489)

Underscoring the significance of the language minority label, Skuttnab-Kangas adds, "many groups strive toward being granted the status of minorities" because that status in international law guarantees rights to education, which "immigrants, migrants, guest workers and refugees do not have" (p. 489; see also May, 1999).

Conclusion: Toward a Definition

The labels and definitions that we apply to heritage language learners are important, because they help to shape the status of the learners and the languages they are learning. Deciding on what types of learners should be included under the heritage language label raises a number of issues related to identity and to inclusion and exclusion. "Who can legitimately be considered a heritage language learner? Which is more important, affiliation with an ethnolinguistic group or proficiency in the target language?" (Wiley & Valdés, 2000, p. iii). In language revitalization efforts, ethnolinguistic affiliation is important: Some learners, with a desire to establish a connection with a past language, might not be speakers of that language yet. For pedagogical purposes, however, Valdés's (2000) definition proves most useful: A heritage language speaker is someone who has been "raised in a home where a non-English language is spoken" and "who speaks or merely understands the heritage language, and who is to some degree bilingual in English and the heritage language" (p. 1). It is this particular learner's unique needs and special sociolinguistic complexity that this book explores.

References

Baker, C., & Jones, S.P. (1998). *Encyclopedia of bilingual education and bilingualism.* Clevedon, UK: Multilingual Matters.

Corson, D. (1999). Community-based education for indigenous cultures. In S. May (Ed.), *Indigenous community-based education* (pp. 8-19). Clevedon, UK: Multilingual Matters.

Fishman, J.A. (1991). *Reversing language shift.* Clevedon, UK: Multilingual Matters.

Horvath, B.M., & Vaughn, P. (1991). *Community languages: A handbook.* Clevedon, UK: Multilingual Matters.

May, S. (1999). Language and education rights for indigenous peoples. In S. May (Ed.), *Indigenous community-based education* (pp. 95-108). Clevedon, UK: Multilingual Matters.

Skutnabb-Kangas, T. (2000). *Linguistic genocide in education or worldwide diversity and human rights?* Mahwah, NJ: Lawrence Erlbaum.

Valdés, G. (1997). Dual-language immersion programs: A cautionary note concerning the education of language minority students. *Harvard Educational Review, 67*(3), 391-429.

Valdés, G. (2000). Introduction. *Spanish for native speakers: AATSP professional development series handbook for teachers K–16* (pp. 1-20). Orlando, FL: Harcourt College.

Wiley, T.G., & Valdés, G. (2000). Editors' introduction: Heritage language instruction in the United States: A time for renewal. *Bilingual Research Journal, 24*(4), iii-vi. Retrieved July 19, 2001, from http://brj.asu.edu/v244/articles/ar1.html

Acknowledgments

I am very appreciative of the valuable editorial advice and suggestions made by Joy Kreeft Peyton and Donald A. Ranard regarding this chapter.

3
Heritage Language Students: Profiles and Possibilities

Guadalupe Valdés
Stanford University

New awareness of language rights and new efforts to right old wrongs have prompted educators around the world to recognize the importance of ethnic and heritage languages. In some countries, this recognition has led to policies that support the teaching of these languages as school subjects to learners with a home background in these languages and as foreign languages to students with no background in them. Supporters of these policies believe that they give these languages both legitimacy and attention.

This recent development offers both new opportunities and new challenges to educators. This paper examines these opportunities and challenges in the context of the United States, where demographic shifts are changing how we think about the teaching of languages that, until recently, were taught exclusively as foreign languages.

Heritage Language Students: A Definition

In the United States, the term *heritage language* has recently come to be used broadly by those concerned about the study, maintenance, and revitalization of non-English languages in the United States. For those individuals interested in strengthening endangered indigenous languages or maintaining immigrant languages that are not normally taught in school, *heritage language* refers to a language with which individuals have a personal connection (Fishman, this volume). It is the historical and personal connection to the language that is salient and not the actual proficiency of individual speakers. Armenian, for example, would be considered a heritage language for American students of Armenian ancestry even if the students were English-speaking monolinguals. In terms of strengthening and preserving Armenian in this country, these students would be seen as having an important personal connection with the language and an investment in maintaining it for future generations. Their motivation for learning Armenian would thus contrast significantly with that of the typical foreign language student.

For foreign language educators, the term *heritage language* student has a different meaning than it does for those concerned with endangered indigenous languages or immigrant languages that are not regularly taught in school. Foreign language educators use the term to refer to a language student who is raised in a home where a non-English language is spoken, who speaks or at least understands the language, and who is to some degree bilingual in that language and in English (Valdés, 2000a, 2000b). For these educators, the heritage language student is also different in important ways from the traditional foreign language student. This difference, however, has to do with developed functional proficiencies in the heritage languages.

It is important to point out that within the profession of foreign language education the use of the term *heritage language speaker* is relatively new. It first became a term of general use in the *Standards for Foreign Language Learning* (National Standards in Foreign Language Education Project, 1996). Up until that time, the Spanish-teaching profession, for example, had primarily referred to these students as native speakers of Spanish, quasi-native speakers of Spanish, or as bilingual students. Dissatisfaction with these terms led to the increased use of other terms, such as *home background speakers* (as used in Australia) and *heritage language speakers* (as used in Canada). As currently used in the United States, the term *heritage language* refers to all non-English languages, including those spoken by native American peoples. It is likely that the field of foreign language education will continue to search for a term that more precisely describes learners who arrive in the classroom with strongly developed proficiencies in their ancestral languages.

The Language Characteristics of Heritage Language Speakers

Bilingualism and Bilingual Individuals

In spite of a growing commitment by some educators to developing the heritage languages of non-English speakers in this country, the challenges surrounding the teaching of these two types of students—those with and those without proficiency in the language—are not simple. In the case of monolingual English-speaking heritage students of some immigrant and indigenous languages, challenges may include making decisions about the variety of the language to be taught, developing a writing system, developing language teaching materials, and identifying remaining speakers of the language, to name a few. For other languages, the major challenge may be to provide instruction that capitalizes on personal connections to the heritage language. In the case of the teaching of heritage languages as academic subjects to students with some proficiency in the language, challenges include determining the range of proficiencies that these students have already developed in the language and understanding the ways to strengthen these proficiencies.

Heritage language students raised in a home where a non-English language is spoken, who speak or only understand the heritage language, and who have some proficiency in English and the heritage language are to some degree bilingual. It is important to point out, however, that for many people—indeed for some scholars—the term *bilingual* implies not only the ability to use two languages to some degree in everyday life, but also the skilled superior use of both languages at the level of the educated native speaker. For individuals who subscribe to this narrow definition of bilingualism, a bilingual person is two monolinguals in one who can do everything perfectly in two languages and who can pass undetected among monolingual speakers of each of these two languages. For scholars who subscribe to a broader definition of bilingualism, the idealized, perfectly balanced bilingual is for the most part a mythical figure that rarely exists in real life. This mythical bilingual is represented in **Figure 1**.

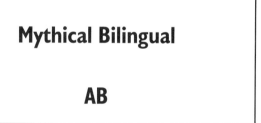

Figure I. The Mythical Bilingual

In Figure 1, same-size letters indicate that this bilingual is equally proficient in languages A and B. This would mean that whatever the individual could do in one language (recite childhood poems, pray, write academic papers, tell jokes, argue with a sibling) that person could do equally well in the other language. While absolutely equivalent abilities in two languages are theoretically possible, individuals seldom have access to two languages in exactly the same contexts in every domain of interaction. Neither do they have opportunities to use two languages to carry out the exact same functions with every person with whom they interact. Thus, they do not develop identical strengths in both languages.

Those who define bilingualism more broadly and whose research involves the investigation of bilingualism in communities where two languages are spoken suggest instead that there are many different types of bilinguals and that bilingual abilities fall along a continuum. From this perspective, bilingualism is seen to be a condition that essentially involves more than one competence, however small it might be. The comparison group against which bilinguals of different types are to be measured is the monolingual group, the group of individuals who have competence in only one language. A native speaker of English who is literate in English and who reads French, for example, is clearly more bilingual than an individual who can read in only one language. Similarly, an individual who is fluent in English and understands spoken Polish has developed dual language abilities very much beyond those of speakers who understand only English. Neither of these individuals is completely bilingual. What is important is that neither of these individuals is completely monolingual either.

Figure 2 illustrates a continuum of bilinguals of different types and with different strengths.

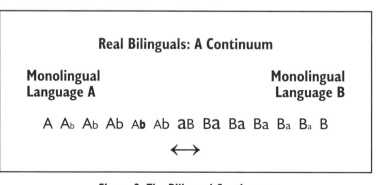

Figure 2. The Bilingual Continuum

In this figure, different letter sizes indicate different strengths in language A and language B in different bilinguals. A bilingual who has recently arrived in the United States, for example, might be represented as Ab (dominant in the heritage language and in the beginning stages of learning English). Similarly, a fourth-generation bilingual could be represented as Ba (dominant in English and still retaining some proficiency in the heritage language.) In minority language communities all over the world, such different types of bilinguals live together and interact with each other and with monolinguals on a daily basis, using one or the other of their two languages.

In addition to varying across bilinguals, bilingualism is best seen as a dynamic condition. Over the course of a lifetime, a single individual's bilingual profile can vary immensely, depending on background experiences and schooling. As **Figure 3** illustrates, an immigrant child, for example, may grow up in a household where mainly Russian is spoken. Over the years, depending on the amount of contact with Russian, that person may become much more English dominant than Russian dominant. It is possible, however, that in older adulthood, perhaps because of marriage late in life to a newly arrived immigrant, that individual will once again use Russian predominantly in everyday life.

Childhood	Adolescence	Adulthood	Older Adulthood
Ab	Ab	aB	Ab

Figure 3. Changes Over Time in Bilingualism

In addition, immigrant bilingualism tends to follow a specific generational pattern. Bilinguals of different generations have different proficiencies in English and in the heritage language. As **Figure 4** illustrates, many first-generation immigrants will remain monolingual in their first language throughout their lives. Others will acquire some English and become incipient bilinguals, but will still be strongly dominant in the heritage language. By the second and third generation, most members of the immigrant community will have acquired English quite well. The majority of these individuals will be, if not English dominant, English preferent. Many, nevertheless, will continue to function in two languages in order to communicate with members of the first generation. Finally, by the fourth generation, most individuals of immigrant background will have become monolingual English speakers. Only a few will retain some competence in the heritage language.

Generation	Possible Language Characteristics	
1st Generation	Monolinguals in Heritage Language A	Incipient Bilinguals Ab
2nd and 3rd Generation	Heritage Language Dominant Ab	English Dominant aB
4th Generation	English Dominant Ba	English Monolingual B

Figure 4. Bilingualism of Different Generations

Language Characteristics of Immigrant Students

Many immigrant students who come to this country as young children enter American schools with little knowledge of English and are classified as limited English proficient (LEP). By the time they arrive in high school and college, however, most will have acquired some English. Some will continue to be heritage language dominant; that is, their overall abilities in the heritage language will be much greater than their English language abilities. Second-, third-, and fourth-generation students, however, will be clearly English dominant. Their strengths in English will very strongly overshadow their abilities in the heritage language.

To make matters even more complex, many immigrant students will often be speakers of nonprestige varieties of their heritage language. They may speak a rural variety of the language or a stigmatized variety associated with non-academic uses of language, or their productive abilities may be limited to a very narrow repertoire of styles and registers. The spoken language of these students may often contain a number of features typical of casual and informal registers of the language that are totally inappropriate in the classroom. Registers, it will be recalled, include very high-level varieties of language, such as those used in university lectures and the writing of academic articles. They also include midlevel varieties, such as those used in newspaper reports, popular novels, interviews, and low-level registers used in intimate and casual conversation. Not all speakers of a given language develop identical linguistic repertoires. High-status groups generally have access to language use in a number of contexts (e.g., academic, religious, administrative) in which the high/formal varieties are used in narrowly prescribed ways. As a result, the linguistic features characterizing the high varieties of language tend over time to characterize the speech of high-status groups as well. Lower-status groups, on the other hand, given their limited access to these same contexts, tend to develop a narrower range of styles in both the oral and the written modes. Their speech is characterized by the use of features normally found in the informal/casual varieties of the language that they use with greater frequency.

Heritage language speakers in the United States, like their monolingual counterparts in their home countries, reflect the complexities of class and access. The linguistic repertoires of upper-middle-class individuals include a broad range of registers including varieties appropriate for those situations (e.g., academia) in which oral language reflects the hyperliteracy of its speakers. The repertoires of individuals of lower-ranked groups, especially those who have had little access to formal education, are much narrower in range and do not normally include ease with hyperliterate discourse. It is important to note, however, that some scholars (e.g., Kroch, 1978) have suggested that other factors, in addition to access to different contexts of language use, have an impact on the differences between the speech of high- and low-status groups in a given society. Kroch argues that dominant social groups tend to mark themselves off from lower-status groups by means of language and that speakers of prestige or high language varieties deliberately work to distance themselves linguistically from the nonelite groups in their society. This would suggest that speakers of prestige varieties consciously and unconsciously work to distance themselves from their nonelite co-nationals. Members of nonelite groups, on the other hand, must consciously work to acquire ways of speaking that characterize the elite groups to which they aspire to belong.

Unlike monolinguals, however, heritage speakers have grown up in bilingual communities in the United States. As in monolingual communities, different registers are used in different situational contexts. What is different, however, is that the high registers of English are used to carry out all formal/high exchanges, while heritage languages and the informal registers of English are used as the low variety appropriate primarily for casual, informal interactions.

In addition to being characterized by diglossia (the functional differentiation of languages) and bilingualism, bilingual communities also reflect the social class origins of their residents. In the case of immigrants from certain countries (e.g., Mexico), evidence suggests that a large majority of persons who emigrate to the United States do not come from the groups with high levels of education. Other immigrants, however, from countries such as Korea and Taiwan are members of the professional and well-educated elite. A further complication in the study of heritage languages spoken in bilingual communities by first-, second-, third-, and fourth-generation immigrants is the fact that these languages—isolated as they are from the broad variety of contexts and situations in which they are used in the home country—are at risk of undergoing a number of significant changes. Some researchers (e.g., de Bot & Weltens, 1991; Maher, 1991; Olshtain & Barzilay, 1991; and Seliger & Vago, 1991) maintain that the immigrant languages attrite and undergo structural loss. This attrition then results in the transferring by immigrants of their mother tongue in a "mutilated" form (de Bot & Weltens, 1991, p. 42) to the next generation of speakers.

In sum, the heritage languages that are spoken in bilingual communities in the United States and acquired by immigrant bilinguals reflect the class origins of their first-generation speakers. If these speakers did not have access to the range of situations and contexts in which formal high varieties of the heritage language are used, the language is characterized by a somewhat narrower range of lexical and syntactic alternatives than is the language of upper-middle-class speakers. Perhaps more importantly, because in these communities the use of the heritage language is restricted to largely low-level functions and private sphere interactions, over time "the immigrant language falls into disuse," as Huffines (1991, p. 125) points out. As a result, many young people in bilingual communities may not acquire a full mastery of the registers and styles characteristic of even working-class monolinguals from the home country.

Figure 5 illustrates the language development that might characterize a particular heritage language speaker.

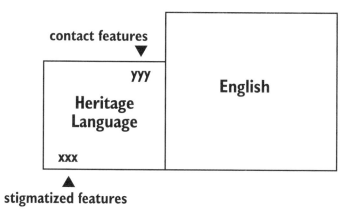

Figure 5. The Language Development of a Bilingual Heritage Language Speaker

As will be noted in this figure, the heritage language is seen to be underdeveloped in comparison to English. Moreover, in this case, the heritage language is characterized by the use of stigmatized features as well as features that are a direct result of contact with English. Functionally, however, this heritage speaker may be able to carry out conversations on everyday topics with ease and confidence and may even be able to understand rapidly spoken language that includes the subtle use of humor. In comparison to students who have acquired the language exclusively in the classroom, the heritage language student may seem quite superior in some respects and quite limited in others. For example, there may be little or no proficiency in reading and writing the language. As is the case with most native speakers of a language, the heritage language speaker "knows" the language and uses a set of internalized grammatical rules but does not have the metalanguage to talk about the grammatical system itself. (See Valdés [1995, 2000a, 2000b] and Valdés &

Geoffrion-Vinci [1998] for discussions of the language characteristics of immigrants and heritage language speakers.)

The Role of Policy and Theory in the Teaching of Heritage Languages: The Case of Spanish

Efforts to develop pedagogies suitable for teaching Spanish to heritage speakers date from the early 1970s, a time when the increasing enrollment of students of Mexican ancestry was felt strongly at the university level in the Southwest. Efforts to develop both theories and policies that might guide the teaching of Spanish as a heritage language, however, have been carried out by isolated individuals at different institutions reacting to problems faced by students in very different programs. As a result, the multiple practices and pedagogies currently being used to teach Spanish to heritage speakers are not directly supported by a set of coherent theories about the role of instruction in the development of language proficiencies in bilingual language learners. Discussions among practitioners at all levels are characterized by strong disagreements about appropriate outcomes and goals of instruction. We find these disagreements even within the current climate of support for heritage language instruction provided by the American Association of Teachers of Spanish and Portuguese (AATSP), the American Council on the Teaching of Foreign Languages (ACTFL), and the National Foreign Language Center, as well as the models of instruction designed in Australia for home background speakers (Ingram, 1994; Scarino, Vale, McKay, & Clark, 1988a, 1988b, 1988c; Valdés, 1995). There has been much debate, for example, about issues such as the following:

- The difference between foreign language and heritage language instruction (Valdés, 1981)

- The implications of the study of linguistic differences for the teaching of Spanish to bilingual students (Floyd, 1981; Guitart, 1981; Solé, 1981)
- The teaching of the prestige or standard variety (Colombi, 1997; García & Otheguy, 1997; Hidalgo, 1987, 1993, 1997; Politzer, 1993; Porras, 1997; Torreblanca, 1997; Valdés, 1981; Valdés, Hannum, & Teschner, 1982; Valdés-Fallis, 1976, 1978)
- The teaching of grammar (Alonso de Lozano, 1981; Lozano, 1981)
- The teaching of spelling (Staczek & Aid, 1981; Valdés Fallis, 1975)
- The teaching of reading and writing (Faltis, 1981, 1984; Teschner, 1981; Villarreal, 1981)
- Testing and assessment (Barkin, 1981; Valdés, 1989; Ziegler, 1981)
- The relationship between theory and practice (Merino, Trueba, & Samaniego, 1993)
- The role of the foreign language teaching profession in maintaining minority languages (Valdés, 1992)
- The development of academic language abilities at both the graduate and the undergraduate levels (Colombi & Alarcón, 1997; D'Ambruoso, 1993; Faltis, 1981, 1984; Faltis & DeVillar, 1993; Gorman, 1993; Hocker, 1993; Merino, Trueba, & Samaniego, 1993; Quintanar-Sarellana, Huebner, & Jensen, 1993; Roca, 1990; Valdés, 1995; Valdés & Geoffrion-Vinci, 1998; Valdés, Lozano, & García-Moya, 1981)

What is missing is a clear educational policy that can guide the goals of language instruction for heritage Spanish-speaking students (as well as heritage speakers of other languages) in the light of current and future economic and social goals. Many Korean and Chinese parents, for example, are urging school systems to give their children high school credit for the study of their heritage languages. At the urging of these parents, the College Board has developed subject matter examinations in these two languages. Growing interest in what were previously considered "minor" languages by students is confirmed by the work recently carried out by Krashen, Tse, & McQuillan (1998). Focusing on both language attitudes and language pedagogies, this work concludes that heritage background students have increasingly positive attitudes toward their ancestral language. If appropriate teaching methods are used, further language study (after English has been well acquired) yields particularly good results after early adolescent rebellion has ended.

What is needed in order to support this growing interest in developing heritage/immigrant language resources is a coherent body of pedagogical theories about what can be accomplished in a classroom setting relative to out-of-school acquisition, functions, and rewards. Very little empirical research about the outcomes of different kinds of instruction is available. There have been no policy discussions at the national or state levels that focus on language education for both monolingual English-speaking *and* heritage background students. Foreign language instruction at the high school level is generally still aimed primarily at monolingual English-speaking, college-bound students, and college and university language instruction is still largely defined by the literature-focused, upper-level courses in which students are eventually expected to enroll. Specific goals have not been established for the teaching of Spanish and other languages as heritage languages, and no policies directly guide the implementation of programs, the training of teachers, and the measurement of outcomes.

Heritage language educators are concerned with such questions as the acquisition of a standard dialect, the expansion of bilingual range, the transfer of reading and writing abilities across languages, and the maintenance of immigrant and other heritage languages. In each of these areas, existing practice is informed to a very limited degree by research carried out on societal and individual bilingualism. Language professionals working in the area of Spanish for Native Speakers (SNS) have utilized descriptions of U.S. Spanish, for example, to prepare materials and to predict difficulties that students will have. They have not yet developed theories, however, about how standard dialects are acquired, how bilinguals expand their range in each language, or how skills transfer across languages. More surprisingly, perhaps, they have not even examined the results of teaching practices in order to draw from those results important insights about both language and language learning.

Direct Instruction and
Spanish Language Maintenance

For many educators engaged in the teaching of Spanish to heritage Spanish speakers, Spanish language maintenance is an important and primary goal. The belief that the formal study of Spanish in high schools and colleges can contribute to the maintenance of the Spanish language among second- and third-generation Chicano and Puerto Rican students is widely held.

Proponents of this position often cite research focusing on bilingualism and on the nature of language maintenance and language shift (e.g., Fishman, 1964, 1991). Indeed, the field of societal bilingualism has contributed important theories about factors that contribute to each of these processes. Similarly, students of individual bilingualism who have researched language loss have examined the linguistic danger signs that point to the general weakening of a bilingual's two languages (Hyltenstam & Obler, 1989; Seliger

& Vago, 1991). What is known is that given societal and residential mobility, it is often difficult to maintain individual bilingualism across generations, even when societal bilingualism is stable. In the case of Spanish speakers, as Hernández-Chávez (1993) carefully documented in his broad review of the literature on such questions, we know that individual language shift is rapid and ongoing.

Theories about how classroom practice can help to delay or reverse language loss have not been developed, however. There is little information available to the practitioner about how certain classroom practices—for example, consciousness raising about language and identity, the teaching of sociolinguistic principles, or the teaching of overall language skills—can contribute to students' views of themselves as lifetime Spanish speakers who will make the effort to transmit the language to their children.

It is important to note that few sociolinguists and students of societal bilingualism are optimistic about developing simple principles about why and how individuals maintain minority languages in bilingual contexts. The variables are many, and the classroom is limited in what can be accomplished against the assimilative pressures of the wider society. Fishman (1991) is most persuasive in arguing that language maintenance depends on transmission across generations. He maintains that schools alone cannot reverse language shift, and he suggests steps that communities need to take to create an environment in which the minority language can both grow and thrive beyond the classroom.

If practitioners believe, however, that they *can* contribute (if only in some small way) to language maintenance, they and applied linguists working with them must answer the following questions in order to develop a theory of classroom approaches to such maintenance:

- What levels of linguistic development correlate with students' desire to maintain Spanish?
- What kinds of interactions with other Spanish speakers at school promote an increased interest among students in continuing to participate in such interactions?
- What can teachers read to promote their understanding of students' linguistic circumstances and a concomitant awareness of the efforts involved in maintaining language?
- Which classroom activities contribute to students' positive attitudes about Spanish for themselves, for their educational institutions, and for their communities?

Responses to such questions would serve as a point of departure for the development of a set of coherent principles about the precise role of language instruction in language maintenance. For the moment, instruction aimed at bilingual speakers of Spanish that purports to support language maintenance is operating according to what are, at best, very tentative hypotheses about the relationship between language instruction and language maintenance.

Direct Instruction and the Acquisition of the Standard Variety of Spanish

The teaching of prestige or "standard" varieties of language to speakers of nonstandard varieties is an area that has received the most attention from researchers. Much attention, therefore, has been given to the discussion of standard and nonstandard varieties of Spanish and the position to be taken by the profession in teaching bilingual students (e.g., Colombi, 1997; García & Otheguy, 1997; Hidalgo, 1987, 1993, 1997; Porras, 1997; Torreblanca, 1997; Valdés-Fallis, 1976, 1978).

The research community, however, has given less attention to the acquisition of second dialects than it has to the teaching and learning of second languages. Existing litera- ture on the relationship between nonstandard dialects and education in Europe (Ammon, 1989; Bailey, 1987; Cheshire, Edwards, Munstermann, & Weltens, 1989; Fishman & Lueders-Salmon, 1972; Gagne, 1983; Rutt, 1962) underscores the fact that although such dialects appear to have been the subject of controversy for many years, there are few existing theories about how standard dialects are acquired by speak- ers of stigmatized varieties. Moreover, while it has always been tempting to view the acquisition of a standard dialect as analogous to the process of acquiring a second language, there are important differences between the two processes.

Individuals learning a second language (even a closely related one) always know whether a particular utterance is or is not a part of their first language. This is not the case when learners are confronted with a standard variety of the language that they speak. As Craig (1988) has argued, nonprestige dialect speakers learning a standard dialect have vocabularies that are essentially identical to vocabularies in the standard language. As Craig has further argued, these learners encounter in the standard variety "four sets or strata of linguistic features" (p. 306). Listed below are Craig's four features, to which I have added a fifth:

1. Features common to both the nonprestige dialect and the standard dialect and normally produced by the non- prestige dialect speaker
2. Features normally not produced in the nonprestige dialect but that are familiar to the learner and possibly produced in situations in which the learner makes an extreme effort to be "correct"
3. Features that the learner would recognize and understand when used in context by prestige dialect speakers but that he or she would be unable (or unwilling) to produce

4. Features totally unknown to the nonprestige dialect speaker
5. Features that are used exclusively in the nonprestige dialect and that are highly stigmatized among prestige variety speakers

In the instructional context, the existence of these five sets of features creates a situation unlike that encountered by the second language (L2) learner. Because of the existence of feature sets (1) and (2), it is often the case that features from set (5) are used by learners when they attempt to speak a standard dialect in the mistaken assumption that these, too, are part of either set (1) or (2).

Concern about the teaching of an educated standard variety of Spanish has been very much at the center of the teaching of Spanish to bilingual Spanish-speaking students in the United States. However, as Politzer (1993) argued, in spite of our knowledge about the complexity of inter- and intraindividual variation, there are no existing theories that can guide practitioners in deciding how to "teach" a standard dialect. Those who hoped to be guided by theories of L2 acquisition now have serious doubts about the parallels to be found between these two very different kinds of acquisition.

In developing language learning theories that might guide the creation of classroom methodology for teaching or bringing about the acquisition of a prestige language variety, questions such as the following need to be answered:

- How is a standard dialect acquired in natural settings?
- What is the order of acquisition of different features?
- How and why do such features become salient to the speaker of the nonprestige variety?
- How do personal interactions contribute to such language awareness?

- How much access to the standard language is necessary before particular features are noticed and acquired?
- What kinds of language exposure provide the most benefit?
- Does avoidance of stigmatized features and production of standard features depend on the development and use of an internal monitor?
- How does the monitor develop?
- How can students be made aware of the dangers of hypercorrection?
- What can be done in the classroom to create an environment in which the standard language can be acquired and the dialect retained for informal, out-of-school uses as it is everywhere else in the world?
- What sets of activities promote language awareness?
- What kinds of language exposure (e.g., reading, writing, viewing and analysis of videos, and studying formal grammar) contribute *most* to the development of sociolinguistic sensitivity and the awareness that some formal styles are inappropriate in certain contexts?

Direct Instruction and the Transfer of Literacy Skills

As compared to the teaching of the standard language or the expansion of bilingual range, the transfer of literacy skills from one language to another appears to be a far more straightforward process. A number of allied fields (e.g., bilingual education and foreign language education) are also concerned about this. The development of theory in this area, then, is already moving forward. In the teaching of Spanish to heritage speakers, however, questions related to this process require a more precise focus. Instructors need to know how different types of skills transfer, how best to bring about an efficient and effective carryover of such skills in both reading and writing, and what kinds of materials best accomplish the task.

Direct Instruction for Heritage Speakers: Theoretical and Pedagogical Challenges

The primary objective of many language departments in this country is to produce students who come very close to monolingual speakers of the language that they teach. When students have no background in the language, the task is generally seen as a difficult one. It is expected that acquiring the language and reaching near-native proficiency will take many years. Moreover, if language-teaching professionals are truthful, they will admit that very few individuals ever reach such a level of proficiency. Such proficiency, when it is achieved, is the result of a rare combination of natural ability, determination, and opportunity. Serious students are thus urged to travel and live in countries where the target language is spoken and to nurture close friendships with native-speaking persons. Instructors impress upon their students that language competencies erode and that maintaining broad abilities in the language will involve a lifetime effort.

While these views about how near-native competencies are acquired seem commonsensical, in reality they are based directly on what is now known about how second languages are acquired. There is a large literature on L2 acquisition that is accessible to language teachers. A great deal less is known about individuals who acquire their first language in bilingual contexts, and almost nothing is known about how a bilingual person's range in each of his or her languages changes and develops over time. We know enough, however, to make us suspect that the process of further development of a first language is fundamentally different from the process of L2 acquisition. The theoretical questions are many, and we have only begun to carry out the kind of research that can help us understand whether and how the process of growth in a "limited" first language actually occurs. We do not yet know how much like monolinguals bilingual speakers can actually become in a natural setting over a lifetime, and we know even less about how this process might work in the high school or university classroom. We have no answers to the question "What is possible for such students in what length of time?"

What needs to be developed is a theory about how heritage language competencies can be expanded in both natural and classroom settings. We can conjecture that expansion of such competencies would involve growth in grammatical, textual, illocutionary, sociolinguistic, and strategic competencies; however, a language learning theory would need to explain how growth in these various competencies takes place. We have little understanding of how individuals reverse or retard individual language shift and of whether and how direct instruction can provide such individuals with resources that will allow them to develop their competencies in the heritage language during their entire lifetimes.

The Development of Pedagogical Theories

In moving toward the development of more coherent pedagogical theories for the teaching of heritage languages, one important option is to draw directly from practices and theories used initially in the teaching of either first or second languages. **Figure 6** illustrates the connections between theories of bilingualism, pedagogical theories, and instructional practices in the teaching of heritage languages. Figure 6 also depicts the connections between pedagogical theories (with sample areas of focus) in first and second language acquisition and development, and pedagogical theories in heritage language teaching.

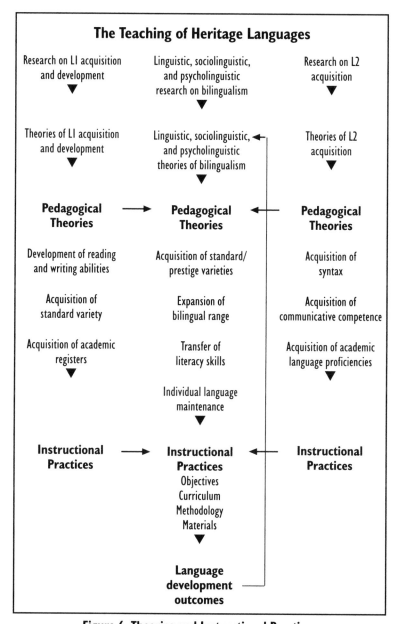

Figure 6. Theories and Instructional Practices

As Figure 6 illustrates, it is important for heritage language educators to continue to examine pedagogical theories and practices in first and second language acquisition and development and to extend the implications of these practices to the teaching of heritage students. Valdés and Geoffrion-Vinci (1998), for example, attempted to understand the development and use of academic registers of Spanish by Chicano students by extending Nemser's (1971) view of "approximative" high registers and evolving competencies originally found in the second language acquisition literature. Some instructors (e.g., Pino, 1997), guided by Heath's (1983) work in conducting community ethnographies with L1 students and teachers, have used this approach with heritage speakers. Finally, several individuals (Politzer, 1993; Valdés, 1981) have pointed out the need for the field of heritage language teaching to review the research on nonstandard varieties of English and the early pedagogies developed for the teaching of standard English (Allen, 1969; Bartley & Politzer, 1972; Feigenbaum, 1970; Stewart, 1970).

As will be noted in Figure 6, research on bilingualism can directly inform the development of various linguistic, sociolinguistic, and psycholinguistic theories of bilingualism. In order to advance the effectiveness of and theoretical foundation for heritage language instruction, we need to develop coherent pedagogical theories for the teaching of heritage languages that are based not only on theories of bilingualism and bilingual language development but also on the actual outcomes of heritage language instruction. Objectives and practices in heritage language instruction must be carefully examined in order to identify successful practices and outcomes that—although not directly based on clear pedagogical theories—may potentially contribute to the development of such theories by providing evidence of the kinds of language development that can take place in classroom settings for bilingual learners.

Similarly, it is important to determine to what degree pedagogical theories and approaches used in the teaching of first or second language learners can be applied to the teaching of heritage speakers. For example, theories of extensive reading (Day & Bamford, 1998), although originally developed with L2 learners in mind, may be effectively used or adapted in expanding the restricted range of registers used by Latinos in this country. Similarly, pedagogical theories of L1 written language development—for example, those used to support the teaching of written academic discourses to unskilled or minority writers (Bizzell, 1986; De & Gregory, 1997; DiPardo, 1993; Fox, 1992; Hill, 1990; Hull, 1991; Lisle & Mano, 1997; McCarthy, 1987; Perl, 1979; Rose, 1985, 1989; Shaughnessy, 1977; Walters, 1994)—may well be used successfully for teaching academic literacies in the heritage language to bilingual learners. We know that some classroom practices in the teaching of heritage languages have been borrowed from L1 and L2 instruction (e.g., the teaching of traditional grammar). It is important, as well, to identify novel adaptations of pedagogical theories and practices (e.g., genre analysis in Swales, 1990; community ethnographies in Heath, 1983; reformulation in Cohen, 1990) drawn from the fields of first and second language development and acquisition that can inform the continued development of theories and practices in the teaching of heritage languages.

A Framework for Planning Instruction for Heritage Language Speakers

Instruction for heritage language speakers who are to some degree bilingual requires that language educators build on these students' existing language strengths. One possible approach is suggested by the new *Standards for Foreign Language Learning* (National Standards in Foreign Language Education Project,1996). The standards were the result of the national standards setting movement and involved members of most of the associations of language educators in the country (i.e., American Association of Teachers of French, American Association of Teachers of German, American Association of Teachers of Italian, American Association of Teachers of Spanish and Portuguese, American Classical League, American Council on the Teachings of Russian, American Council on the Teaching of Foreign Languages, Central States Conference on the Teaching of Foreign Languages), and Joint National Committee for Languages. Because the standards writing team included from its inception individuals actively engaged in the teaching of heritage languages, the standards offer a view of the goals of language study that are of direct relevance to those of us concerned with this instruction. The goals of foreign language study that serve as the organizing framework for the standards are presented in **Figure** 7.

Goal I.
Communicate in Languages Other Than English

Goal 2.
Gain Knowledge and Understanding of Other Cultures

Goal 3.
Connect With Other Disciplines and Acquire Information

Goal 4.
Develop Insight into the Nature of Language and Culture

Goal 5.
Participate in Multilingual Communities
at Home and Around the World

Figure 7. National Standards for Foreign Language Learning—
Goals of Foreign Language Study

As will be noted, the goals of language study as presented by the standards go far beyond the ACTFL Proficiency Guidelines (ACTFL, 1986). The standards perspective on language learning views language study as resulting in the ability to function in the target language. Students who study language will communicate with others, will explore other disciplines using the target language, and will use it to participate in multilingual communities in this country and abroad. Moreover, through their study of language, students will learn about culture itself as well as about the nature of language.

What is evident from this discussion of the goals of language study is that even though linguistic abilities are still seen as central to the acquisition of language, no longer is there a preoccupation with the four skills—listening, speaking, reading, and writing—as separate language abilities. More importantly, for the purposes of this paper, the standards allow us to think about instruction for heritage language speakers in an entirely new way. In examining the above five goals, for example, it is clear that no matter how much they already know, heritage speakers must continue to focus on Goal 1. They must continue to develop a greater bilingual communicative range. The other four goals, moreover, are equally important. Heritage speakers need to gain knowledge and understanding of other heritage language cultures (Goal 2). They need to use the heritage language to connect with other disciplines and to acquire new information (Goal 3). They need opportunities to develop even more insights than they already have into the nature of language and culture (Goal 4). Finally, they must be encouraged to become lifelong learners of the language by participating in multilingual communities at home and around the world (Goal 5).

The presentation of the communications goal (Goal 1) as outlined in the standards is of particular relevance to our understanding of the unique language strengths of heritage language speakers. Because of the importance of Goal 1 to the teaching of language to heritage speakers, I will discuss it at some length and describe the view of communication that is presented in the standards document.

From the point of view of the standards, communication in a language involves much more than simply speaking and listening. The standards recognize three "communicative modes" and place primary emphasis on the context and purpose of the communication. As illustrated in **Figure 8**, these three modes are *interpersonal, interpretative,* and *presentational.* Each mode involves a particular link between language and the ways in which interaction takes place. Moreover, various skills, such as listening and speaking or reading and writing, occur together within a single mode of communication.

Interpersonal	Interpretive	Presentational
• Face to face communication • Written communication with individuals who come into personal contact	• Receptive communication of oral or written messages	• Spoken or written communication for an audience
• Speaking • Listening • Reading • Writing	• Listening • Reading • Viewing	• Speaking • Writing

Figure 8. The Three Communication Modes

Note. Adapted from Figure 5, "Framework of Communicative Modes," in *Standards for Foreign Language Learning: Preparing for the 21st Century,* by the National Standards in Foreign Language Education Project, 1996, p. 33.

As will be noted, the above conceptualization takes the position that communication is carried out in both oral and written language. It involves both productive and receptive skills. The spoken language may be informal in certain types of interpersonal interactions and much more formal in others. Interpersonal communication, for example, may involve the written language as in the writing of informal notes to members of the family. It may also involve conversing with strangers, making requests, apologizing, or simply establishing personal contact. It requires linguistic, sociolinguistic, and pragmatic knowledge.

The interpretive communication mode involves understanding what is communicated by others in both oral and written texts. When students read literary texts, for example, or listen to lectures in the language they are studying, they are engaged in interpretive communicative activities. The abilities required for engaging in this type of communication are primarily the receptive skills of reading and listening.

The presentational oral communication mode involves communication with a group of listeners or readers. It can take place in both written and oral language. As will be evident, oral communication in the presentational mode is quite different from oral communication in the interpersonal mode. In the presentational mode, there is little opportunity to read body language and to clarify or reformulate. Oral communication in the presentational mode is in fact much like formal written communication in this same mode and requires a sense of the audience as well as planning and preparation in presenting an argument, explaining, or summarizing information.

For students with a home background in the language studied, the standards framework of communication modes provides a useful way of conceptualizing both learners' strengths and needs. As I pointed out above in the description of the language characteristics of such students, heritage learners may enter formal language instructional programs with considerable ability in the interpersonal mode. However, they may not have completely developed the interpretative and presentational communication modes. While many heritage learners are quite fluent in oral interpersonal language, many need to develop a greater bilingual communicative range. They need to develop their interpersonal skills in order to interact with a broad range of individuals of different backgrounds and ages for a variety of purposes. In terms of the interpretive and presentational communication modes, heritage language speakers need to learn how to read skillfully in the heritage language, to interpret subtle meanings found in both oral and written texts, and to present information in both oral and written forms intended for audiences with which they do not have immediate contact.

As will be evident from work with these communication modes, using a standards-based perspective, instruction directed at heritage language speakers can move beyond a focus on prescriptive grammar, transfer of skills, and basic language maintenance. This kind of instruction can directly contribute to the expansion of bilingual range in that it can help students grow in their competence to carry out face-to-face interactions, comprehend live and recorded and extended oral texts, comprehend written texts, and use language in written and oral form to present information to groups of listeners or readers.

Toward the Establishment of a New Profession

Heritage language speakers present new challenges for the field of foreign language education. Most teachers have not been trained to work with students who already speak or understand the target language or who have a strong connection with it. Similarly, language teachers brought in from countries where the languages are spoken have little or no idea about bilingualism and about the language competencies of heritage students who have been raised in this country. For individuals and groups concerned about the role of instruction in maintaining or revitalizing heritage languages, the basic pedagogical issues, however, are similar to those of foreign language instruction. The challenge involves understanding the needs of minority language communities and of particular groups of learners and adapting or developing pedagogical approaches that can bring about the best results.

In this paper, I have attempted to describe the characteristics of language students who are raised in homes where the language is still spoken and who speak a language that is commonly taught at the secondary and postsecondary levels. The pedagogical challenges I have discussed, the need for theory, and the suggested framework based on the current standards for foreign language learning apply primarily to heritage students with this kind of profile. I would argue, however, that lessons learned from the many years of struggling to legitimize the teaching of heritage languages as academic subjects to students who have developed proficiencies outside of school may not be entirely irrelevant to those groups whose situations are significantly different. Many of the same political and pedagogical challenges will be faced by other heritage language groups in the existing English-only context.

As we move to the establishment of a heritage language teaching profession, it is important that we keep in mind that what brings us together is our commitment to the study and teaching of non-English languages in this country to students who have a personal investment in these languages. As we work together, it is important that we discuss with each other details about the specific challenges of instruction in various heritage languages. If we are to build on each other's experiences, we need to share answers to questions such as the following:

- What are the characteristics of the community in which the heritage language was or is spoken?
- Does the heritage language teaching effort involve language revitalization or language maintenance?
- How many school- and college-age students have functional proficiencies in the heritage language?
- What kinds of language backgrounds do these students bring to the classroom? (Are they first-, second-, or third-generation? Are they biliterate?)
- What kinds of strengths in those languages do they bring?
- Are members of the community interested in developing, maintaining, or revitalizing the heritage language?
- Do individual students wish to develop or maintain the heritage language?
- How large is this group?
- Are these students willing to request instruction in the language, if not available, and to apply pressure on the academic institution to respond to their request?
- Is the heritage language commonly taught as an academic subject in schools or colleges in the community? Should it be?
- What kinds of support are available to carry out such instruction and to plan pedagogical practices?
- Is an out-of-school teaching context likely to be more effective?
- Are teachers of the heritage language available?
- Are pedagogical materials available?

- Are teacher preparation efforts in place or likely to be put in place?
- In cases where instruction in the heritage language is already part of a school or college program, are heritage language speakers well placed in existing language sequences?
- How well can students' strengths be developed by existing instruction?
- What are legitimate and valid language development goals for these students?
- What kinds of special courses have to be developed to bring about those goals?
- Are school and college faculty interested in heritage language students and willing to work closely with them?
- Can school and college administrators be persuaded to support the teaching of the heritage language?

Sharing such information, cataloguing ways in which challenges have been addressed, and examining why efforts have been successful or unsuccessful will directly benefit others who are working to bring about the continued development and maintenance of heritage languages.

Heritage language speakers bring with them many strengths and many different abilities, and heritage communities are very different from each other. In preparing ourselves to teach heritage students, we must see their strengths, value them, and take joy in the fact that in spite of negative sentiments toward non-English languages in this country, many languages are alive and well. To be successful in helping to maintain these languages, we must firmly resolve as a profession that we will learn from each other, that we will share what we learn, and that we will endeavor to extend lessons learned by others to our own contexts. We must continue to find strength in the fact that we value heritage languages and heritage language speakers and that we are convinced that language maintenance efforts are vitally important to our country and to our society.

References

Allen, V.F. (1969). Teaching standard English as a second dialect. *Florida Foreign Language Reporter, 7,* 123-129, 164.

Alonso de Lozano, L. (1981). Enseñanza del subjuntivo a hispanohablantes. In G. Valdés, A.G. Lozano, & R. García-Moya (Eds.), *Teaching Spanish to the Hispanic bilingual: Issues, aims, and methods* (pp. 140-145). New York: Teachers College Press.

American Council on the Teaching of Foreign Languages (ACTFL). (1986). *Proficiency guidelines.* Yonkers, NY: Author.

Ammon, U. (1989). Teaching materials for dialect speakers in the Federal Republic of Germany: The contrastive booklets. In J. Cheshire, V. Edwards, H. Munstermann, & B. Weltens (Eds.), *Dialect and education: Some European perspectives* (pp. 234-241). Clevedon, UK: Multingual Matters.

Bailey, R.W. (1987). Teaching in the vernacular: Scotland, schools and linguistic diversity. In C. Macaffee & I. Macleod (Eds.), *The nuttis schell: Essays on the Scots's language presented to A.J. Aitken* (pp. 131-142). Aberdeen, Scotland: Aberdeen University Press.

Barkin, F. (1981). Evaluating linguistic proficiency: The case of teachers in bilingual programs. In G. Valdés, A.G. Lozano, & R. García-Moya (Eds.), *Teaching Spanish to the Hispanic bilingual: Issues, aims, and methods* (pp. 215-234). New York: Teachers College Press.

Bartley, D.E., & Politzer, L. (1972). *Practice-centered teaching training: Standard English for speakers of non-standard dialects.* Philadelphia: The Center for Curriculum Development.

Bizzell, P. (1986). What happens when basic writers come to college. *College Composition and Communication, 37,* 294-301.

Cheshire, J., Edwards, V., Munstermann, H., & Weltens, B. (Eds.). (1989). *Dialect and education: Some European perspectives.* Clevedon, UK: Multilingual Matters.

Cohen, A. (1990). *Language learning.* New York: Newbury House.

Colombi, M.C. (1997). Perfil del discurso escrito en textos de hispanohablantes: Teoría y práctica. In M.C. Colombi & F.X.

Alarcón (Eds.), *La enseñanza del español a hispanohablantes: Praxis y teoría* (pp. 175-189). Boston: Houghton Mifflin.

Colombi, M.C., & Alarcón, F.X. (Eds.). (1997). *La enseñanza del español a hispanohablantes: Praxis y teoría.* Boston: Houghton Mifflin.

Craig, D.R. (1988). Creole English and education in Jamaica. In C.B. Paulston (Ed.), *International handbook of bilingualism and bilingual education* (pp. 297-312). New York: Greenwood Press.

D'Ambruoso, L. (1993). Spanish for Spanish speakers: A curriculum. In B.J. Merino, H.T. Trueba, & F.A. Samaniego (Eds.), *Language and culture in learning: Teaching Spanish to native speakers of Spanish* (pp. 203-207). London: Falmer Press.

Day, R.R., & Bamford, J. (1998). *Extensive reading in the second language classroom.* Cambridge, UK: Cambridge University Press.

De, E.N., & Gregory, D.U. (1997). Decolonizing the classroom: Freshman composition in a multicultural setting. In C. Severino, J.C. Guerra, & J.E. Butler (Eds.), *Writing in multicultural settings* (pp. 118-132). New York: Modern Language Association.

de Bot, K., & Weltens, B. (1991). Recapitulation, regression, and language loss. In H.W. Seliger & R.M. Vago (Eds.), *First language attrition* (pp. 31-51). New York: Cambridge University Press.

DiPardo, A. (1993). *A kind of passport: A basic writing adjunct program and the challenge of student diversity.* Urbana, IL: National Council of Teachers of English.

Faltis, C.J. (1981). Teaching Spanish writing to bilingual college students. *NABE Journal, 6,* 93-106.

Faltis, C.J. (1984). Reading and writing in Spanish for bilingual college students: What's taught at school and what's used in the community. *The Bilingual Review/La Revista Bilingüe, 11,* 21-32.

Faltis, C.J., & DeVillar, R.A. (1993). Effective computer uses for teaching Spanish to bilingual native speakers: A socioacademic perspective. In B.J. Merino, H.T. Trueba, & F.A. Samaniego (Eds.), *Language and culture in learning: Teaching Spanish to native speakers of Spanish* (pp. 160-169). London: Falmer Press.

Feigenbaum, I. (1970). The use of non-standard English in teaching standard: Contrast and comparison. In R.W. Fasold & R. Shuy (Eds.), *Teaching standard English in the inner city* (pp. 87-104). Washington, DC: Center for Applied Linguistics.

Fishman, J.A. (1964). Language maintenance and language shift as fields of inquiry. *Linguistics, 9,* 32-70.

Fishman, J.A. (1991). *Reversing language shift: Theoretical and empirical foundations of assistance to threatened languages*. Clevedon, UK: Multilingual Matters.

Fishman, J.A., & Lueders-Salmon, E. (1972). What has sociology of language to say to the teacher? On teaching the standard variety to speakers of dialectal or sociolectal varieties. In C.B. Cazden, V.P. John, & D. Hymes (Eds.), *Functions of language in the classroom* (pp. 67-83). New York: Teachers College Press.

Floyd, M.B. (1981). Language variation in southwest Spanish and its relation to pedagogical issues. In G. Valdés, A.G. Lozano, & R. García-Moya (Eds.), *Teaching Spanish to the Hispanic bilingual: Issues, aims, and methods* (pp. 30-45). New York: Teachers College Press.

Fox, T. (1992). Repositioning the profession: Teaching writing to African American students. *Journal of Advanced Composition, 12*, 291-303.

Gagne, G. (1983). Norme et enseignement de la langue maternelle. In E. Bedard & J. Maurais (Eds.), *La norme linguistique* (pp. 463-509). Paris: Le Robert Quebec.

García, O., & Otheguy, R. (1997). No sólo de estándar se vive el aula: Lo que nos enseñó la educación bilingüe sobre el español de Nueva York. In M.C. Colombi & F.X. Alarcón (Eds.), *La enseñanza del español a hispanohablantes: Praxis y teoría* (pp. 156-174). Boston: Houghton Mifflin.

Gorman, S. (1993). Using elements of cooperative learning in the communicative foreign language classroom. In B.J. Merino, H.T. Trueba, & F.A. Samaniego (Eds.), *Language and culture in learning: Teaching Spanish to native speakers of Spanish* (pp. 144-152). London: Falmer Press.

Guitart, J. (1981). The pronunciation of Puerto Rican Spanish in the mainland: Theoretical and pedagogical considerations. In G. Valdés, A.G. Lozano, & R. García-Moya (Eds.), *Teaching Spanish to the Hispanic bilingual: Issues, aims, and methods* (pp. 46-58). New York: Teachers College Press.

Heath, S.B. (1983). *Ways with words: Language, life and communication in communities and classrooms*. Cambridge, UK: Cambridge University Press.

Hernández-Chávez, E. (1993). Native language loss and its implications for revitalization of Spanish in Chicano communities. In B.J. Merino, H.T. Trueba, & F.A. Samaniego (Eds.), *Language and culture in learning: Teaching Spanish to native speakers of Spanish* (pp. 58-74). London: Falmer Press.

Hidalgo, M. (1987). On the question of "standard" vs. "dialect": Implications for teaching Hispanic college students. *Hispanic Journal of the Behavioral Sciences, 9*(4), 375-395.

Hidalgo, M. (1993). The teaching of Spanish to bilingual Spanish-speakers: A "problem" of inequality. In B.J. Merino, H.T. Trueba, & F.A. Samaniego (Eds.), *Language and culture in learning: Teaching Spanish to native speakers of Spanish* (pp. 82-93). London: Falmer Press.

Hidalgo, M. (1997). Criterios normativos e idiología lingüística: Aceptación y rechazo del español de los Estados Unidos. In M.C. Colombi & F.X. Alarcón (Eds.), *La enseñanza del español a hispanohablantes: Praxis y teoría* (pp. 109-120). Boston: Houghton Mifflin.

Hill, C.E. (1990). *Writing from the margins: Power and pedagogy for teachers of composition.* New York: Oxford University Press.

Hocker, B.C. (1993). Folk art in the classroom. In B.J. Merino, H.T. Trueba, & F.A. Samaniego (Eds.), *Language and culture in learning: Teaching Spanish to native speakers of Spanish* (pp. 153-159). London: Falmer Press.

Huffines, M.L. (1991). Pennsylvania German: Convergence and change as strategies of discourse. In H.W. Seliger & R.M. Vago (Eds.), *First language attrition* (pp. 125-137). New York: Cambridge University Press.

Hull, G. (1991). Remediation as social construct: Perspectives from an analysis of classroom discourse. *College Composition and Communication, 42*(3), 299-329.

Hyltenstam, K., & Obler, L. (Eds.). (1989). *Bilingualism across the lifespan: Aspects of acquisition, maturity, and loss.* Cambridge, UK: Cambridge University Press.

Ingram, D.E. (1994). Language policy in Australia in the 1990's. In R.D. Lambert (Ed.), *Language planning around the world: Contexts and systemic change* (pp. 69-109). Washington, DC: National Foreign Language Center.

Krashen, S., Tse, L., & McQuillan, J. (1998). *Heritage language development.* Culver City, CA: Language Education Associates.

Kroch, A.S. (1978). Toward a theory of social dialect variation. *Language in Society, 7*, 17-36.

Lisle, B., & Mano, S. (1997). Embracing a multiculural rhetoric. In C. Severino, J.C. Guerra, & J.E. Butler (Eds.), *Writing in multicultural settings* (pp. 12-26). New York: Modern Language Association.

Lozano, A.G. (1981). A modern view of teaching grammar. In G. Valdés, A.G. Lozano, & R. García-Moya (Eds.), *Teaching Spanish to the Hispanic bilingual: Issues, aims, and methods* (pp. 81-90). New York: Teachers College Press.

Maher, J. (1991). A crosslinguistic study of language contact and language attrition. In H.W. Seliger & R.M. Vago (Eds.), *First language attrition* (pp. 67-84). New York: Cambridge University Press.

McCarthy, L. (1987). A stranger in strange lands: A college student writing across the curriculum. *Research in the Teaching of English, 21*, 233-267.

Merino, B.J., Trueba, H.T., & Samaniego, F.A. (Eds.). (1993). *Language and culture in learning: Teaching Spanish to native speakers of Spanish*. London: Falmer Press.

National Standards in Foreign Language Education Project. (1996). *Standards for foreign language learning: Preparing for the 21st century*. Yonkers, NY: Author.

Nemser, W. (1971). Approximative systems of foreign language learners. *International Review of Applied Linguistics, 9*, 115-123.

Olshtain, E., & Barzilay, M. (1991). Lexical retrieval difficulties in adult language attrition. In H.W. Seliger & R.M. Vago (Eds.), *First language attrition* (pp. 139-150). New York: Cambridge University Press.

Perl, S. (1979). The composing processes of unskilled college writers. *Research on the Teaching of English, 13*(4), 317-336.

Pino, C.R. (1997). La reconceptualización del programa de español para hispanohablantes: Estrategías que reflejan la realidad sociolingüística de la clase. In M.C. Colombi & F.X. Alarcón (Eds.), *La enseñanza del español a hispanohablantes: Praxis y teoría* (pp. 65-82). Boston: Houghton Mifflin.

Politzer, R.L. (1993). A researcher's reflections on bridging dialect and second language learning: Discussion of problems and solutions. In B.J. Merino, H.T. Trueba, & F.A. Samaniego (Eds.), *Language and culture in learning: Teaching Spanish to native speakers of Spanish* (pp. 45-57). London: Falmer Press.

Porras, J.E. (1997). Uso local y uso estándar: Un enfoque bi-dialectal a la enseñanza del español para nativos. In M.C. Colombi & F.X. Alarcón (Eds.), *La enseñanza del español a hispanohablantes: Praxis y teoría* (pp. 190-197). Boston: Houghton Mifflin.

Quintanar-Sarellana, R., Huebner, T., & Jensen, A. (1993). Tapping a natural resource: Language minority students as foreign language tutors. In B.J. Merino, H.T. Trueba, & F.A. Samaniego (Eds.), *Language and culture in learning: Teaching Spanish to native speakers of Spanish* (pp. 208-221). London: Falmer Press.

Roca, A. (1990). Teaching Spanish to the bilingual college student in Miami. In J.J. Bergen (Ed.), *Spanish in the United States: Sociolinguistic issues* (pp. 127-136). Washington, DC: Georgetown University Press.

Rose, M. (1985). The language of exclusion: Writing instruction at the university. *College English, 47,* 341-359.

Rose, M. (1989). *Lives on the boundary.* New York: Penguin.

Rutt, T. (1962). *Didaktik der Muttersprache.* Frankfurt, Germany: Verlag Morita Diesterweg.

Scarino, A., Vale, D., McKay, P., & Clark, J. (1988a). *Australian language levels guidelines: Book 1. Language learning in Australia.* Adelaide, South Australia: Australian National Curriculum Development Center. (ERIC Document Reproduction Service No. ED 340 199)

Scarino, A., Vale, D., McKay, P., & Clark, J. (1988b). *Australian language levels guidelines: Book 2. Syllabus development and programming.* Adelaide, South Australia: Australian National Curriculum Development Center. (ERIC Document Reproduction Service No. ED 340 200)

Scarino, A., Vale, D., McKay, P., & Clark, J. (1988c). *Australian language levels guidelines: Book 3. Method, resources, and assessment.* Adelaide, South Australia: Australian National Curriculum Development Center. (ERIC Document Reproduction Service No. ED 340 201)

Seliger, H.W., & Vago, R.M. (1991). The study of first language attrition. In H.W. Seliger & R.M. Vago (Eds.), *First language attrition* (pp. 3-15). New York: Cambridge University Press.

Shaughnessy, M. (1977). *Errors and expectations.* New York: Oxford University Press.

Solé, Y. (1981). Consideraciones pedagógicas en la enseñanza del español a estudiantes bilingües. In G. Valdés, A.G. Lozano, & R. García-Moya (Eds.), *Teaching Spanish to the Hispanic bilingual: Issues, aims, and methods* (pp. 21-29). New York: Teachers College Press.

Staczek, J.J., & Aid, F.M. (1981). *Hortografía himortal*: Spelling problems among bilingual students. In G. Valdés, A.G. Lozano, & R. García-Moya (Eds.), *Teaching Spanish to the Hispanic bilingual: Issues, aims, and methods* (pp. 146-156). New York: Teachers College Press.

Stewart, W.W. (1970). Foreign language teaching methods in quasi-foreign language situations. In R.W. Fasold & R. Shuy (Eds.), *Teaching standard English in the innner city* (pp. 1-19). Washington, DC: Center for Applied Linguistics.

Swales, J.M. (1990). *Genre analysis: English in academic and research settings*. Cambridge, UK: Cambridge University Press.

Teschner, R.V. (1981). Spanish for native speakers: Evaluating twenty-five Chicano compositions in a first-year course. In G. Valdés, A.G. Lozano, & R. García-Moya (Eds.), *Teaching Spanish to the Hispanic bilingual: Issues, aims, and methods* (pp. 115-139). New York: Teachers College Press.

Torreblanca, M. (1997). El español hablado en el Suroeste de los Estados Unidos y las normas lingüísticas españolas. In M.C. Colombi & F.X. Alarcón (Eds.), *La enseñanza del español a hispanohablantes: Praxis y teoría* (pp. 133-139). Boston: Houghton Mifflin.

Valdés, G. (1981). Pedagogical implications of teaching Spanish to the Spanish-speaking in the United States. In G. Valdés, A.G. Lozano, & R. García-Moya (Eds.), *Teaching Spanish to the Hispanic bilingual: Issues, aims, and methods* (pp. 3-20). New York: Teachers College Press.

Valdés, G. (1989). Testing bilingual proficiency for specialized occupations: Issues and implications. In B.R. Gifford (Ed.), *Test policy and test performance: Education, language and culture* (pp. 207-229). Boston: Kluwer Academic.

Valdés, G. (1992). The role of the foreign language teaching profession in maintaining non-English languages in the United States. In H. Byrnes (Ed.), *Languages for a multicultural world in transition: 1993 Northeast Conference Reports* (pp. 29-71). Skokie, IL: National Textbook Company.

Valdés, G. (1995). The teaching of minority languages as "foreign" languages: Pedagogical and theoretical challenges. *Modern Language Journal, 79*(3), 299-328.

Valdés, G. (2000a). Introduction. In *Spanish for native speakers. AATSP professional development series handbook for teachers K–16, Volume 1* (pp. 1-20). New York: Harcourt College.

Valdés, G. (2000b). Teaching heritage languages: An introduction for Slavic-language-teaching professionals. In O. Kagan & B. Rifkin (Eds.), *Learning and teaching of Slavic languages and cultures: Toward the 21st century* (pp. 375-403). Bloomington, IN: Slavica.

Valdés, G., & Geoffrion-Vinci, M. (1998). Chicano Spanish: The problem of the "underdeveloped" code in bilingual repertoires. *Modern Language Journal, 82*(4), 473-501.

Valdés, G., Hannum, T.P., & Teschner, R.V. (1982). *Cómo se escribe: Curso de secundaria para estudiantes bilingües.* New York: Scribners.

Valdés, G., Lozano, A.G., & García-Moya, R. (Eds.). (1981). *Teaching Spanish to the Hispanic bilingual: Issues, aims, and methods.* New York: Teachers College Press.

Valdés-Fallis, G. (1976, December). Language development versus the teaching of the standard language. *Lektos*, 20-32.

Valdés-Fallis, G. (1978). A comprehensive approach to the teaching of Spanish to bilingual Spanish-speaking students. *Modern Language Journal, 43*(3), 101-110.

Valdés Fallis, G. (1975). Teaching Spanish to the Spanish-speaking: Classroom strategies. *System, 3*(1), 54-62.

Villarreal, H. (1981). Reading and Spanish for native speakers. In G. Valdés, A.G. Lozano, & R. García-Moya (Eds.), *Teaching Spanish to the Hispanic bilingual: Issues, aims, and methods* (pp. 157-168). New York: Teachers College Press.

Walters, K. (1994). Writing and education. In H. Hunther (Ed.), *Schrift und Schriftlichkeit: Ein interdisziplinarisches Handbuch internationaler Forschung* [Writing and its use: An interdisciplinary handbook of international research] (pp. 638-645). Berlin: Walter de Gruyter.

Ziegler, J. (1981). Guidelines for the construction of a Spanish placement examination for the Spanish-dominant Spanish-English bilingual. In G. Valdés, A.G. Lozano, & R. García-Moya (Eds.), *Teaching Spanish to the Hispanic bilingual: Issues, aims, and methods* (pp. 211-214). New York: Teachers College Press.

Shaping the Field

4
300-Plus Years of Heritage Language Education in the United States

Joshua A. Fishman
Yeshiva University, Bronx, New York
Stanford University
New York University

All of us—individuals, societies, cultures, and nations alike—live by our fondest myths, beliefs whose importance transcends their value as truth. One of the myths held in the United States is that our Pilgrim fathers first left England and resettled in the Netherlands, then left the Netherlands for Plymouth Rock because their children were becoming monolingual Dutch speakers and losing their command of English. Whether this is pure myth or has some confirmed truth, it is beyond doubt that since the time of the Pilgrims, millions upon millions of refugees and immigrants have arrived on America's shores with strong hopes of maintaining the ethnolinguistic traditions that defined them to themselves, to their neighbors, and to their God.

If we define heritage languages as those that (a) are LOTEs (languages other than English), in Michael Clyne's usage (1991, p. 3), and that (b) have a particular family relevance to the learners, then we will find schools devoted to teaching these languages and to developing literacy and promoting further education through these languages among the indigenous, the colonial, and the immigrant groups that have come to this country by choice and good fortune or by force and the winds of cruel history.

Indigenous Heritage Languages

We have no record of heritage languages in the United States before the arrival, on foot and by boat, of the Amerindians. Amerindian schools were initially the schools of life, the noninstitutional means by which the young were socialized into the daily rounds, beliefs, and practices that constituted the culture of their parents. Such enculturation still goes on, of course, but increased contact with others (conquerors, settlers, and governmental officials) has led Amerindian educators to create their own brick and mortar institutions—formal schools associated with literacy or, as is increasingly common, biliteracy in an Indian language and in English. Given the sad state of intergenerational cultural transmission—particularly, mother tongue transmission—in most Amerindian groups today, it is instructive that never before in this century has such a high proportion of American Indian children been engaged in heritage language schooling, from prenursery to college institutions, under tribal control or with tribal input (McCarty, Watahomigie, & Yamamoto, 1999; McCarty & Zepeda, 1998.)

Despite a discouraging history of intermittent governmental intrusion (in blatant disregard of treaty obligations), many Amerindians have managed to liberate their lives and their educational institutions from outside influences that deprecate their values, beliefs, and community ties. The conference series Stabilizing Indian Languages (Cantoni, 1996; Reyhner, 1997, 1998); the annual summer American Indian Language Development Institute, housed at the University of Arizona (see McCarty, Yamamoto, Watahomigie, & Zepeda, 1997); the Mentor–Apprentice Program in California (see Hinton, 1994); and the slowly but steadily growing number of Amerindian junior colleges offering indigenous languages are all evidence that heritage language concerns are alive among Amerindians, whether or not they will be supported by local, state, or federal funds. The fact that an Indian teacher, researcher, and poet, Ofelia Zepeda, was a recipient in 1999 of a MacArthur ("Genius") Award is a sign that at least in some mainstream quarters Amerindian interests and welfare are finally considered to be in the public interest.

The combination of Indian primum mobile (they were here first) and mainstream guilt feelings over past injustices to Indians have finally resulted in much greater language consciousness among Amerindians themselves and more sympathy among mainstream authorities and foundations for Amerindian heritage education. It is unfortunate that we often wait until matters become extreme before paying attention to them and taking ameliorative steps that are in everyone's best interest. The improved state of affairs with regard to Amerindian heritage education does not derive from a mainstream conviction that Amerindian societies that preserve their own languages are better off—richer, healthier, less dislocated, less alienated and hopeless, and, therefore, less problem-prone. Rather, it is a result of what Amerindians themselves have accomplished in terms of heritage language revitalization, acquisition, and maintenance.

Colonial Heritage Languages

Heritage language education for speakers of colonial languages—nonindigenous languages that were already established here before the United States of America came into being—usually have neither the justification of primum mobile nor mainstream guilt to support them. Indeed, some have already lost contact with their colonial roots, and their current existence in the United States is an outgrowth of immigrant reinforcement rather than colonial origins. In this category are found such small language groups as Dutch (introduced in the 17th century into Manhattan and for miles along the Hudson River in New York State); Swedish and Finnish (Sweden and

Finland were at times under single rule, and many immigrants from these countries were bilingual Swedish–Finnish speakers even before coming to our shores); and Welsh. All of these languages have long since faded away as intergenerationally transmitted vernaculars in the United States, leaving only place names to remind us of their erstwhile presence. We also find such worldwide giants as French, Spanish, and German. It speaks volumes about our lack of appreciation for heritage languages that there has been almost no intergenerational mother tongue language transmission among the speakers of this trio of languages, who can trace their roots back to colonial times. Certainly the Franco-Americans in New England and Louisiana have only rarely been able to transmit their language across generations, and the success of Spanish speakers in the rural, small-town Southwest is only insignificantly greater. It is recent immigration that largely explains the present prevalence of Spanish, not only in the country as a whole but even in the same small towns in the agricultural Southwest to which the forebears of today's residents came hundreds of years ago.

Only German in its Pennsylvania German incarnation can claim significant intergenerational mother tongue transmission. It holds the distinction of being the only colonial language with an uninterrupted, though not completely unaltered, tradition of heritage language community life and, therefore, of heritage schooling in the United States. Once again, it is to internal forces that we must turn to fathom the ability of Pennsylvania German groups to maintain their language across generations. That ability (not unlike the ability among some Amerindian groups and ultraorthodox Jews) is primarily attributable to their jealously guarded physical and cultural distance from the American mainstream. Without some kind of self-imposed cultural boundaries, there would be virtually no colonial heritage language education in the United States today, notwithstanding the huge numbers (relative to total population size) that were once involved in heritage language education and the obvious governmental, commercial, and cultural value of these languages for America's own well-being. This fact is well worth keeping in mind as we turn next to the immigrant languages and their associated heritage language efforts.

Immigrant Heritage Languages

How can we hope for a national agenda on immigrant heritage language education—one that supports the acquisition, retention, and active use of immigrant languages in private and public life—when we consider the sad experiences of indigenous and colonial heritage language maintenance? The colonial languages lacked the assets of the indigenous languages (primum mobile and mainstream guilt), but at least three of them enjoyed the advantages of huge numbers and worldwide utility. In contrast, most immigrant languages have lacked even these advantages, although the major ones—French, German, Spanish, Italian, Polish, and Yiddish—claimed around one million or more speakers in the United States during almost all of the 20th century. Whether widely spoken or not, immigrant languages have rarely been regarded as a national resource, and for the most part have suffered the same sad fate here that immigrant languages typically suffer around the world. Even so, as a testament to the human spirit, the immigrant languages, large and small, have refused to fade quietly away. The determination of immigrants to develop and maintain heritage language schools for their children should have been documented by the U.S. Department of Education or by the separate state departments of education. However, as far as these official agencies were concerned, no such schools have existed, unless they have been cited for lack of bathrooms, windows, or fire escapes.

Already in the late 19th and early 20th centuries, when immigration to the United States was still in full swing, heritage language schools made important contributions to American education and the development of education-related laws. Among the most instructive benchmark languages to follow in those early days is German, not only because it was for so long the largest immigrant language in the United States, and of major importance in the world at large (particularly in the areas of science, commerce, and diplomacy), but also because it was one of the most controversial. In 1886, the German American writer K. W. Wolfradt published a study showing that in the United States 280,000 children were studying German in 2,066 German ethnic heritage elementary schools (cited in Kloss, 1966, p. 234). That these figures are not out of line is clear from the Commissioner of Education's 1902 Report of the year 1900–1901 (Viereck, 1902, cited in Kloss, 1966, p. 234), which notes that that there were 3,984 such schools with 318,000 students. In addition to the above, the number of public elementary schools that taught German also grew during this period because a large proportion of their students were of German immigrant extraction. By the end of the 19th century, as public schools rapidly multiplied and spread, particularly throughout the Midwest, the number of schools that taught German and that were officially German–English bilingual public elementary schools began to equal the number of nonpublic ethnic heritage schools. The legal basis for such public elementary schools was explicitly incorporated into state education law in many states. An example is the Nebraska education law of 1913, just before the outbreak of World War I, which permitted such bilingual public schools to be established (in English plus any other language) when requests to do so were received from the parents of 50 pupils in urban areas.

German is also a good example of how U.S. foreign policy and other national interests can affect heritage language education. World War I led to such severe antiforeigner (and particularly anti-German) propaganda that many ethnic heritage schools were closed, both voluntarily and by state directives.

Legislation against foreign language instruction, aimed particularly at the elementary education level, both public and private, was passed. *Meyer vs. Nebraska* (1924, 262, US 390) is the U.S. Supreme Court decision that overthrew such legislation, on the grounds that it constituted unjustified state intrusion into the educational preferences of parents and the professional freedom of teachers to practice a legally certified occupation. The Nebraska state government's argument that early exposure to a living foreign language was injurious to the national loyalty and to the intellectual development of children was explicitly rejected by the Supreme Court as contrary to reason and unsupported by evidence. Thus, Nebraska lawmakers and German educators were involved in both the high and low points of ethnic heritage education in the United States. Although the Supreme Court came to the rescue of parents and teachers in connection with the constitutionality of ethnic heritage language education, the atmosphere was already poisoned. We did not fully recover for another quarter century, when minority civil rights were more positively located on the national agenda.

Before the Ethnic Revival

It was my good luck to come of age as a sociolinguistic researcher in the late 1950s and early 1960s, just when the Sputnik scare moved various federal agencies to recognize that heritage languages might make an important contribution to the national interest, even important enough, it turned out, for some funding to be directed toward trying to understand just how much of a resource these languages constituted, at individual and institutional levels. As a result, I was able to undertake a national study to determine by myself what the government had studiously ignored. This 1960–1963 study (Fishman, 1966) was the first modern call to conserve and foster our nation's heritage language resources by developing capacity in the various heritage languages before they were assimilated out of existence. I located 1,885 ethnic community schools operating in dozens of different languages, most of them Southern and Eastern European. Undoubtedly, there were several hundred more that I had failed to uncover or that had hidden from me, in fear of government-related probing during what were still the McCarthyite Cold War years. I cannot say that any public agency was really interested in my research, other than the FBI, which paid me a visit to see if any of these schools were communist dominated. When I replied that I hadn't the slightest idea, nor would I ever have, I lost the FBI's interest as well.

After the Ethnic Revival

From 1980 through 1983, the National Science Foundation, the National Institute of Education (now the Office of Educational Research and Improvement), and the National Endowment for the Humanities all demonstrated that the argument of my 1966 book—that heritage languages were a national resource that should be preserved and encouraged—had finally gotten through, at least to those organizations. They enabled me to repeat and extend my study of nearly 20 years earlier (Fishman, 1985). By then, I was both a more experienced and a better-known researcher. I knew where to look for heritage language schools, and, perhaps, some of them understood by then that I was a trustworthy researcher as well. Perhaps even more important, this took place after the ethnic revival of the mid- to late-1960s, and by then heritage language schools were a more self-confident breed. They were being maintained by a younger generation of advocates who were more secure in their own ethno-American identities. Although I identified 6,553 schools at that time (1985, pp. 243–244), I still had the impression that there were 1,000 or more that I had not located. Once more I felt the need for a stable government interest that would realize the value of up-to-date files, and I happily deposited mine at the National Clearinghouse for Bilingual Education in the hope that such interest would materialize. Alas, that was not to be. Like all files, the longer my school data just sat there, the less useful they became, as schools moved, closed, and changed addresses, programs, and affiliations. To my knowledge, that was the last nationwide study of heritage language schools in the United States. Just as the second study came 20 years after the first, so another 20 years is about to elapse since the second. A new benchmark study would now be extremely welcome. With what other national resource would we wait 20 years to find out its status? It is my hope that a call for such an updated benchmark study will go out from our ranks and reach the ears of those who are concerned that we maximize, rather than trivialize, our country's heritage language resources.

The Early 1980s

The more than 6,500 heritage language schools that I located in the early 1980s, all of them outside of the public sector, involved 145 languages, 91 of which were Amerindian, with Chinese, French, German (including Pennsylvania German), Greek, Hebrew, Italian, Japanese, Korean, Polish, Portuguese, Spanish, Ukrainian, and Yiddish accounting for approximately 90% of the total number of schools. Note that Asian languages had become nationally important for the first time, as a result of the rise of legal immigration from China and South Asia after World War II. The century's "big six" languages (French, German, Italian, Polish, Spanish, and Yiddish) were all present and prominent in the ranks of heritage language school sponsors. Every state in the Union was represented. Another noteworthy finding was the high correlation between the number of schools associated with any particular language and the number of local religious units (churches, mosques, synagogues, and temples) associated with that language, giving us a clear insight into what has thus far been the major and most durable support for heritage language schooling in the United States.

One other point about our heritage language schools in the early 1980s bears mentioning: They varied greatly as to the amount of time spent on language instruction per se. Day schools (about a quarter of the total) both devoted most time to language study and most frequently used their heritage languages as media for other areas of substantive instruction. Those schools with the longest curriculum (again, the day schools) also tended to claim a higher proportion of graduating students who spoke the language moderately well or better (which only a third or so of the responding schools claimed). The 1960 to 1980 growth rate for heritage language schools was 228%, compared to a growth rate of 63% for public schools and 24% for Catholic schools as a whole. Clearly, the heritage language schools constituted an educational sector whose social significance goes beyond heritage language instruction. Has their rate of growth continued? Has their image as successful transmitters of heritage languages improved? What would be the roughly equivalent number of years of study needed in public high schools in these languages to reach the level of moderate spoken facility or better? These would be important questions to answer if we have in mind following the recent Australian model of providing public high school credit for heritage language study (Fishman, 1991, pp. 262–269).

Can the Two Worlds Be Bridged?

Thus far, we have perused heritage language study, particularly since the end of World War II, as if it were totally unrelated to the world of public school language study. The last large-scale link between public schools and heritage language education that we have examined pertained to the study of German before World War I. In recent years, however, there have been two other links between heritage language education and the public schools. The first pertains to Spanish. The second pertains to a longish list of smaller heritage language groups that have succeeded in establishing links and cooperative programs with local public school authorities, often doing so with more success than the Spanish groups did. Let us look at both of these attempts to bridge what would otherwise be two isolated worlds, heritage language schools and public schools, taking first the case of Spanish in American elementary and secondary school education.

Spanish in the 1990s

It took decades before it was recognized that Spanish was the most popular foreign language in American high schools and colleges, effectively replacing French and all but obliterating German in most departmental offerings (Huber, 1996). A good proportion of Spanish language students (estimates as high as 25% beyond the first year of study seem reasonable) already speak Spanish, and certainly understand it, when they show up in our mainstream classrooms. Efforts are being made to develop special teacher training programs to cope more adequately with these students (many of whom speak Spanish more fluently but less "correctly" than their teachers); to prepare appropriate curricula, lesson plans, and course materials for them; and, above all, to keep our attention focused on the important community roles and responsibilities that these students and their parents play in relation to the future of Spanish in their own lives and in the commercial, diplomatic, intellectual, and cultural life of the country as a whole.

Although various parallels exist with German in the late 19th and early 20th centuries, there are many differences as well. There is no huge religious sector backing Spanish now, as there once was for German, the Catholic Church having become a more mainstream American (and less immigrant) church. Indeed, there may be fewer community-maintained Spanish heritage language schools today than there were in 1980, when there were around 250, and incomparably fewer than existed for German a century ago. Latinos have been incorporated into the American public school system so fully that they may have neglected cultural institutions of their own. Dependent on the American school system for Spanish language education, Latino parents have not organized to push for more suitable Spanish courses for their native (or near-native, quasi-native, or submerged-native) Spanish-speaking children. Furthermore, unlike most German-speaking parents in the last century, Spanish-speaking parents frequently have low literacy skills. This affects their comfort level in negotiating with school authorities for more appropriate courses for their children; questions regarding their legal status serve to further complicate the situation. Finally, low literacy within the Latino speech community reflects negatively on the entire image of Spanish in American society. Rather than being viewed as the literary and standardized language that it has been for centuries, Spanish is widely viewed as the dialectally splintered and socially stigmatized language of lower-class illiterates. As a result, it is severely undervalued as a language resource. For the sake of the entire country's enrichment, its New World dialects need to be recognized as legitimate, thereby fostering its grassroots and intergenerational maintenance. This type of attention (involving appropriate instructional programs, placement, and evaluation) is only just beginning to be seriously pondered.

Other Heritage Languages and the American Public School

The picture is somewhat different on the middle-class side of the heritage language street, whether the languages involved pertain to more visible or less visible minorities. I first became aware that something new was afoot in 1956, when I became a research associate (and later vice president for research) at the College Entrance Examination Board. The first test development project to which I was assigned was an English language listening test, and the second was an achievement test for Hebrew. The latter was requested by community groups fostering Hebrew as a heritage language, both in the public high schools and in private heritage language schools, most of which were attached to local synagogues or other religious organizations. Students studying in all-day schools (Yeshivas) were exposed to the language (or to its closely related cousin, Judeo-Aramaic) through the intensive study of religious classical texts, everyday, for many hours, for a period of 8 to 12 years. For some of the students, Hebrew was also the medium of instruction in their other Judaic studies. Public high school (and, more rarely, public elementary school) students were exposed to the language only through secular texts and topics, for far fewer hours per day, and for far fewer years of study. Since both groups of students had to be tested for their Hebrew language achievement in connection with college entrance, a variety of different language testing instruments, as well as different sets of norms, had to be prepared to accommodate students of widely different educational and community backgrounds. That was my first experience in dealing with differing community profiles in connection with heritage vernacular and heritage classical languages.

Since then, other middle-class groups have succeeded in convincing public school and college authorities to recognize their respective heritage languages in one way or another. In Palo Alto, California, next door to Stanford University, heritage language schools teach Arabic, Chinese, Japanese, and Korean, as well as French, German, Hebrew, Persian, and Spanish. Some of these schools meet (rent-free or at nominal cost) in public school or university quarters. The students who attend these heritage language courses for a specified number of years can receive high school foreign language credit for doing so. In many cases, they can also be examined on College Entrance Examination Board tests for college admission, and then they can complete or go beyond their college's foreign language requirement by taking further courses in their heritage language. In many cases (particularly where Japanese and Korean are concerned), the parents of these students are literate in the heritage languages involved. The standardized varieties of these languages are, therefore, part of the home heritage that students bring to their language study. Dialect versus standard and classical versus vernacular problems may be more common for Arabic and Chinese, but in those cases, too, community heritage language schools are commonly available to students before their graduation from high school. Although none of these cases has been researched (let alone researched well), the contrasts between these languages and Spanish as a heritage language—with respect to both school–community cooperation and community profiles (parental income, education, and exposure to literacy in their own standard varieties)—need to be fully appreciated.

Conclusion

If we want to foster the language resources of our country, we cannot do so by dealing only with the smaller and relatively problem-free cases. Other languages will come and go as catastrophes continue to plague different parts of the globe. (Witness the influx of speakers of Albanian, Arabic, Bosnian, Croatian, Kurdish, Persian, Russian, Ukrainian, and Vietnamese, just to mention several recently arriving languages.) However, our geographic location is the best guarantee that while other languages may come and go (most Kosovar Albanians, for example, are now returning to their homeland), Spanish will keep on arriving on our shores forever. We must face up to this opportunity quickly, constructively, and inventively. We in the United States are now more multilingual than we have been for quite a while. We are perhaps even more so than we were in the latter part of the 19th century, when European immigration was at its height and 10% of the white population was German speaking, even though further mass immigration from Germany had already ended.

The goal of promoting heritage language proficiency will revitalize our entire approach to non-English language instruction. It will not only give us more individuals proficient in these languages, it will also dignify our country's heritage language communities and the cultural and religious values that their languages represent. It will help language instruction to connect with cultural and intellectual creativity, which it has often been speciously distant from. It will help connect instruction with business and governmental needs for expertise in the languages involved. Finally, it will help us break out of the penumbras of fear and contention that English-only and anti-bilingual education policies have cast on heritage languages, as Valdés (1995) has pointed out. These languages will be brought into the scholarly and professional orbits of our schools and colleges, away from the battlefield that public elementary and secondary bilingual education has become, in large part because of the ties to poverty and politics that heritage languages are perceived to have. We all embrace English and accept its crucial importance in this country. But our country and our educational systems also have other needs—in science and in math, in history and in literature, in world consciousness and in world sensitivity. We desperately need competence in languages—to become "a language competent society," in Tucker's phrase (1991)—and our huge and varied heritage language resources have a definite role to play in achieving such competence.

Along with the contributions that industry, government, and language teaching are already making in this connection, we must find and refine the ways and means of bringing these heritage languages into the educational "main tent," where our national well-being is given its most serious attention and most ample support. This will not be easy to do because we have shamelessly neglected our heritage languages for far too long. However, we are beginning the intellectual, tactical, pedagogical, and organizational struggle to give these languages the support they deserve, and we may well be remembered by posterity for having done so.

References

Cantoni, G. (Ed.). (1996). *Stabilizing indigenous languages.* Flagstaff, AZ: Northern Arizona University, Center for Excellence in Education.

Clyne, M. (1991). *Community language.* Cambridge, UK: Cambridge University Press.

Fishman, J.A. (1966). *Language loyalty in the United States.* The Hague, Netherlands: Mouton.

Fishman, J.A. (1985). *The rise and fall of the ethnic revival.* Berlin: Mouton de Gruyter.

Fishman, J.A. (1991). *Reversing language shift: Theoretical and empirical foundations of assistance to threatened languages.* Clevedon, UK: Multilingual Matters.

Hinton, L. (1994). *Flutes of fire: Essays on Califonia Indian languages.* Berkeley, CA: Heyday Press.

Huber, B.J. (1996). Variation in foreign language enrollments through time (1970-1990). *ADFL Bulletin, 27*(2), 57-84.

Kloss, H. (1966). German-American language maintenance efforts. In J.A. Fishman (Ed.), *Language loyalty in the United States.* The Hague, Netherlands: Mouton.

McCarty, T.L., Watahomigie, L.J., & Yamamoto, A.Y. (Eds.). (1999). Reversing language shift in indigenous America [Special issue]. *Practicing Anthropology, 21*(2).

McCarty, T.L., Yamamoto, A., Watahomigie, L.J., & Zepeda, O. (1997). In J. Reyhner (Ed.), *Teaching indigenous languages: Proceedings of the 1997 Stabilizing Indigenous Languages Conference* (pp. 85-104). Flagstaff, AZ: Northern Arizona University, Center for Excellence in Education.

McCarty, T.L., & Zepeda, O. (Eds.). (1998). Indigenous language use and change in the Americas [Special issue]. *International Journal of the Sociology of Language, 132.*

Reyhner, J. (Ed.). (1997). *Teaching indigenous languages: Proceedings of the 1997 Stabilizing Indigenous Languages Conference.* Flagstaff, AZ: Northern Arizona University, Center for Excellence in Education.

Reyhner, J. (Ed.) (1998). *Revitalizing indigenous languages: Proceedings of the 1998 Stablilizing Indigenous Languages Conference.* Flagstaff, AZ: Northern Arizona University, Center for Excellence in Education.

Tucker, G.R. (1991). Developing a language competent American society: The role of language planning. In A.G. Reynolds (Ed.), *Bilingualism, multilingualism, and second language learning.* Hillsdale, NJ: Lawrence Erlbaum.

Valdés, G. (1995). The teaching of minority languages as "foreign languages": Pedagogical and theoretical challenges. *Modern Language Journal, 79,* 299-328.

Viereck, L. (1902). *German instruction in American schools. Report of the Commissioner of Education for 1900-01* (pp. 531-708). Washington, DC: U.S. Government Printing Office.

Wolfradt, K.W. (1886). Die Statistik des Deutsch-Amerikanischen Schulwessens. *Deutscher Pionier, 18,* 50-55.

5
Policy Formation and Implementation

Terrence G. Wiley
Arizona State University

From a public policy perspective, the effort to maintain and develop heritage languages poses a number of challenges. Historically, this effort has largely been left to the resources and desires of heritage communities. Throughout much of U.S. history, given the dominance and spread of English, there has been a three-generation shift to English among immigrant groups (Veltman, 1983). The historic pattern among immigrant language groups has been for the first generation to acquire some English but remain dominant in the native tongue; the second generation to become bilingual but with more highly developed language and literacy skills in English; and the third generation to be English speaking with little functional ability in the language of their grandparents. In recent decades, there is some evidence that the shift to English is occurring more rapidly among some immigrant populations.

In the United States, as in other countries with histories of large immigrant populations, the discussion of heritage language maintenance and development has largely focused on immigrants, despite the presence of indigenous language groups. The English-speaking majority in this country has often viewed the loss of heritage languages as a kind of rite of passage into the dominant culture (see Kloss, 1971). Obviously, this view should be antithetical to a nation that prides itself on its diversity and on the preservation of individual liberties.

This chapter reviews the historical role of state and federal governments and local communities in heritage language preservation efforts. It looks at the impact of different government policies on these efforts and recommends a bottom-up, community-based approach to program development that takes advantage of government support when it is available and is closely attuned to local sociolinguistic realities.

The Role of the State and Federal Governments

The role of state and federal governments in the formation of heritage language policies is an area of contention. The implications of federal bilingual education policy for heritage language instruction, for example, have been the subject of considerable disagreement and misunderstanding. Some opponents of federally and state-funded bilingual education believe its goal is what Noel Epstein (1977) called "affirmative ethnicity" (promoting languages other than English or cultures considered to be outside the American mainstream), and contend that it is improper for the government to promote any single language other than English. On the opposite side of the issue, some bilingual education advocates have criticized federal policy and federal transitional bilingual education programs in particular for being instruments of a "monolingual policy with the goal of Anglification" (Ruíz, 1995, p. 78; see also Lyons, 1995).

To understand the current policy environment for speakers of heritage languages, we need to understand the historical experiences of different groups of heritage language speakers. In his groundbreaking study of language policy in the United States, Kloss (1977/1998) observed that in response to heritage languages the government can take several policy stances— promotion, accommodation, tolerance, or suppression. According to Kloss, the U.S. government has typically neither promoted nor suppressed heritage languages, preferring instead a laissez-faire position of tolerance: Communities that have the resources and the desire to maintain their ancestral languages may do so without government interference—but without its help, either.

This position has varied from time to time and from group to group. The U.S. government's position toward the languages of European immigrants has generally been one of tolerance, Kloss concluded. One notable exception to this tendency occurred in the World War I era, when speakers of German and other languages were persecuted, and most states removed or restricted German in the curriculum (Toth, 1990; Wiley, 1998). A few years after the war, however, in a constitutional test of language rights, *Farrington v. Tokushige* (1927), the U.S. Supreme Court affirmed the right to promote heritage language instruction through private and community-based efforts (Wiley & Valdés, 2000).

With federal funding for Title VII transitional bilingual programs, implemented in the late 1960s, the federal government's position toward some heritage languages shifted to accommodation. Since the late 1970s, however, English-only critics of bilingual education have attacked federally funded programs, viewing them as promoting other languages over English. In California, the country's most linguistically diverse state, English-only legislation has severely restricted transitional bilingual education programs.

If tolerance was the predominant stance toward European immigrant languages, the experience of Native Americans was marked by overt attempts to eradicate their languages and cultures, especially in the late 19th and early 20th centuries, when the federal government prohibited the use of Native American languages in government-run Native American boarding schools. Other groups, such as speakers of Hawaiian, experienced a similar fate (Benham & Heck, 1998).

In recent years, an important symbolic shift in policy has occurred for Hawaiian and Native American languages. Since 1978, Hawaiian has been an official language, along with English, in Hawaii, and in 1987, the State Board of Education approved a pilot proposal for Hawaiian medium schools. Despite the vicissitudes of state support and retrenchment, Wilson (1999) concludes,

> The overall effect of the various Hawaiian language programmes established by law has been very significant if only to greatly increase the number of people who can speak Hawaiian and the involvement of Hawaiians in the public schools system. . . . Furthermore, against all odds and albeit still at a rudimentary level, a new population that speaks Hawaiian as its dominant language, at least in some circumstances, has been created and is growing. (pp. 106-107)

For indigenous languages in general, noteworthy policy shifts have occurred at the federal level. In 1990, the federal government passed the Native American Languages Act, which emphasizes the uniqueness and value of indigenous languages and the responsibility of the government to redress its past attempts to exterminate them (Schiffman, 1996). Schiffman has taken a dim view of the passage of this act, concluding that it was mostly a case of "locking the barn door after the horse" had been stolen, because "now that Native-American languages are practically extinct, and pose no threat to anyone anywhere, we can grant them special status" (p. 91). However, McCarty and Watahomigie (1999) take a more optimistic view of the Native American Languages Act. They conclude that although funding for educational programs has been meager, it has "supported some of the boldest new attempts at language renewal" (p. 91). They add,

> Indigenous language education programmes are not the only resource that can be marshaled in this effort. But, given the immensity of the language-loss crisis, they and their personnel constitute critical assets which cannot be overlooked. Cultivating these assets is a process that *can* be influenced by external institutions. (p. 91)

McCarty and Watahomigie cite a number of successful indigenous language programs that have been implemented with federal bilingual education funding (see McCarty & Watahomigie, 1999, for elaboration).

Ruíz (1995) also sees some cause for optimism, despite problems with official policy. "If, in fact, federally funded bilingual education programs in American Indian communities have served purposes of language renewal and reversal of language shift, it is testimony to the ingenuity and dedication of staffs of these programs, not the policy itself" (p. 79). Given the history of language policies related to Native Americans, Ruíz suggests that policies supporting bilingual education should be developed now to counteract the possibility that government efforts might restrict federal bilingual education programs in the future. He argues that "language policy planning decisions made now will help communities achieve the continuity of tradition that has served them well up to now" (1995, p. 79).

Endoglossic and Exoglossic Language Policies

In his critique of federal bilingual education policy, Ruíz (1995) makes a distinction among *endoglossic*, *exoglossic*, and *mixed* language policies. "Endoglossic policies are those that give primacy to and promote an indigenous language of the community" (p. 75), while exoglossic policies promote languages of wider communication. Mixed policies attempt to promote both.

Ruíz characterizes this nation's federal bilingual education policy as exoglosssic, given its emphasis on promoting English. In the United States, unlike some countries, indigenous and immigrant languages are local and regional and do not serve as languages of wider communication. Policies that support community-based language education are the most likely to achieve the goal of revitalizing endangered indigenous heritage languages, while exoglossic policies could promote the learning of languages such as Spanish for wider communication. Exoglossic policies have been used in Europe to promote the use of specific languages in the European Economic Community (EEC). Thus far, there have been no programs to promote Spanish as a language of the North American Free Trade Agreement (NAFTA), even though Mexico is a major partner in the agreement.

The Need for Well-Informed Heritage Language Policies

For those concerned about the loss of proficiency in languages other than English in the United States, public policy endorsements and initiatives to promote heritage language development are welcome (Fishman, 1991). However, as Horvath and Vaughn (1991) have argued, unless those who make and implement policies consider the "possible ways in which languages can vary sociolinguistically, misunderstandings can result" (p. 2). Citing an Australian example, they describe how a well-intended effort to promote community languages backfired:

> An Egyptian teacher was hired to teach Lebanese children; although Egypt and Lebanon are both Arabic-speaking countries, the spoken languages of these two speech communities are not mutually intelligible although the formal spoken and written language is. So much for starting with the language that the children speak. Administrators quickly learned that Serbo-Croatian was not a single language; Croatians are particularly adamant that their language is separate and distinct from Serbian no matter what the linguists might have to say about it. Suddenly, the Anglo-Celtic population was shocked to learn that most of the Italian migrants did not speak Italian; they spoke "dialect." (p. 3)

Similar examples of mismatch between the assumptions of policymakers and program implementers, on the one hand, and the perceptions of language learners, on the other, have occurred in the United States, where some school districts have recruited teachers of Spanish from Spain to instruct Mexican and Central American immigrant children whose community language varieties vary greatly from those of their teachers.

These examples underscore the importance of understanding the sociolinguistic profiles of the heritage communities to be served as well as the language attitudes and social judgments of those in the majority language community toward their own and related language varieties. Several ways of categorizing heritage languages have been recommended to develop these profiles. They include the social uses and functions of the languages, their historical development, and their relationship to other language varieties (Horvath & Vaughn, 1991).

In order to formulate a viable heritage language policy, the sociolinguistic context of a given heritage language must be understood, particularly as it relates to the dominant language(s) of wider communication. For example, "If we start with a language, e.g., Welsh, and describe only its history or dialect variants, we might fail to notice that most if not all speakers of Welsh also speak English, and it is likely that English would be the dominant language for most" (Horvath & Vaughn, 1991, p. 8). In the United States, many Spanish–English bilinguals likewise have greater facility in English. Thus, when designing programs for heritage language speakers of Spanish or other languages in the United States, it is necessary to attempt to compensate for the stronger linguistic vitality of English (see Baker, 2001, for a discussion of *linguistic vitality*).

In some communities, heritage languages may include language varieties that are mutually intelligible with a written standard that also serves as the language of schooling, but in other communities, the spoken form and the written standard may differ greatly. Historically, immigrants to the United States

105

from Germany and Italy spoke regional dialects, some of which were closer to the national standard of the source countries than others. Proficiency in the national standard tended to correlate with access to and success in formal schooling. For members of these communities, formal schooling in the standard language variety provided a means to maintain linkages with the prestige variety but not always with the community variety of the language.

Similar issues exist among contemporary U.S. populations. Regarding the issue of which variety of a heritage language should be taught in school, the tendency is to teach the school standard, which may vary greatly from the variety of home and community. In some sociolinguistic contexts, the discrepancies are pronounced, and the results unfortunate. For example, a third-generation descendent of Chinese ancestors who studies Mandarin is not necessarily in a better position to communicate with her Cantonese-speaking grandmother than she was before she studied the language.

Conclusion

For those committed to the maintenance and development of heritage languages, history suggests that the best strategy is to use government policies to promote heritage languages during favorable times and to rely on community-based efforts over the long term. As Hornberger (1997) and McCarty & Watahomigie (1999) argue, there is a role for externally supported programs and top-down policies as long as they are supported by bottom-up efforts in the home and community.

References

Baker, C. (2001). *Foundations of bilingual education and bilingualism* (3rd ed.). Clevedon, UK: Multilingual Matters.

Benham, M.K.P., & Heck, R.H. (1998). *Culture and educational policy in Hawai'i: The silencing of native voices*. Mahwah, NJ: Lawrence Erlbaum.

Epstein, N. (1977). *Language, ethnicity, and the schools*. Washington, DC: Institute for Educational Leadership.

Farrington, Governor of Hawaii v. Tokushige, 273 U.S. 284, 298 (1927).

Fishman, J.A. (1991). *Reversing language shift*. Clevedon, UK: Multilingual Matters.

Hornberger, N.H. (1997). Language planning from the bottom up. In N.H. Hornberger (Ed.), *Indigenous literacies in the Americas: Language planning from the bottom up* (pp. 357-66). Berlin: Mouton de Gruyter.

Horvath, B.M., & Vaughn, P. (1991). *Community languages: A handbook*. Clevedon, UK: Multilingual Matters.

Kloss, H. (1971). Language rights of immigrant groups. *International Migration Review, 5*, 250-268.

Kloss, H. (1998). *The American bilingual tradition*. McHenry, IL, and Washington, DC: Delta Systems and Center for Applied Linguistics. (Original work published 1977)

Lyons, J. (1995). The past and future directions of federal bilingual-education policy. In O. García & C. Baker (Eds.), *Policy and practice in bilingual education: Extending the foundations* (pp. 1-15). Clevedon, UK: Multilingual Matters. (Reprinted from *Annals of the American Academy of Political and Social Sciences 508*, pp. 66-80, 1990)

McCarty, T.L., & Watahomigie, L.J. (1999). Indigenous community-based language education in the USA. In S. May (Ed.), *Indigenous community-based education* (pp. 79-94). Clevedon, UK: Multilingual Matters.

Ruíz, R. (1995). Language planning considerations in indigenous communities. *Bilingual Research Journal, 19*(1), 71-81.

Schiffman, H. (1996). *Linguistic culture and language policy*. London: Routledge.

Toth, C.R. (1990). *German–English bilingual schools in America: The Cincinnati tradition in historical context*. New York: Peter Lang.

Veltman, F. (1983). *Language shift in the United States.* Berlin: Mouton.

Wiley, T.G. (1998). The imposition of World War I English-Only policies and the fate of German in North America. In T. Ricento & B. Burnaby (Eds.), *Language and politics in the United States and Canada* (pp. 211-241). Mahwah, NJ: Lawrence Erlbaum.

Wiley, T.G., & Valdés, G. (2000). Editors' introduction: Heritage language instruction in the United States: A time for renewal. *Bilingual Research Journal, 24*(4), iii-vi. Retrieved July 2001 from http://brj .asu.edu/v244/articles/ar1.html

Wilson, W.H. (1999). The sociopolitical context of establishing Hawaiian-medium education. In S. May (Ed.), *Indigenous community-based education* (pp. 95-108). Clevedon, UK: Multilingual Matters.

6
Professional Opportunities for Heritage Language Speakers

María Carreira, California State University, Long Beach
Regla Armengol, Center for Applied Linguistics

3.9   Average number of languages spoken by senior business executives in the Netherlands.

3.4   Average number spoken by senior business executives in Sweden.

2.6   Average number spoken by senior business executives in Japan.

1.5   Average number spoken by senior business executives in the United States.

(Southwest Airlines *Spirit*, October, 2000, p. 158)

While learning a second or third language has long been considered good for mental discipline and understanding of other cultures (Schultz, 1998), the expansion of the global community and marketplace has made proficiency in languages other than English a necessity rather than a luxury. As the demand for skilled multilingual professionals continues to skyrocket, the United States faces the challenge of producing a workforce that not only communicates in many languages, but also understands the nuances of many cultures.

One solution to this demand is to look to speakers of heritage languages and to consider the sophisticated expertise in language and knowledge of culture that they bring to the professional arena. Many have developed a level of language proficiency and depth of cultural understanding that would be difficult to replicate in even the most advanced second language learner. Moreover, proficiency in more than one language expands thinking, improves the ability to understand the views and values of others, and promotes creativity and productivity (Curtain & Pesola, 1994). Employers who value workers able to see problems from multiple perspectives and communicate with clients and colleagues from other cultures may view heritage language speakers as an excellent source of skills not easily found in our society.

This chapter looks at the professional opportunities that our rapidly changing economy now offers to individuals proficient in two or more languages. It provides a representative, rather than an exhaustive, survey of these opportunities, focusing on those professions with a demonstrated critical need for a multilingual workforce. Naturally, languages with large communities of speakers such as Spanish, Mandarin, and Cantonese afford a greater range of professional opportunities than those with fewer numbers of speakers, and it is on these languages that we focus our discussion. Less commonly spoken languages, however, can provide excellent opportunities for employment in areas where concentrated groups of such speakers can be found. Moreover, in some sectors of government it is in the less commonly spoken languages that the need for proficiency is most urgent (Brecht & Rivers, 2000).

Professional Needs and Opportunities

Nearly every sector of our increasingly global economy and culturally diverse workforce needs multilingual, cross-culturally aware workers. This chapter explores those sectors where the needs and opportunities are greatest—in government, business, media and communications, the performing arts, healthcare, and education.

Government

Heritage language speakers possess a range of linguistic skills that are critically needed by the government, both within the nation and abroad. As Brecht and Rivers (2000) note in their analysis of U.S. language needs and national security, "Globalization, democratization, and sole superpower status have imposed on the United States a range and scale of language needs that are unprecedented in the country's history" (p. 119).

As the largest employer of professionals whose work includes foreign language use, the federal government has a rapidly expanding need for professionals who speak a wide range of foreign languages (Brecht & Rivers, 2000). The work of 67 federal agencies depends in part on proficiency in more than 100 languages. At the Department of Defense alone, roughly 30,000 jobs require language proficiency in some 70 languages. Other departments and agencies with a rapidly rising demand for professionals proficient in languages other than English include the Department of State, the Department of Justice, the CIA, the Department of Health and Human Services, the Department of Treasury, the Department of Commerce, the National Security Agency, and the Library of Congress. Many of these departments and agencies have been unable to meet their foreign language needs, especially in the less commonly taught languages. At the Federal Bureau of Investigation, for example, the shortage is particularly acute in Arabic, Chinese, Farsi, Japanese, Korean, Russian, Spanish, Turkish, and Vietnamese (Margaret Gulotta, personal communication, January 10, 2001).

So critical is the demand for foreign language proficiency that some government agencies offer special incentives to individuals who are proficient in more than one language. Department of Defense agencies offer incentive pay for linguists, and applicants to the FBI greatly improve their chances of being hired for some positions if they are proficient in a language other than English (John Tolarski, personal communication, January 8, 2001).

The demand for foreign language proficiency in state and local governments is also great. The need is especially critical in law enforcement. Police officers able to communicate with an increasingly diverse population are essential to successful law enforcement in many areas of the nation. Like many other police departments around the country, the Los Angeles Police Department (LAPD) suffers a shortage of trained bilingual personnel. In order to recruit more such workers, the LAPD offers an incentive of a 2.75% salary increase for officers who speak Spanish or one of a number of Asian languages, with a 5% increase for officers who can also demonstrate reading and writing abilities in these languages (Hillary Rappe, personal communication, January 19, 2001).

Court interpreters are also in great demand throughout the country. Currently, California's courts use eight languages: Arabic, Cantonese, Japanese, Korean, Portuguese, Spanish, Tagalog, and Vietnamese. The state has witnessed a rise in the use of these languages recently, and plans to add five more languages—Armenian, Cambodian, Mandarin Chinese, Punjabi, and Russian ("2000 Language Need," 2000). Through the California Judicial Council, the state is working with schools and universities to create more educational opportunities for bilingual students interested in careers in judicial interpreting (Weinstein & Liu, 2000).

In Arizona, New Mexico, and Utah, where Navajo-speaking victims, defendants, and witnesses need interpreters in 30% to 40% of court cases, there is a shortage of bilingual professionals proficient enough in both languages to translate cultural and linguistic nuances and to handle highly specialized material ("Language, Culture Create Need," 2000).

Business

The business sector reports a greater need than ever for individuals with highly developed skills in two or more languages. *The San Francisco Examiner* notes,

The inability to find skilled workers is costing U.S. companies millions in potential revenue, according to a survey of 300 executives . . . by Selected Appointments North America. . . . When asked which skill was most lacking, 43 percent cited foreign language skills, followed by technical (15 percent), creativity (13 percent), and problem solving [skills] (13 percent). ("Companies worry," 1998)

The need for language skills in business is well illustrated by considering the specific need for Spanish language skills. As Kraul (2000), writing in *The Los Angeles Times,* reports,

Countless U.S. companies are feeling the Latino talent pinch, not only to staff their operations in Mexico and Central and South America, but to serve the 35-million-strong Latino market at home, a sector whose population, purchasing power and businesses are growing faster than that of the U.S. as a whole. (p. B1)

The shortage of Spanish-speaking workers will undoubtedly become more acute as some of this nation's largest corporations invest significant resources to attract the lucrative Hispanic market in the United States. As these efforts proliferate, they create a rich and complex infrastructure of goods and services in Spanish.

In a sign of the vital importance of the U.S. Hispanic market, *Selecciones*, Reader's Digest's Spanish language version, announced recently that it is revamping its content and format to make the magazine more relevant to this population ("Reader's Digest Seeks," 2001). In a similar move, in November 2000, HBO launched the Latino channel with a focus on the diversity of Latino culture in the United States (Vazquez, 2000).

Other large corporations are recognizing the importance of this market. Recently Procter & Gamble launched an advertising venture aimed at gaining Spanish-speaking consumers' trust, and as part of this effort, a new magazine, *Avanzando Con Tu Familia* (*Moving Ahead With Your Family*), was delivered to 4.5 million households (Artze, 1999). In 1998, Sears, Roebuck and Company spent about $25 million on advertising aimed at Hispanics. Sears was one of the first companies to market credit cards directly to Hispanics, an effort that helped it build a substantial U.S. database of Hispanic consumers. Sears's quarterly magazine, *Nuestra Gente* (*Our People*), which features articles about Hispanic celebrities alongside fashions, has a circulation of about 700,000. In the fall of 1998, Target Corporation launched *Familia*, its own magazine for Hispanics, sending it to 750,000 Hispanic households in California (Artze, 1999).

Many American companies are also expanding their Latino employee base as a strategy to attract a larger Hispanic market. US West, the telecommunications company, has a workforce that is 12% Hispanic and has a Mexican American CEO. Another company that is hiring Latinos to build Hispanic business is Allstate Insurance Company, which in 1995 formed the Hispanic Business Team, composed primarily of Hispanic employees. Since the formation of this team, Allstate has built a national network of 2,400 agencies serving customers in Spanish. It has published more than 300 Spanish language materials and instituted a national bilingual toll-free number.

With the globalization of business, individuals proficient in languages spoken in countries that the United States does business with are uniquely positioned to take advantage of their bilingual and bicultural skills. With a wide range of Spanish-speaking countries represented in this country, the United States is in a very real sense a microcosm of the entire Spanish-speaking world, and those who can communicate in this microcosm have distinct advantages in the global market. "Hispanic small businesses have a special role to play in Latin America with their familial and cultural connections," states Jorge Muñoz, former head of the U.S. government's Overseas

Private Investment Corporation (OPIC). "They have the right characteristics for globalization, and they are more flexible about meeting the needs of the foreign business" (Vidueira, 1999).

Naturally, these advantages are not confined to U.S. Hispanics. Susan Au Allen, president of the U.S. Pan-Asian American Chamber of Commerce, notes, "Minority-owned businesses often have the language ability, and the social and business connections to the countries abroad. . . . They could be key allies in developing products for these new markets and in building marketing infrastructures and alliances" (Lin, 2000). Wendy Cai, winner of the Asian Women in Business award for the year 2000, capitalizes on her knowledge of five Chinese dialects: "When I go to China, I'm able to participate in business meetings conducted in the local dialect. People in the room loosen up, and it makes negotiations much easier" (Chepesiuk, 2001).

From 1987 to 1997, Asian-owned businesses in the United States grew 180%. Since 1992, loans to Asian American businesses backed by the Small Business Administration increased more than 350% ("U.S. Business Group Launches," 2000). Despite this strong growth in Asian American business, Asian Americans remain underrepresented among the ranks of business owners. For this reason, several initiatives have recently been launched to increase Asian American participation in the business world. Asian Business Co-Op and the Asian American Association have undertaken two particularly noteworthy efforts. These organizations perform a wide range of important services, including providing training, facilitating loans, and storing a database of social and demographic trends vital to Asian American businessmen. (Contact information for these and other organizations can be found at the end of this chapter.)

The value of a multilingual, multicultural workforce is keenly felt in the area of marketing. A survey conducted in

1999 by Multicultural Marketers found that nearly all of the 45 firms that they surveyed had increased their efforts to market to ethnic consumers. Furthermore, these companies anticipated that their budgets for these efforts would increase by more than 10% over the next 5 years. The study notes that the ethnic media in general, and the Asian and Spanish media in particular, constitute an effective and essential way for American corporations to promote their products among immigrants (Skriloff, 2000).

Market research also reveals that Spanish language telemarketing and advertising represent an indispensable way for American companies to reach U.S. Hispanics. Indeed, marketing surveys have found that advertising movies to Hispanics in Spanish is even effective in promoting English language movies among this population (Romney & Eller, 2001). Creating promotional materials that are both appropriate and effective with U.S. Hispanics, however, is not a simple task. *The Hispanic Business Journal* reports, "Marketers are finding they cannot simply translate direct marketing materials from English to Spanish and expect the Hispanic consumer to respond. The information that marketers send to the Hispanic consumer through the mail has to sound authentic and should not be translated verbatim from English" (Artze, 2001).

Telemarketing companies that understand this country's ethnic communities and can communicate with them in culturally and linguistically authentic ways are in high demand. One such company is Asian American Telemarketing (ATT), a business that offers telemarketing services in six Asian languages (Mandarin, Cantonese, Japanese, Korean, Tagalog, and Vietnamese) and in English. Some of the Fortune 100 companies that rely on ATT for their ethnic needs include MCI, AT&T, Sprint, DHL, and AirTouch.

Media and Communications

As news media and communications companies continue to respond to demographic changes, the need for journalists in the United States who can communicate in languages other than English continues to grow. In order to move successfully into historically untapped markets, mass communications companies will have to expand their multilingual workforce.

Currently, many journalists working in the United States for Spanish language newspapers, television, and radio stations are imported from Latin America and Spain. However, Spanish language media organizations are all too aware of the limitations of foreign-educated journalists when it comes to covering local issues and communicating with U.S. Hispanics. According to Miriam Galicia Duarte, *La Opinion*—Los Angeles's largest, and the nation's oldest, Spanish language newspaper—wants to hire bilingual candidates who were raised and educated in Los Angeles and are familiar with local government and politics (personal communication, May 5, 2000).

The Spanish language news media and entertainment industries in the United States represent a burgeoning business. According to the Arbitron ratings service, more than 550 of America's 12,800 radio stations broadcast in Spanish, making it now possible to hear Spanish language radio in 44 states. Los Angeles' two major radio stations are Spanish language stations. The Spanish language network giants *Univisión* and *Telemundo,* seen by millions throughout the Spanish-speaking world and the United States, have their headquarters in Miami, as does the HBO Latin American Groups, the leading cable and satellite programming distributors in Latin America and the Caribbean (Lynch, 2000).

Newspapers in cities with a large Spanish-speaking population realize that they cannot survive without this group as a subscriber base. In 1997, *The Chicago Tribune* created *¡Exito!,* a

Spanish language weekly tabloid. Two years later *The Los Angeles Times* launched the Latino Initiative to increase its coverage of the area's Hispanic community (De Los Santos, March, 1999).

In addition to the news media, three industries with critical language needs stand out in the field of communications. These are the satellite and cable industries, Internet companies, and companies that provide over-the-phone interpreting and translation services.

Recent advances in communication technology have given satellite and cable companies the capacity to add international channels to their menus, thereby increasing their subscriptions among foreign language speakers in the United States. In 1999, more than 350 cable systems across the country launched foreign language channels targeting various subgroups of America's immigrant population. EchoStar's Dish Network currently offers more than 50 foreign language channels, including five channels in its South Asian package, five channels in Arabic, and extensive programming in Portuguese, Russian, and Serbo-Croatian. Hong Kong-based Phoenix Satellite offers Mandarin language programming from China, Taiwan, and Hong Kong catering to U.S. audiences (Romney, 2001). These and other efforts by cable companies to attract the lucrative immigrant market in the United States will create the need for a multilingual workforce that can understand and communicate with this market's various subgroups.

Companies, many of them mainstream American conglomerates, have come to understand that to be competitive in e-commerce they must be able to communicate in cyberspace in many languages. According to *Hispanic Business Magazine*, Miami is now the financial, business, and trade center of Latin America. It is also this region's capital of e-commerce (Reveron, 2001). *The Los Angeles Times* reports that the shortage of bilingual workers is particularly acute among Internet companies launching operations in Latin America. To attract workers, some Internet companies and businesses that specialize in e-commerce have raised salaries by as much as 50%. Even with recent downsizing trends among Internet companies, these businesses continue to reach out to individuals whose cultural and linguistic skills will help them develop their client base abroad. By all predictions, this trend will continue well into the future (Kraul, 2000).

More and more, American companies are relying on over-the-phone interpreting to meet their foreign language needs. With a workforce of more than 1,200 interpreters, AT&T LanguageLine, which offers interpreting in 140 languages, 7 days a week, 24 hours a day, is the world's largest provider of this service. This company employs a full-time workforce of hundreds of trained interpreters that provide over-the-phone services to some of this nation's largest companies in the fields of finance, healthcare, tourism, transportation, and law enforcement. LanguageLine reports an immediate need for interpreters in a number of languages, including Cantonese, Farsi, Haitian Creole, Hmong, Italian, Mandarin, and Spanish. Wages for interpreters are competitive, benchmarked against the highest standards in the industry (http://www.LanguageLine.com).

Performing Arts and the Motion Picture Industry

Recent trends in entertainment preferences by Americans suggest that the conditions are favorable for ethnic productions and talent. The box office success of the movie, *Crouching Tiger, Hidden Dragon*; the immense popularity enjoyed by actors such as Michelle Yeoh, Lucy Liu, Andy Garcia, and Jennifer Lopez; and the critical acclaim earned by directors such as Ang Lee, John Woo, Thi Thanh Nga, and Moctezuma Esparza are proof that ethnic themes can be of interest to American audiences and can produce profits for studios.

The success of these and other individuals is creating new opportunities for ethnic talent in Hollywood. According to producer and director Moctezuma Esparza, "There is, in fact, a critical mass of Latinos forming in the industry. The numbers are just coming to a point where people are just beginning to feel like there is a community—and that didn't exist 5 years ago at all" (Muñoz & Braxton, 2001). Similarly, Vietnamese American director Thi Thanh Nga, the youngest recipient of the Women in Film Award of the Director's Guild of America, notes, "When I was a teenager struggling for work as an actress, Asian American Screen Actors Guild members took up only two pages in the Academy book. Nowadays our glossy photos fill up dozens of pages in the Academy book. . . . The long march isn't complete, but maybe we do see the hint of light at the end of the Hollywood tunnel" (Thanh Nga, 1995).

One of the most important contributions made by ethnic entertainers in Hollywood is their effort to educate colleagues and the general public about immigrant America. Thi Thanh Nga has become a powerful voice in Hollywood against Asian stereotypes in movies and television. Cuban American screenwriter Cynthia Cidre is a champion of Hispanic culture. "I try to say in a good way that Hispanic means that we speak Spanish—it does not mean we are a race. There are Hispanics who are white, who are Chinese, who are black. We represent all cultures and a mixing of cultures. And they get it for the moment" (Muñoz & Braxton, 2001).

As the performing arts and motion picture industries respond to increasingly diverse markets, the need to find scripts and roles that authentically portray experiences of individuals and groups who speak languages other than English continues to increase. Good actors, writers, and filmmakers must be well read and exposed to different cultural experiences. Heritage language speakers have the ability to understand stories from the inside of a group's experience. Scriptwriters and actors who have been exposed to rich and varied language and cultural experiences are able to capture the nuances of roles in a way that avoids caricatures and stereotypes.

Healthcare

In *Best Careers for Bilingual Latinos*, Graciela Kenig notes that more than half of the 30 fastest-growing professions in this country are in the healthcare industry. In these professions, there is a critical need for bilingual doctors, nurses, and therapists who can communicate with patients with limited or no English language skills. This need is particularly acute in states and urban areas with large immigrant populations (Kenig, 1999).

As the U.S. Department of Human Health and Services (2000) reports,

> Compelling evidence that race and ethnicity correlate with persistent, and often increasing, health disparities among U.S. populations demands national attention. Indeed, despite notable progress in the overall health of the nation, there are continuing disparities in the burden of illness and death experienced by blacks, Hispanics, American Indians and Alaska Natives, and Pacific Islanders, compared to the U.S. population as a whole. The demographic changes that are anticipated over the next decade magnify the importance of addressing disparities in health status.

When it comes to disease prevention, the importance of understanding the health practices and beliefs of immigrant populations is underscored in a document released in 1998 by the U.S. Department of Health and Human Services and the Office of Minority Health ("Quality Health Care," 1998):

> Individual providers and their organizations must be knowledgeable about the patient population they serve. The predictors of disease and effectiveness of treatments often vary by subpopulation, so effective medical care rests on understanding these differences.

One way that different states have responded to the call to improve healthcare for ethnic minorities is to enact laws requiring healthcare providers to offer language assistance to those with limited English. For example, New Jersey requires drug and alcohol treatment facilities to provide interpreter services. In Massachusetts, every acute care hospital must provide interpreter services. California laws mandate that intermediate care facilities must use interpreters to ensure adequate communication between staff and patients (http://www.hhs.gov/ocr/lep/appb.html).

With its large immigrant base, California faces serious linguistic challenges in tending to patients with limited English. *The Los Angeles Times* reports that this state's ability to provide adequate healthcare to Hispanics is being compromised by a dire shortage of doctors who can communicate with the growing Spanish-speaking population (Hayes-Bautista & Stein, 2000). Although Latinos make up about 30% of this state's population, Latino physicians account for fewer than 5% of its total number of physicians. This situation has created a veritable health crisis for the state, increasing the risk of infectious diseases not just among Hispanics but among the general population as well.

Latino physicians offer more than just the ability to communicate accurately with Spanish-speaking patients. Their cultural sensitivity to the needs and fears of Latino patients make them essential to providing appropriate healthcare to this population. In view of this, *The Los Angeles Times* anticipates that "if more Latinos apply to medical schools, more are bound to be admitted. Admissions committees can judiciously increase the applicant pool by giving greater weight to skills and knowledge that better serve the state's changing demographic profile than the highest possible MCAT scores" (Hayes-Bautista & Stein, 2000).

California also faces a number of linguistic and cultural challenges in serving the healthcare needs of its sizable Asian immigrant populations. *The Spirit Catches You and You Fall Down*, an award-winning book about the experiences of a Hmong refugee family in a hospital in Merced, California, vividly chronicles the tragic consequences of linguistic and cross-cultural misunderstanding (Fadiman, 1998).

Asian Health Services (AHS), a community health center in Alameda County that provides medical care, health education, and counseling to the Asian and Pacific Islander population, estimates that more than 90% of its 12,000 patients require special language assistance when seeing a healthcare professional. Of these, more than half speak Cantonese and Mandarin, and the rest speak a variety of Asian languages, including Cambodian, Filipino, Korean, Laotian, and Vietnamese. Linda Okahara, the director of the Language and Cultural Access Program at AHS, notes that the ability to offer culturally and linguistically appropriate services is "fundamental to our mission of providing adequate healthcare to the Asian and Pacific Islander population of this area" (personal communication, January 8, 2001).

In fact, U.S. laws consider appropriate linguistic representation to be so fundamental to the task of providing adequate healthcare that the 1964 Civil Rights Act considers language rights to be civil rights. A memorandum issued by the U.S. Office for Civil Rights (1998) reminds healthcare providers of this.

> The language barriers experienced by these LEP [Limited English Proficient] persons can result in limiting their access to critical public health, hospital and other medical and social services to which they are legally entitled and can limit their ability to receive notice of or understand what services are available to them. Because of these language barriers, LEP persons are often excluded from programs or experience delays or denials of services from recipients of Federal assistance. Such exclusions, delays or denials may constitute discrimination on the basis of national origin, in violation of Title VI.

Rainof (2000) illustrates the catastrophic consequences of inadequate linguistic representation for immigrant patients with limited English skills.

> In "Worlds and Words Apart" (*Los Angeles Times*, November 6, 2000, Health Section) Jane E. Allen writes of patients given injections without explanations, of cases cited during an interview by Thomas Perez, Director of the OCR at HHS, "of a South Carolina hospital's practice of denying epidural anesthesia during childbirth to patients who could not speak English. Doctors there said that if there were complications, the women wouldn't be able to communicate," and other horrors. Two physicians, in the latest issue of *JAMWA* (*Journal of the American Medical Women's Association*, Vol. 55, No. 5, pp. 294-295, Fall 2000), report in an article titled "Language Barriers to Informed Consent and Confidentiality: The Impact on Women's Health" that "Evidence that language barriers have a direct effect on health care delivery is growing." Errors in interpretation in psychiatric interviews, for instance, "led to misdiagnoses." This language barrier is especially problematic in women's health: "At the beginning of the year I had this woman who spoke Arabic, and I wanted to do a few things, including a mammogram, pelvic exam, and Pap smear. This was hard to do given that her young son was the interpreter . . . so we didn't do it." (p. 8)

In his groundbreaking interpreter training work with Hispanic high school students, Rainof has found that when it comes to making a career choice, these students want more than just money and prestige. They want to make a difference by ensuring equal access to the legal system and adequate healthcare to the Latino community (Alexander Rainof, personal communication, January 8, 2001). The healthcare industry is brimming with opportunities for heritage language speakers who want to contribute to the well-being of their community, as primary caretakers, counselors, or interpreters.

Education

For the bilingual heritage language speaker, professional opportunities in education abound, whether in a dual language, English as a second language, foreign language, or general education setting. A recent headline in *The Washington Post*, "Schools Desperate for Foreign-Language Teachers" (Wax, 2000), highlights the widespread foreign language teacher shortage. The article enumerates the long list of school districts that cannot find enough foreign language teachers to meet the unprecedented demand for foreign language classes. According to a survey by the Center for Applied Linguistics, the number of foreign language students in elementary schools increased by nearly 10% from 1987 to 1997 (Rhodes & Branaman, 1999). It is evident that in a booming global economy, more students want to learn foreign languages than ever before.

At the same time, demographic shifts have significantly altered the makeup of the K–12 student population. All over the nation, city school districts are experiencing rising numbers of English language learners. In addition, school districts in parts of the nation that never imagined that they would face the challenges of educating a diverse student population find themselves with classrooms brimming with students from other countries (Lucas, 1997). Unfortunately, the supply of teachers from diverse language and cultural backgrounds has not kept pace with this surge in student diversity. A survey by the National Education Association (1997) found that more than 90% of teachers in 1995-1996 were White. The need for teachers who share cultural backgrounds with their students, understand their students' linguistic and cultural orientation, and can speak languages other than English has never been higher.

According to a national survey conducted in 2000 by the Council of the Great City Schools, an organization representing the needs of urban schools, schools in urban areas educate between 40% and 50% of the students who are not proficient in English and about 50% of minority students (Recruiting New Teachers, Inc., Council of the Great City Schools, & Council of the Great City Colleges of Education, 2000). Nearly 68% of the districts surveyed in this study identified a current demand for bilingual and ESL teachers.

According to this study, in the next decade, urban schools will need to hire some 700,000 new teachers who are qualified to meet the challenges of teaching America's diverse student population. To meet this demand, urban schools are adopting a number of recruitment strategies that include offering special incentives, such as housing assistance, relocation benefits, loan forgiveness programs, and tuition assistance for graduate work. In geographical areas where the need for teachers is particularly acute, school districts are turning to other countries to supply teachers in critical areas of instruction, such as English as a second language, foreign languages, math, and science. *The New York Times* reports,

> There are now thousands of foreign teachers . . .in American classrooms. As school administrators struggle to cope with a teacher shortage that ranks among the worst in history, principals and superintendents are increasingly looking overseas for at least a temporary fix. Where it was once uncommon to cross state lines in pursuit of new teachers, recruiters now do not blink at crossing oceans. ("Facing a Teacher Shortage," 2001)

While recruiting abroad may provide temporary relief from the current teacher shortage, foreign instructors often lack the bicultural knowledge and bilingual skills necessary for teaching students in this country. Although these teachers are undoubtedly highly proficient in the home language and culture, they lack familiarity with this country's educational system and with the experiences of its immigrant populations, a point that S.C. Wang (1996) makes in her study of Chinese language schools in the United States (see also Wang & Green, this volume):

> The problem lies in the fact that most of the teachers in Chinese language schools are native Chinese, with no experience with the American education system. . . . Biculturalism for these teachers is essential; it is vital that they understand how the American education system works. This knowledge is indispensable because the teaching and promotion of the Chinese language and culture are occurring in the social and political contexts of the United States. (p. 65)

Many foreign-educated teachers also lack a full understanding of the challenges inherent in straddling two linguistic systems. Thus, they may inadvertently undermine the fragile linguistic self-esteem of heritage language speakers through the use of educational practices designed for monolingual students. Valdés (1997) underscores this point:

> The so-called home background, residual, and quasi-native speaker about whom these professionals are concerned are not simply imperfect speakers of Spanish who have fallen short of the monolingual norm. Rather, they are complex individuals who are fundamentally different from monolinguals. As opposed to monolingual speakers of Spanish who grow up in societies where Spanish is the sole or primary language, bilingual Hispanics in the United States are members of the communities where a single language (be it English or Spanish) does not suffice to meet all communicative needs. (p. 29)

For these reasons, heritage language classes are often best taught by heritage language speakers who have lived in the United States or by native English-speaking instructors with the highest levels of cultural and linguistic proficiency in the target language. Of course language proficiency alone does not constitute excellent pedagogy. Heritage language teachers must also be well versed in language theory and effective pedagogy. As S.C. Wang (1996) notes, although most of the Chinese heritage language teachers are "well educated, creative, and dedicated," they "need training in language teaching theory, pedagogy, and assessment" (p. 65). In addition, they need training in sociolinguistics, dialectology, and historical linguistics (Carreira, 2000).

As the number of heritage language students at all educational levels continues to escalate nationwide, the demand for individuals with expertise in issues pertaining to the education of this population will also increase. Sue Suggs, principal of La Escuela Bilingüe Pioneer in La Fayette, Colorado, notes that

> a fully bilingual staff, ranging from teachers, administrators, and office personnel is essential to creating a learning environment where the cultural and linguistic needs of all students and parents are fully met and where the value of the Spanish language and Latino cultures is fully recognized. Every single person that we hire is bilingual. (personal communication, June 12, 2001)

The shortage of culturally and linguistically appropriate educational materials for heritage language students has also created a demand for bicultural and bilingual writers and editors. Krashen (1998) identifies lack of language input, in the form of conversational interaction, books, and media, as one of the most significant barriers to language development. Spanish teachers surveyed by Pino (1997) named materials development as the single most urgent need in their Spanish for Spanish speakers classes. S.P. Wang (1996) reveals the inadequacy of the foreign textbooks currently in use by most Chinese heritage language programs in the United States and urges Chinese language instructors to develop and edit supplemental teaching materials to meet the needs of heritage language students of Chinese in this country.

The lack of appropriate materials for teaching heritage languages is felt particularly in the less commonly taught languages. For example, like most Arabic instructors, Professor Najib Redouane at California State University, Long Beach must create his own teaching materials for heritage Arabic speakers, with little in the way of instructional or commercial resources to build on (personal communication, May 31, 2001). A survey by the Southwest Educational Development Laboratory (Fuentes, 1999) indicates that Native American language programs have similar challenges: "Materials are produced by the teacher, as textbooks and other materials have not been developed for classroom purposes . . . and were not made available."

Publishers are beginning to take note of the commercial value of the heritage language market. *Diversity.com,* an online publication that reports on America's ethnic markets, notes that the popularity of Spanish language and bilingual children's books that are culturally relevant to U.S. Hispanics is at an all-time high. At the same time, the need for authors and editors who can create materials for this market is acutely felt.

From teaching and publishing to careers in school administration and counseling, the field of education is brimming with opportunities for heritage language speakers. Given the current and projected shortages of professionals in these fields, educators, researchers, and policy makers must make it a priority to recruit and train heritage language speakers for careers in education.

Model Programs

Some heritage language education programs focus on developing language proficiency for real-world professional needs and opportunities.

With funding from the U.S. Department of Education's Office of Bilingual Education and Minority Languages Affairs (OBEMLA), Project ASPIRE! in Florida provides bilingual paraprofessionals with support to move up the career ladder into certified teaching positions (Stebbins & Jameson, 2000). Recruitment, inservice training, assistance with college and university admission, and a tuition reimbursement program are components of this program.

In Venice, California, Venice High School offers training for prospective journalists who want to work in this country's growing Spanish language media market. The training includes coursework and hands-on experience producing a monthly Spanish language newspaper. It is offered through the school's Bilingual Business and Finance Academy, a program that focuses on building job skills.

Also in Southern California, California State University Long Beach and five local high schools teamed up to create an intensive interpreter training class for 25 Latino high school students. The class, offered in the fall semester of 2000, focused on developing language skills and on educating students about opportunities in translation and interpretation. During the semester, representatives from the Judicial Council of California and the California Court Interpreters Association made presentations to the class. In a measure of the success of the program, a good number of the participants stated in an end-of-course questionnaire that they intended to apply to the university and pursue a B.A. in translation.

A growing number of heritage language programs are focusing on the professional opportunities available to bilingual Americans as a way to instill pride in students and to encourage them to pursue advanced studies in their home language. The Heritage Language Literacy Club at Bailey's Elementary School for the Arts and Sciences in Fairfax County, Virginia, teaches students as early as the fourth grade that proficiency in more than one language is a financial asset (Benning, 2001). In this innovative afterschool Spanish literacy program, students in the upper-elementary grades are employed as tutors to beginning language learners. Tutors earn their wages in the form of stipends toward college, which are awarded after the successful completion of the school year.

In addition to providing students with potentially valuable professional and academic skills, successful heritage language programs recognize the importance of instilling a social conscience in students, so they will lend their bilingual and bicultural skills to social improvements. The Rose and Alex Pilibos Armenian School in Los Angeles, California, for example, offers an integrated K–12 curriculum in English and Armenian. In addition to stressing high academic standards, this school exposes students to their Armenian heritage while preparing them to make a contribution to American society. The school's philosophy statement represents a model for heritage language instruction in the United States:

> The ultimate vision is to produce Armenian-Americans who are anchored by their ethnic identity and strong system of values and will use those assets to instrumentally contribute to the development, enhancement, and multi-level enrichment of the United States. A firm foundation upon which to base their future development, as well as a sense of community and belonging, is instilled in the students through a structured, disciplined environment and their participation in a myriad of community outreach programs. ("Focus on Learning," 1997)

Conclusion

One way to expand the available pool of professionals who are highly proficient in languages other than English is to preserve and nurture the heritage languages that abound in many immigrant communities. To do that, we will need to change fundamental attitudes. In the United States, the language of status is English, and the majority group culture is Anglo European. Consequently, children learn early on that their heritage language and culture are of lower status than the majority language and culture. These negative attitudes adversely affect the preservation of heritage languages, especially in areas where no formal schooling in these languages is available.

The message that speaking multiple languages affords social status and is financially rewarding will challenge the widespread belief among immigrant parents and their children that their cultural and linguistic heritage must be sacrificed in order to succeed in the larger society. Programs that hone the cultural and linguistic skills of bilingual Americans while boosting their self-confidence not only enrich their lives and provide them with valuable skills for the workforce, but also preserve America's vast linguistic and cultural resources.

References

2000 language need and interpreter use study. (2000, September 29). Sacramento, CA: Walter R. McDonald & Associates, Inc. Retrieved from http://www.courtinfo.ca.gov/programs/courtinterpreters/documents/needusestudy.pdf

Artze, I. (1999, September). Targeting Hispanic consumers: U.S. companies have taken notice of Latinos' growing purchasing power. *Hispanic Magazine.* Retrieved from http://www.Hispaniconline.com/buss&finn/bussres/target.html

Artze, I. (2001, May). Marketing to show empathy. *Hispanic Business Journal.* Retrieved from http://www.Hispaniconline.com/buss&finn/bussres/empthy.html

Benning, V. (2001, January 21). Program mixes fun and fluency. *The Washington Post*, p. C9.

Brecht, R.D., & Rivers, W.P. (2000). *Language and national security in the 21st century: The role of Title VI/Fulbright-Hays in supporting national language capacity*. Dubuque, IA: Kendall/Hunt.

Carreira, M. (2000). Validating and promoting Spanish in the U.S.: Lessons from linguistic science. *Bilingual Research Journal, 24*, (3), 423-442.

Chepesiuk, R. (2001, January 29). Asian American women in e-business. *Asian Week*. Retrieved from http://www.asianweek.com/2001_01_12/section_business.html

Companies worry about skills gap. (1998, May 3). *The San Francisco Examiner*, p. J1.

Curtain, H., & Pesola, C.A. (1994). *Languages and children: Making the match* (2nd ed.). White Plains, NY: Longman. (ERIC Document Reproduction Service No. ED 376 717)

De Los Santos, N. (1999, March). The Los Angeles Times launches the Latino initiative. *Hispanic Magazine*, p. 16.

Facing a teacher shortage, American schools look overseas. (2001, May 19). *The New York Times*. Retrieved from http://www.nytimes.com

Fadiman, A. (1998). *The spirit catches you and you fall down*. New York: Farrar Straus & Giroux.

Focus on learning, self study: Rose and Alex Pilibos Armenian School. (1997). Paper presented to the Western Association of Schools and Colleges Accrediting Commission for Secondary Schools, Pilibos Armenian School, Los Angeles, CA.

Fuentes, N. (1999). *Profiles of native language education programs*. Austin, TX: Southwest Educational Development Laboratory. Retrieved from http://www.sedl.org/pubs/lc05/welcome.html

Hayes-Bautista, D., & Stein, R. (2000, October 1). A shortage that's killing Latinos. *The Los Angeles Times*. Retrieved from http://www.latimes.com/services/site/archives

Kenig, G. (1999). *Best careers for bilingual Latinos*. Chicago: VGM Career Horizons.

Krashen, S. (1998). Heritage language development: Some practical arguments. In S. Krashen, L. Tse, & J. McQuillan (Eds.), *Heritage language development* (pp. 3-14). Culver City, CA: Language Education Associates.

Kraul, C. (2000, June 25). Latino talent pinch hobbling U.S. firms' expansion plans. *The Los Angeles Times*, p. B1.

Language, culture create need for Navajo speakers. (2000, December 31). *The Los Angeles Times*, p. A23. Retrieved from *http://www.latimes.com/services/site/archives*

Lin, P. (June 8, 2001). Diversity—A necessary business tool in sync with the needs of today and the future. Retrieved from http://www.uspaacc.org/article.htm

Lucas, T. (1997). *Into, through, and beyond secondary school: Critical transitions for immigrant youths*. McHenry, IL, and Washington, DC: Delta Systems and Center for Applied Linguistics.

Lynch, A. (2000). Spanish-speaking Miami in sociolinguistic perspective: Bilingualism, recontact, and language maintenance among the Cuban-origin population. In A. Orca, (Ed.), *Research on Spanish in the United States, linguistic issues and challenges* (pp 271-283). Sommerville, MA: Cascadilla Press.

Muñoz, L., & Braxton, G. (2001, January 6). An accent on progress. *The Los Angeles Times* (Calendar section). Retrieved from http://www.latimes.com/services/site/archives

National Education Association. (1997). *Status of the American public school teacher, 1995-96*. West Haven, CT: Author. Retrieved from http://www.nea.org/nr/status.pdf

Pino, C.R. (1997). La reconceptualización del programa de español para hispanohablantes: Estrategías que reflejan la realidad sociolingüística de la clase. In M.C. Colombi & F.X. Alarcón (Eds.), *La enseñanza del español a hispanohablantes: Praxis y teoría* (pp. 65-82). Boston: Houghton Mifflin.

Quality health care for culturally diverse populations: Provider and community collaboration in a competitive marketplace. (1998). Retrieved from http://www.DiversityRx.org/CCCONF/98/INDEX.html

Rainof, A. (2000). *Language rights are civil rights: Recent developments in the area of medical interpretation and translation*. Unpublished manuscript.

Reader's Digest seeks to attract Hispanics. (2001, January 9). Retrieved from http://www.HispanicBusiness.com/news/newsbyid.asp?id=2808

Recruiting New Teachers, Inc., Council of the Great City Schools, & Council of the Great City Colleges of Education. (2000, January). *The urban teacher challenge: Teacher demand and supply in the great city schools*. Belmont, MA: Author. Retrieved from http://www.cgcs.org/reports/2000/RNT-0101.pdf

Reveron, D. (2001, Jan/Feb). Miami: The capital of Latin American e-commerce. *Hispanic Business Magazine*. Retrieved from http://www.Hispanicbusiness.com/news/newsbyid.asp?id=3014

Rhodes, N.C., & Branaman, L.E. (1999). *Foreign language instruction in the United States: A national survey of elementary and secondary schools*. McHenry, IL, and Washington, DC: Delta Systems and Center for Applied Linguistics.

Romney, L. (2001, January 15). TV talks to immigrant markets. *The Los Angeles Times*. Retrieved from http://www.latimes.com/services/site/archives

Romney, L., & Eller, C. (2001, January 9). In Disney experiment, Spanish prefer English. *The Los Angeles Times* (Business). Retrieved from http://www.latimes.com/services/site/archives

Schultz, R.A. (1998, Fall). Foreign language education in the United States: Trends and challenges. *K–12 Foreign Language Education, The ERIC Review, 6*(1), 6-12.

Skriloff, L. (2000). *Survey of multicultural marketers finds a bright future for ethnic marketing*. Los Angeles, CA: Multicultural Marketing Resources.

Stebbins, C., & Jameson, J. (2000, March). *Opportunities for paraprofessionals through in-service and college*. Paper presented at the meeting of Teachers of English to Speakers of Other Languages, Vancouver, British Columbia, Canada.

Thanh Nga, T. (1995). The long march from Wong to Woo: Asians in Hollywood. Retrieved from http://www.lib.berkeley.edu/MRC/LongMarch.html

US business group launches Asian outreach. (2000, February 21). *The Times of India*. Retrieved from http://www.timesofindia.com/210200/21inte1.htm

U.S. Department of Health and Human Services. (2000, August 30). HHS provides written guidance for health and human services providers to ensure language assistance for persons with limited English skills. *HHS News*. Retrieved from http://www.hhs.gov/news/press/2000pres/20000830.html

U.S. Office for Civil Rights. (1998, January 29). *Guidance memorandum: Title VI prohibition against national origin: Discrimination—Persons with limited-English proficiency*. Washington, DC: U.S. Office for Civil Rights. Retrieved from http://www.hhs.gov/OCR/lepfinal.htm

Valdés, G. (1997). The teaching of Spanish to bilingual Spanish-speaking students: Outstanding issues and unanswered questions. In M.C. Colombi & F. Alracón (Eds.), *La enseñanza del español a hispanohablantes* (pp. 8-37). Boston: Houghton Mifflin.

Vazquez, R. (2000, September). HBO to launch new Spanish language channel. Retrieved from http://latinoculture.about.com/library/publicity/blmktHBOLatino1.htm

Vidueira, J.R. (1999, December). Leader of globalization: George Muñoz promotes American business overseas. *Hispanic Magazine.* Retrieved from http://www.hispanicmagazine.com/1999/dec/CoverStory/index.html

Wang, S.C. (1996). Improving Chinese language schools: Issues and recommendations. In X. Wang (Ed.), *A view from within: A case study of Chinese heritage community language schools in the United States* (pp. 63-68). Washington, DC: National Foreign Language Center.

Wang, S.P. (1996). Academic curriculum. In X. Wang (Ed.), *A view from within: A case study of Chinese heritage community language schools in the United States* (pp. 21-26). Washington, DC: National Foreign Language Center.

Wax, E. (2000, July 4). Schools desperate for foreign-language teachers. *The Washington Post,* p. A9.

Weinstein, H., & Liu, C. (2000, November 1). Courts to add interpreters in five more languages. *The Los Angeles Times.* Retrieved from http://www.latimes.com/services/site/archives

Additional Resources
Publications, Professional Organizations, and Web Sites on Professional Opportunities for Bilinguals

Books

Kenig, G. (1999). *Best careers for bilingual latinos*. Chicago: VGM Career Horizons.

Oakes, E. (Ed.). (1997). *Big book of minority opportunities*. Chicago: Ferguson.

Stith, A. (1999). *How to build a career in the new economy: A guide for minorities and women*. Toronto, Ontario, Canada: Warwick.

Wong, A.M. (1999). *Target: The U.S. Asian market, A practical guide to doing business*. Palos Verdes, CA: Pacific Heritage Books.

Law Enforcement

The Federal Bureau of Investigation (FBI)
http://www.fbi.gov
This site, the official web site of the Federal Bureau of Investigation, includes press releases, employment opportunities with the FBI, programs, and resources for students and teachers.

Translation and Interpretation

The National Association of Judiciary Interpreters and Translators (NAJIT)
http://www.najit.org
This site provides a database of more than 800 interpreters and translators, searchable by language, location, credentials, etc. It also provides access to PROTEUS, the quarterly newsletter of NAJIT and answers to frequently asked questions about court interpreting.

The Translators and Interpreters Guild
http://www.trans-interp-guild.org
This site provides information to professional and prospective translators and interpreters on professional training, jobs, and health insurance.

Business

The Asian American Association and The Asian Business Co-Op
http://www.aan.net
This is the web site for the Asian Business Co-Op, the holding company of the Asian American Network (AAN). The site provides information on jobs, as well as links to Asian American businesses in Southern California.

Asian American Chamber of Commerce
http://www.asianchamber.org
This organization provides business consulting and technical assistance to members. The web site is a resource center for members to network and market their products and services.

Hispanic Business
http://www.HispanicBusiness.com
This bimonthly English language publication features information on all aspects of Latino/Hispanic business in the United States, including promising careers, scholarships, and the best companies for Latinos.

Hispanic Employment Program Managers Home Page
http://www.hepm.org
This organization helps Hispanics identify job opportunities in the federal government and the private sector.

Hispanic Organization of Professionals and Executives (HOPE)
1700 17th St NW Suite 405-2009
Washington DC 20009
HOPE is the largest national organization of Hispanic professionals and executives.

National Society of Hispanic MBA's
http://www.nshmba.org
This Hispanic MBA professional network offers a wide range of benefits to its members, particularly in networking, scholarships, and information related to the Hispanic business community.

Russian American Chamber of Commerce
http://www.russianamericanchamber.org
The Russian American Chamber of Commerce promotes U.S. business in Russia. Its web site provides expertise and guidance to American companies in Russia.

U.S. Hispanic Chamber of Commerce
http://www.ushcc.com
This web site includes a directory of U.S. Hispanic businesses, a newsletter, and information on business conventions and training opportunities of interest to Hispanics.

U.S. Pan-Asian American Chamber of Commerce (USPAACC)
http://www.uspaacc.org
This nonprofit organization represents the interests of Asian Americans in the sciences, arts, sports, education, entertainment, community, and public service. The site includes business news, press releases, useful links, and a national directory of members.

Media and Communications

Association of Hispanic Advertising Agencies (AHAA)
http://www.ahaa.org
This is the premier trade organization for U.S. Hispanic advertising agencies. Its web site offers information about conferences and meetings and analyses of demographic information pertinent to advertising to U.S. Hispanics.

The National Association of Hispanic Journalists
http://www.nahj.org
This web site for Hispanic journalists offers access to *Latino Reporter*, a daily newsletter analyzing issues of interest to the U.S. Latino communities. Other valuable resources include links to newspapers, student programs, and career resources.

National Association of Hispanic Publications
http://www.nahp.org
This association includes more than 400 senior-level staff from newspapers, magazines, and newsletters. The site promotes Hispanic media by providing incentives for Hispanics to enter the media and by attracting advertisers to support Hispanic media.

Performing Arts and the Motion Picture Industry

National Hispanic Academy of Media, Arts & Sciences
Nhamas@hotmail.com
This organization of Latinos working in film, television, radio, and print media does not have a web site, but further information is available through the e-mail address given above.

Healthcare

Center for Multicultural and Multilingual Mental Health Services
http://www.mc-mlmhs.org
This center provides support to mental health professionals who work cross-culturally and cross-linguistically. Its web site offers information on different health topics, including interpreter and professional training issues. It also features an online library and a referral service for health care providers serving minority communities in the Chicago area.

Health Care Interpreter Training Survey and Contact List
http://www.ahschc.org/traindir2.htm
This site provides an overview of interpreter training programs in the United States and Canada, along with contact information.

The Kaiser Family Foundation
http://www.statehealthfacts.kff.org
This site offers comprehensive and up-to-date health information for all 50 states, the District of Columbia, and U.S. territories. It also includes health policy information on a broad range of issues including managed care, health insurance coverage, Medicaid, Medicare, women's health, minority health, and HIV/AIDS.

National Coalition of Hispanic Health and Human Services Organizations (COSSMHO)
http://www.Hispanichealth.org
This site includes job opportunities, education and funding information, conference reports, and web links related to Hispanic health issues.

National Council on Interpretation in Health Care
NCIHC-list@diversityRx.org
This electronic discussion group allows participants whose dominant language is other than English to raise issues, ask questions, and share information related to medical interpretation and access to adequate healthcare.

Resources for Cross Cultural Health Care
http://www.DiversityRx.org
This site offers policymakers, healthcare providers, and consumer representatives resources to learn about language and cultural competence in healthcare, design better programs and policies, and to network with colleagues and experts.

Education

The California Center for Teaching Careers
http://www.calteach.org
This is a one-stop information and referral service for prospective teachers and recruiters in California. It includes information on credential programs in California, national exams, and job opportunities.

Council of the Great City Schools
http://www.cgcs.org
This organization consists of the nation's largest urban public school systems and is governed by superintendents and board of education members from 58 cities across the country. Its web site offers a variety of reports and studies pertaining to the education of minorities in urban areas.

Future Teachers of Chicago
http://www.coe.ilstu.edu/c+idept/mmp/ftc/what.htm
This is a collaborative of 9 Chicago area universities, 5 city colleges, and over 40 schools. This web site features information on recruiting, motivating, and preparing minority students for careers in education.

Recruiting New Teachers, Inc.
http://www.rnt.org
This site is sponsored by a national nonprofit organization that aims to recruit teachers and raise the status of the teaching profession.

We Color Education Minority Teacher Education Scholarship Program
http://www.coe.ufl.edu/FFMT/info.html
This organization aims to increase the number of minority teachers in Florida by offering scholarships and guidance to African Americans, Asians and Pacific Islanders, American Indians, and Latino/ Hispanics interested in careers in education.

Acknowledgments

We are grateful to the following individuals who served as members of the Heritage Languages in America conference panel on Professional Opportunities for Heritage Languages Speakers and provided much of the information for this chapter: Harold Cannon, professional actor and professor, California State University, Long Beach; Margarita Cannon, producer and casting agent, partner, Velasco & Associates; Terence Geoghegan, attorney, Fairfield & Freeman; Margaret Gulotta, Chief of Language Services, Federal Bureau of Investigation; and Julio Morán, Executive Director, The Chicano News Media Organization.

Educational Issues

7
Heritage Language Communities and Schools: Challenges and Recommendations

Carol J. Compton
University of Wisconsin–Madison

Heritage language communities and schools are the source of incalculable riches for their members, their students, and the entire country. The linguistic diversity that these communities and schools support and preserve is important intellectually, economically, politically, and culturally. It is a strength to be cherished. By beginning the study of heritage languages at an early age, members of these communities can acquire a depth and breadth of language skills that can result in the development of serious scholars of language and area studies and of well-educated, multilingual adults.

However, members of heritage language communities face challenges as they seek to preserve and pass on their linguistic and cultural legacies to their children. This chapter examines the challenges related to establishing and maintaining community heritage language schools and offers recommendations for addressing those challenges. Many of the points made are synthesized from comments made during a discussion on heritage language communities and schools at the first National Conference on Heritage Languages in America in 1999.

Heritage Language Communities

Heritage language communities include indigenous and immigrant groups that speak languages other than the dominant national language. Thus, in the United States, a heritage

145

language community is one that uses a language other than English.

These communities have grown dramatically in recent years. According to the 2000 census, nearly 18% of U.S. residents age 5 and older speak a language other than English at home (U.S. Census Bureau, 2001). While a small percentage of this population speaks only a heritage language, most are bilingual, though not necessarily biliterate.

Although there are clear differences in the situation and histories of indigenous and immigrant language communities, many of the current sociocultural and sociolinguistic issues they face are similar. For instance, support for heritage language communities from political decision-makers at the international, national, state, and local levels can affect the quality and amount of educational opportunities that heritage communities can provide to their members. What Shoji and Janhunen (1997) note in their discussion of indigenous languages is true for other heritage languages as well:

> Through a proper policy of language enhancement, these intellectual benefits of multilingualism could be made available for both the majorities and the minorities. (p. 226)

As Michael Yang, Director of the Immigrant and Refugee Policy Coalition for the Urban Coalition in Minneapolis/St. Paul, Minnesota, points out, ethnic communities "are a driving force and our policy makers need to understand that we are here" (Carlson, 2001, p. B4).

Heritage Language Schools

In the United States, ethnic groups have historically set up and maintained educational institutions to support the teaching of their languages and cultures (Bradunas, 1988; Fishman, this volume). Today, with immigration at its highest since the turn of the 19th century, the number of community heritage language schools is on the rise. Each week, hundreds of heritage language classes are taught in community schools and classrooms throughout the United States and Canada. Chinese language schools in the United States alone have enrolled nearly 83,000 students in more than 600 schools (Chao, 1996, p. 7).

Many of these schools are supported and operated by members of the heritage communities. Others are sponsored jointly by the heritage community and a local public school or community college. Such cooperation between heritage language communities and public schools can often help to ensure the survival of heritage language classes for some languages.

Students vary widely in their ages, backgrounds, and interests. Heritage language classes may be open to all ages, from preschoolers to seniors, or they may be designed for a particular age group. For example, a recent survey conducted in Tucson, Arizona, found that separate Hebrew classes were available for adults, for students in Grades 1 through 8, and for high school students (Oldfield, 1998). The Tucson Chinese School, on the other hand, had students ranging in age from 6 to 60, but the majority were in the 6 to 16 age range.

Not all students who participate in these classes are from the heritage community. As a result, it is not always easy to define clearly just what a heritage language community class or program is. Only 6 of the 11 language programs described in the Tucson report appear to be exclusively heritage language community programs; the other 5 were offered through public or private schools and colleges but were designed for heritage language learners.

Student motivations for studying heritage languages vary greatly and have been discussed in the literature (Bradunas & Topping, 1988; Campbell & Rosenthal, 2000; Feuerverger,

1991). Motivations may include the desire to preserve and improve the use of the home language, the wish to understand and develop cultural values, an interest in exploring self-identity, the desire to be bilingual, and the desire to belong to a community. Younger students may participate because their parents require them to do so, while older students may want to meet foreign language requirements or to use the language in careers such as teaching, missionary work, or business. Adoptive parents or those who have married into the community may participate to meet their own or their children's social needs. Community-building, political activism, and the need for social support and comfort are other motivating factors for attending heritage language schools.

Staff in these schools may consist of administrators, teachers, interns, parents, and other community members. Sometimes staff receive a salary; sometimes they work on a voluntary basis. Teachers vary in the amount of professional preparation they bring to their work; many, however, have received little or no preservice or inservice training. For some of the larger heritage languages, there are regional or national language, cultural, or religious organizations in which teachers may participate. Such groups as the Islamic Society of North America, the National Council of Associations of Chinese Language Schools, the American Indian Language Development Institute, and the Korean Schools Association may provide support to heritage language teachers and administrators in the form of materials, training, or advice.

Heritage language classes generally focus on language skills (listening, speaking, reading, and writing) and culture. Courses in religion, civic involvement, literature, and history may be taught as well. Sometimes language varieties, language attitudes, and language learning strategies are taught. Courses on parenting, grandparenting, and traditional cooking may also be offered. Classes are generally held in community centers, churches, and temples. Local public and private schools are other common sites.

Challenges

Establishing and maintaining effective heritage language classes and schools involves a great deal of work and dedication on the part of community members. Challenges for heritage community schools include raising public awareness, cultivating broad-based support, improving articulation with other groups and institutions, improving curriculum and materials, developing teachers, and fostering support among parents and elders.

Raising Public Awareness

Raising public awareness about heritage languages, classes, and schools is crucial to strengthening the overall quality and impact of heritage language teaching and learning. The public needs to understand that through these language programs learners can maintain and develop their proficiency in the language, and, as a result, serve as local, national, and international linguistic resources. Shoji and Janhunen (1997) urge us "to spread positive information about linguistic diversity to all those who have the power to do something in order to save this diversity" (p. 226).

Raising public awareness is needed because the public is often unaware of the wide range of language learning opportunities available through heritage community programs, particularly in urban areas throughout the United States. For instance, Oldfield (1998), in a survey of heritage language programs in the Tucson, Arizona, area, found that more than 11 different languages were being taught at the time, at least 2 other languages had been taught recently, and plans were underway to offer classes in 3 more languages in the near future.

Part of the difficulty in raising public awareness about the variety, quality, and extent of heritage language education in the United States is a lack of data for most languages on what heritage language classes are being offered, to whom, at what levels, and where. The difficulty of obtaining this information is one of the challenges facing researchers and program implementors. Another is keeping available information up to date, since heritage community language class offerings vary from year to year depending on a variety of factors. The size of a particular heritage population in a given area; the availability of teachers and materials; the presence of recent arrivals; and the motivation in the community for keeping linguistic, religious, and cultural traditions alive are but some of the factors that affect the ability of a community to provide heritage language classes. In order for language educators to obtain and maintain public support for heritage language schools, the public needs to be made aware and reminded of their existence and value.

Cultivating Broad-Based Support

There is a need to cultivate financial and volunteer support for community heritage language programs. Obtaining funding from government sources and human service and site support from local schools and colleges can be important to program quality and growth. Heritage and nonheritage members of the local community can provide some of the financial and volunteer support needed to strengthen language classes. Contributions from parents of their time and money have also long been important to the success of many community language schools.

Seeking support from other countries related to the heritage community is another approach that some heritage communities have found useful. For example, representatives from the Tucson Chinese School attended conferences on Chinese language teaching sponsored by the Taiwan Cultural Affairs Office (Oldfield, 1998).

Another way to increase support and visibility is for heritage language communities and associations to organize at the state or provincial level. An example of such an effort is the British Columbia Heritage Language Association (BCHLA) in Canada. A nonprofit organization established in 1982, the BCHLA

> serves as the umbrella body for approximately 150 other organizations involved in the teaching of international languages. The association represents all levels of language instruction and education for over 30,000 students of international languages outside the public school system. . . Currently, 159 heritage language schools are being partially funded (for classroom resources) through the Heritage Language Program of the Ministry Responsible for Multiculturalism and Immigration. (BCHLA, 2001)

Many of BCHLA's primary objectives match those expressed by participants in the 1999 Heritage Languages in America conference. They include teacher training, curricula and materials development, research, course accreditation and teacher credentialing, and the development of a communication network on heritage language education at the provincial and national levels. Similar heritage language organizations can be found in other provinces in Canada. Such umbrella organizations can play an important role in supporting and promoting heritage language teaching and learning.

Improving Articulation with Other Groups and Institutions

As Xueying Wang (1996) has indicated, there is a "need for a new era of collaborative, collective work between the heritage communities and mainstream educational institutions" (p. 89). For some heritage language groups, such efforts are already well underway. Awarding students credit for language courses taken at heritage community institutions has been established at the school district level for some heritage languages (Liu, 1996). Other groups work with the cultural sections of the embassies of the countries of origin to establish standards that fit with those in the home countries. Still other groups have worked with universities or public schools to establish curricula that enable students to obtain high school or university credits for their studies (Chen, 1996).

In some areas of the United States, college and university students are working together with local heritage communities to see that classes in heritage languages are included in institutions of higher education and in K–12 school settings. At the K–12 level, there is a movement to get approval from school districts or states to award credit for language study at heritage schools that meet district and state curriculum standards. There is growing interest in heritage language classes at the college and university level as well. For example, during the last 25 years, we have seen increasing numbers of Southeast Asian Americans entering our colleges and universities. Some have been able to acquire literacy skills in their languages through temple and heritage community classes. Others, however, having grown up in communities where such opportunities did not exist, are seeking to learn more about their own languages and cultures and are asking university administrators to provide such programs for them (Compton, 1984, 2000).

Heritage language classes and programs are strengthened not only by articulation with public schools and universities but also by collaboration with religious institutions, consulates, embassies, and the media. At the 1999 Conference on Heritage Languages in America, one participant raised the example of an embassy sending a professional team of teachers to work with the local heritage language schools. The team brought with them books on the culture, history, and religion in the heritage language. Such interaction with teachers and professionals from the country of origin can help to bring local heritage language teachers up to date on the current state of the language and culture in the country.

A wealth of material is available from many of the countries whose languages are taught in heritage language programs. Newspapers, magazines, tapes, CDs, radio programs on the Internet, television programs, videotapes, and movies are available for many languages and may provide appropriate supplementary materials for heritage language classes. Sometimes cultural staff at consulates and embassies will facilitate the acquisition of these materials.

For some languages, a wide range of material is available commercially in the United States. For example, Sridhar (1997) discusses the availability of South Asian language films at video stores and Indian grocery stores in New York City. He also points out that newspapers and magazines published in India and elsewhere in languages such as Bengali, Gujarati, Hindi, Punjabi, and Urdu are sold by local merchants. Depending upon the needs and size of local heritage communities, similar access to heritage language materials is available in cities across North America. For heritage students who have grown up in media-rich American culture, such authentic materials can greatly enrich their language learning experiences.

Improving Curriculum and Materials

Improving the quality and scope of the curricula and materials used in heritage language schools and classes has been of great concern to heritage language educators. Many language groups have developed extensive materials appropriate for their students, and some have reached the point where they may be able to expand the curriculum of their schools to include more advanced courses in literature, culture, translation, and interpreting. Other groups lack basic textbooks for introducing reading and writing to heritage language learners. For some languages, materials for teaching vocabulary and intermediate speaking and listening skills are outdated or non-existent, and good dictionaries may be out of print or not yet developed.

All programs, in planning language and cultural activities for children, youth, and adults, need to give some thought to generational differences—how the language is used and learned by different generations. Some language programs are developing age-appropriate curricula to reflect the different linguistic needs of learners who are at different points in the life cycle. As Pelz (1991) notes in discussing the use of Yiddish in community cultural programs for older adults,

> The life-review process of the elderly does not redefine their being in terms of their youth or resolve old conflicts; rather, it allows a reintegration of past experience and emotion into their ever-changing lives. (p. 204)

One Swedish American woman has described her and her older sister's exposure to Swedish in childhood as an aid to their study of Swedish in their late sixties: "We seemed to have an echo in our heads when we came to learn the language later" (E.A. Meisch, personal communication, July 12, 2001). Classes for older adult learners with past heritage language experience need to reflect and build upon that "echo."

Sometimes it may take international efforts to produce the materials needed to support heritage language teaching. An example of such an effort is the international project to revise and update a dictionary of the Odawa dialect of Ojibwe being undertaken by American and Canadian scholars (Wolff, 2000). Compiler R.J. Valentine hopes that the dictionary will aid Ojibwe language teaching and learning

> by offering a rich vocabulary, with many examples of usage, with a relatively standard way of spelling, so that teachers can share materials more easily, and students at

all grade levels will encounter consistency as they progress in their study. (Wolff, 2000)

Professionals teaching in some languages (e.g., the Japanese National Standards Task Force, 1998) have worked to develop a national curriculum and standards. Such standards can facilitate articulation between community programs and those offered in the K–16 level. These standards also can provide goals and guidelines for the development of curriculum and materials for heritage community schools.

Staff in programs teaching languages that do not have national organizations might seek guidance and support for curriculum and materials development from faculty at nearby institutions of higher education or from teachers and staff in local school districts. They might also wish to review examples of standards developed for other languages, such as those prepared by the National Standards in Foreign Language Education Project (1996). They might also consult curricula for Spanish and Chinese available online (see, for example, the heritage language resource collection at the Center for Applied Linguistics, www.cal.org/heritage, and the instructional materials collection of the National Foreign Language Center's LangNet Project, www.nflc.org/activities/projects/langnet).

Strategies and instruments for assessing the skills of heritage language learners in listening, speaking, reading, and writing are still in the developmental stages. Because the linguistic characteristics of heritage language learners differ significantly from those of nonheritage learners of the same language (Campbell & Rosenthal, 2000; Valdés, this volume), new approaches to placement, testing, teaching, and learning for heritage language students are crucial. Handbooks and materials on language-specific language learning strategies are also needed. Information and techniques described in such books as *How to Be a More Successful Language Learner* (Rubin & Thompson,

1994) might provide a starting point for the development of such materials.

Language learning modules are being developed for Hausa, Korean, Swahili, and Yoruba through a grant from the Fund for the Improvement of Postsecondary Education (FIPSE) to the National Council of Organizations of Less Commonly Taught Languages (NCOLCTL). When they are completed, these modules will be available at NCOLCTL's web site (www.councilnet.org). Though these modules are intended for second language learners, it is quite possible that many of them will be adaptable to the needs of heritage language learners. At the very least, these modules may provide ideas for the development of similar materials for heritage language classes.

The use of computer technology has been incorporated into the heritage language curriculum of some schools, but there is still great potential for expanding its uses and applications in heritage schools. Though some kinds of technology may be too expensive for smaller schools and classes, there are many ways that the Internet can be used to supplement classroom study of heritage languages. For example, web-based courses may be developed for heritage language study at sites such as www.blackboard.com. "About one-third of all college courses now use the internet as part of the syllabus. ... Twenty-three percent of all courses are using web pages for class materials" (National Education Association, 1998, p. 1). In addition, heritage language students can become involved in Internet-based language learning activities such as the Lakota language Internet chat room mentioned by Brooke (1998).

Warschauer and Meskill (2000) suggest a number of uses of computer technology for second language teaching and learning that would be appropriate for heritage language teaching as well. For some languages, there are excellent opportunities on the web. For example, Southeast Asian heritage language learners and teachers can find a wealth of useful linguistic and cultural information about Burmese, Indonesian,

Khmer, Lao, Tagalog, Thai, and Vietnamese at www.seasite .niu.edu, a site developed by faculty at Northern Illinois University's Center for Southeast Asian Studies with support from government grants. This site contains interactive language activities, instructional tools, and cultural information. Distance education may be another option for increasing the teaching and learning of some of the least commonly taught heritage languages (Taff, 1997).

Developing Teachers

What do teachers in heritage language schools need to know to teach effectively? What do they need to know about the languages and cultures they are teaching, their students, and the instructional curricula, materials, assessments, and methodologies for teaching various levels of students? The answers to these questions can help us develop preservice and inservice heritage language teacher training models. Community heritage language schools could then hire teachers whose preparation and training were close to that of the models. National language groups might wish to design heritage teacher recruitment programs and develop a heritage language recruitment center in order to hire the most qualified teachers available and to increase the number of heritage students participating in their schools, language camps, and summer language institutes.

Exploring the issue of professional development for heritage language teachers, Schwartz (this volume) outlines what can be done through university-level teacher training programs to prepare teachers to work with heritage students in language classes in the K–12 system and in institutions of higher education. The training components she recommends, which include content knowledge from the relevant fields and pedagogical skills, also would serve teachers in community heritage language programs. Many classes in these programs are now being taught by teachers who have not had opportunities to participate in or to complete such teacher training programs.

For community heritage language programs with little or no budget for teacher professional development, it may be necessary to seek out low-cost, inservice teacher training opportunities in local community schools and institutions of higher education. For instance, heritage language school staff might be encouraged to participate in the summer workshops for teachers available through a nearby National Foreign Language Resource Center or at local universities or community colleges. State foreign language conferences often offer useful workshops and presentations that could expand heritage language teachers' knowledge. Teachers in heritage language schools could be made aware of state or national language and cultural organizations that support the teaching of their specific languages or language teaching in general. As Shuhan Wang (1996) points out in discussing the needs of teachers in Chinese community language schools,

> national and regional teacher training institutes are of fundamental importance. These institutes could provide the training these teachers need to meet the certification requirements. A high quality program would also raise standards for instruction and help in the creation of agreed upon standards. (p. 66)

In addition to finding opportunities for inservice teacher training, it is important to develop in school administrators and parents an awareness of teachers' needs and of ways that parents and administrators can support classroom teaching.

Fostering Support Among Parents and Elders

Thoughtful involvement of parents and elders in the planning and teaching of the language and in the celebration of cultural events can strengthen and deepen the heritage lan-

guage program and its impact in the community. The participation of parents and elders has long been an integral part of
many community heritage language programs. Some classes
may actually have an elder as a teacher. Davis (1988), who did
research on Hupa language schools, noted that one of the
women on staff was "the most revered teacher because she is
a native speaker, an elder, and a Medicine Woman" (p. 311).

However, the involvement and roles of parents and elders
must be carefully designed, for, as Davis notes, there can be

> jealousy over the control of "heritage," over the "cor-
> rect" forms of the selective knowledge to be passed on,
> over doctrinal methods of teaching the sacred knowl-
> edge, and especially over the "authenticity" of the
> teacher. (p. 311)

Some parents and elders did not have access to literacy
skills in their first language in their youth. Thus, they themselves may be the first to request the development of heritage
language literacy classes. One such project took place in Fresno,
California, where Hmong parents asked for instruction in
Hmong literacy skills because it was considered necessary in
order to preserve traditional culture (Kang, Kuehn, & Herrell,
1996). The parents felt that an increasing rift had developed
between them, their culture and values, and their children. In
decisions concerning the first language literacy curriculum,
Hmong parents were the main source of information. While it
remains to be seen whether parents who have acquired native
language literacy can influence their children's later decision to
become literate in the language, it is clear that the desire to pass
the heritage language on to the next generation was a strong
motivating factor for some Hmong parents.

> We must learn and keep Hmong literacy before our cul-
> ture disappears. It's very important to teach our children

how to read, write and speak Hmong so that we have a way of preserving our culture. We want to write down beautiful stories about our culture, things that happen in our country, in Hmong, for our children. (Kang, Kuehn, & Herrell, 1996)

For heritage languages, whether written down recently or long ago, literature exists; poetry, puns, proverbs, and riddles abound. It is often the parents and the elders who have the knowledge and capacity to share through storytelling, drama, and song significant aspects of the literary and cultural traditions of a people. Encouraging and carefully designing opportunities for participation by parents and elders in community heritage language schools can increase interest in these programs and improve their quality.

Recommendations

In the previous section, I discussed areas of need in the burgeoning field of community heritage language education. In this section, I offer some specific actions that the field can take to establish and strengthen the effectiveness of heritage language communities and schools.

- Gather baseline data about heritage language communities and schools. Such data would include recent immigration trends, heritage community resettlement patterns, and the location of heritage language communities and schools.
- Carry out descriptive studies of heritage language communities, schools, teachers, and learners. Since some studies on these topics have already been conducted, it would be useful to have a clearinghouse devoted to heritage language teaching and learning, which would serve as a repository for such research. This clearinghouse could also provide information on materials available to support heritage language teaching.

- Disseminate, publicize, and share heritage language information through web sites and listservs on the Internet and through other media, including print publications, film, radio, and television. A strong effort needs to be made to ensure the quality and accuracy of the information being shared and to correct inaccurate information as soon as possible.
- Develop web-based exchange centers for heritage language schools. These centers might contain curricula and materials for all heritage languages; booklets and handbooks on setting up, running, and teaching in heritage language programs and schools; and up-to-date information about programs and schools across the United States.
- Develop umbrella organizations at the regional and national levels that focus on language policy and that bring heritage language communities together. Such organizations could serve as advocates for issues of concern to heritage language communities and schools. They might include subgroups such as heritage language school administrators, language teachers, curriculum and materials developers, and literature and culture specialists.
- Improve articulation between heritage community language programs and language departments in the K–12 system, as well as with language and area studies programs in institutions of higher education.
- Work with library and information specialists in universities, community colleges, public schools, and public libraries to develop collections and materials to support the maintenance and growth of local heritage languages.

In addition, there is much that each of us as language professionals can do individually. We can speak up for multilingualism whenever possible, share our resources, use technology to develop heritage language materials (including templates) to be distributed as inexpensively as possible, and involve our students in language research projects. In addition, meeting in small groups with other heritage language professionals at larger conferences such as the American Council on the Teaching of Foreign Languages (ACTFL), the American Educational Research Association (AERA), the Linguistic Society of America (LSA), and the National Association for Bilingual Education (NABE) will facilitate the exchange of ideas and the development of collaborative projects.

Conclusion

Heritage language schools in America continue to be a vibrant force in our communities for preserving and developing the linguistic and cultural traditions of our heritage languages. The role that these schools play in supporting multilingualism and linguistic diversity is significant. However, heritage language school staff often face overwhelming challenges to keeping their classes going. There are important ways in which state and national language education policy, leadership, and financial support could assist heritage school staff in providing effective instruction in the heritage languages of America. As Shoji and Janhunen (1997) note, "the future of any language is in the mouths of its youngest speakers" (p. 227). Our community heritage language schools have an important role to play in ensuring that young and old alike will continue to learn and speak the diverse languages of America.

References

Bradunas, E. (1988). Introduction. In E. Bradunas & B. Topping (Eds.), *Ethnic heritage and language schools in America* (pp. 13-27). Washington, DC: Library of Congress.

Bradunas, E., & Topping, B. (Eds.). (1988). *Ethnic heritage and language schools in America*. Washington, DC: Library of Congress.

British Columbia Heritage Language Association (BCHLA). (2001). *BCHLA mission/objectives*. Retrieved from http://www.bchla.org/bchla1a.html and http://www.bchla.org/bchla/bchla1.html

Brooke, J. (1998, April 9). Indians strive to save their languages. *The New York Times*, pp. A1, A22.

Campbell, R.N., & Rosenthal, J.W. (2000). Heritage languages. In J.W. Rosenthal (Ed.), *Handbook of undergraduate second language education* (pp. 165-184). Mahwah, NJ: Lawrence Erlbaum.

Carlson, C. (2001, July 3). Immigrants becoming new political force in Minnesota. *St. Paul Pioneer Press*, p. B4.

Chao, T.H. (1996). Overview. In X. Wang (Ed.), *A view from within: A case study of Chinese heritage community language schools in the United States* (pp. 7-13). Washington, DC: National Foreign Language Center.

Chen, R.S. (1996). Obtaining credit from local school districts. In X.Wang (Ed.), *A view from within: A case study of Chinese heritage community language schools in the United States* (pp. 51-57). Washington, DC: National Foreign Language Center.

Compton, C.J. (1984). Quality in language skills. In R.A. Morse (Ed.), *Southeast Asian studies: Options for the future* (pp. 95-105). Washington, DC: The Wilson Center East Asia Program.

Compton, C.J. (2000). *Language teachers and heritage communities: Working together for the less commonly taught languages.* Paper presented at the annual meeting of the American Association for Applied Linguistics, Vancouver, British Columbia, Canada.

Davis, L. (1988). Hupa Indian language schools. In E. Bradunas & B. Topping (Eds.), *Ethnic heritage and language schools in America* (pp. 285-315). Washington, DC: Library of Congress.

Feuerverger, G. (1991). University students' perceptions of heritage language learning and ethnic identity maintenance. *The Canadian Modern Language Review/La Revue Canadienne des langues vivantes, 47*, 660-677.

Japanese National Standards Task Force. (1998). *Standards for Japanese language learning.* Unpublished manuscript.

Kang, H-W., Kuehn, P., & Herrell, A. (1996). The Hmong literacy project: Parents working to preserve the past and ensure the future. *The Journal of Educational Issues of Language Minority Students, 16*(2), 1-10. Retrieved from http://www.ncbe.gwu.edu/miscpubs/jeilms/vol16/jeilms1602.htm

Liu, J. (1996). Awarding credit through testing: The case of the San Francisco Unified School District. In X.Wang (Ed.), *A view from within: A case study of Chinese heritage community language schools in the United States* (pp. 59-61). Washington, DC: National Foreign Language Center.

National Education Association. (1998). *NEA Advocate, 1*(2), 1.

National Standards in Foreign Language Education Project. (1996). *Standards for foreign language learning: Preparing for the 21st century.* Yonkers, NY: Author.

Oldfield, A.C. (1998). *Heritage language program initial survey—Tucson, Arizona.* Unpublished survey conducted January-February 1998 on behalf of The Critical Languages Program at The University of Arizona.

Pelz, R. (1991). Ethnic identity and aging: Children of Jewish immigrants return to their first language. In J.R. Dow (Ed.), *Language and ethnicity: Focusschrift in honor of Joshua A. Fishman* (pp. 183-205). Philadelphia: John Benjamins.

Rubin, J., & Thompson, I. (1994). *How to be a more successful language learner: Toward learner autonomy* (2nd ed.). New York: Heinle & Heinle.

Shoji, H., & Janhunen, J. (1997). Conclusion. In H. Shoji & J. Janhunen (Eds.), *Northern minority languages: Problems of survival* (Senri Ethnological Studies No. 44, pp. 225-227). Osaka, Japan: National Museum of Ethnology.

Sridhar, K.K. (1997). The languages of India in New York. In O. Garcia & J.A. Fishman (Eds.), *The multilingual apple: Languages in New York City*. New York: Mouton de Gruyter.

Taff, A. (1997). Learning ancestral languages by telephone: Creating situations for language use. In J. Reyhner (Ed.), *Teaching indigenous languages* (pp. 40-45). Flagstaff, AZ: Northern Arizona University, Center for Excellence in Education.

Wang, S.C. (1996). Improving Chinese language schools: Issues and recommendations. In X. Wang (Ed.) *A view from within: A case study of Chinese heritage community language schools in the United States* (pp. 63-67). Washington, DC: National Foreign Language Center.

U.S. Census Bureau. (2001). *Census 2000 supplementary survey: Profile of selected social characteristics.* Retrieved from http://factfinder.census.gov/home/en/c2ss.html

Wang, X. (1996). Forging a link: Heritage community language schools and the formal education system. In X. Wang (Ed.), *A view from within: A case study of Chinese heritage community language schools in the United States* (pp. 77-89). Washington, DC: National Foreign Language Center.

Warschauer, M., & Meskill, C. (2000). Technology and second language teaching. In J.W. Rosenthal (Ed.), *Handbook of undergraduate second language education* (pp. 303-318). Mahwah, NJ: Lawrence Erlbaum.

Wolff, B. (2000, November 29). Project to help preserve Ojibwe language. *Wisconsin Week*. Retrieved August 23, 2001, from http://www.news.wisc.edu/wisweek/view.msql?id=5575

8
Heritage Language Students in the K–12 Education System

Shuhan C. Wang, Department of Education, State of Delaware
Nancy Green, Long Beach Unified School District, California

> We can leave the oil in the ground, and it will still be there to use in a hundred years; the more we use it, and the more we use it unwisely, the less we have of it later. Just the opposite is true of language and culture. The more we use these, the more we have of them; but the longer we neglect their use, the closer we are to extinguishing them. That has already happened for some languages, and we may be starting to see the consequences. The world will one day end, but the overriding cause is more likely to be a shortage of human resources like language and culture than a shortage of physical resources like coal and oil. (Ruíz, 1981, p. 28, cited in Hornberger, 1997, p. 8)

There is a growing recognition in the United States that the nation's non-English languages are valuable resources both for individuals and for the society as a whole (Brecht & Ingold, 1998; Fishman, Nahirny, Hofman, & Hayden, 1966/1978; Hornberger, 1997; Ruíz, 1984). Unlike natural resources, however, linguistic resources can be exhausted by negligence and lack of use, as Ruíz (1981, p. 28) and Hornberger (1997, pp. 6-8) warn.

Nearly 3 decades ago, the National Council of State Supervisors of Foreign Languages (NCSSFL) noted in a position paper on language education that "if the United States is to remain a world leader, it must develop for its citizens the opportunities to learn to communicate adequately in many tongues and in the context of many cultures" and called for the "orderly development of native or ancestral languages" in addition to English (NCSSFL, 1977). Today, at the beginning of a new century and a new millennium, NCSSFL reaffirms its support for greater linguistic and cultural diversity in the United States through the development of the country's heritage languages (Wang & Garcia, 2001).

For language educators in the primary and secondary school systems who are committed to this goal, certain questions arise. What are heritage languages, and who are the heritage language speakers in our schools? What are heritage language speakers' needs and goals, and how can the K–12 school system meet their needs and help them achieve their goals? This chapter explores theoretical and practical considerations in responding to these questions. The issues raised are neither comprehensive nor conclusive, but rather are designed to serve as catalysts for further discussion and debate.

In exploring these issues, we use Cooper's (1989) language planning framework. Cooper defines language planning as "deliberate efforts to influence the behavior of others with respect to the acquisition, structure, or functional allocation of their language codes" (p. 183). By combining theories from four disciplines, he proposes a descriptive framework, "an accounting scheme" (pp. 58-98), in which he proposes the following matrix for language planning: "What actors attempt to influence what behaviors, of which people, for what ends, under what conditions, by what means, through what decision-making process, with what effect?" (p. 98). By considering heritage language speakers in the K–12 education system from the perspective of this matrix, we can begin the task of untangling the complex issues related to heritage language speakers and heritage language learning.

What Behaviors of Which People

Since in our case "what behaviors of which people" refers to the language use behaviors of heritage language speakers, we need first to define the terms heritage language and heritage language speaker in the K–12 context. As pointed out in the introduction to this volume and by Van Deusen-Scholl (2000), the term heritage language has not yet been precisely defined. As a starting point for our discussion, we have adopted Fishman's definition (this volume), according to which a heritage language is a non-English language with a particular family relevance to the learner.

The heritage language population in the United States covered by this definition is thus huge and heterogeneous. Fishman categorizes heritage languages into three major groups, according to each group's sociohistorical background in the United States (Fishman, 1991, this volume). The first group is made up of the indigenous heritage languages, such as Hualapai, Navajo, and Yup'ik, spoken by Amerindians (Fishman, 1991; Hornberger, 1997; McCarty & Zepeda, 1995). The second group comprises what Fishman calls the colonial heritage languages—such as Dutch, French, and German—that were established here before the United States declared its independence. The third group, immigrant languages, comprises the many languages that immigrants have brought with them over the past 2 centuries. Because Spanish is both a colonial and an immigrant language, coupled with the fact that its speakers outnumber any other heritage language groups, it presents the most challenging case among the heritage language groups in the United States.

For Valdés, it is the heritage language speaker's bilingual proficiency in the heritage language and in English that is important. For the purposes of her discussion, a heritage language speaker is an individual "who is raised in a home where a non-English language is spoken, who speaks or at least understands the language, and who is to some degree bilingual in that language and in English" (this volume, p. 38). As Valdés points out, there is a wide range of language proficiency among this population. They may be monolingual English speakers with only a rudimentary knowledge of their heritage language and culture, or they may be monolingual heritage language speakers with little or no proficiency in English. Within our school systems, most heritage language speakers fall somewhere along the continuum of language abilities between these two ends.

If we combine Fishman's and Valdés's definitions of heritage language speakers and apply them to the K–12 context, we can divide heritage language students into three major categories: students who are new arrivals or migrants; foreign-born students who arrived at a young age but have been in U.S. schools for several years; and U.S.-born students of immigrant or indigenous ancestry. A heritage language student may be placed in a bilingual, English as a second language, or foreign language program in our schools. Which kind of program a student is placed in depends on different factors, including length of time in this country, national place of birth, proficiency in English, academic achievement, availability of a particular heritage language course, and student interest and need.

What Actors Attempt to Influence

Heritage language education overlaps two traditionally separate fields, bilingual education and foreign language education. These fields have been seen as separate because their learners and educational goals have been seen as different. The education of heritage language speakers may offer new opportunities for educators in these two fields to begin a dialogue leading to collaboration and cooperation.

A growing number of language educators believe it is time for the United States to reexamine its language policies and its orientation to both bilingual and foreign language education (for a detailed discussion of U.S. language policy, see Kloss, 1977/1998; Ruíz, 1984). The primary goal of bilingual education has been proficiency in English, not bilingualism (Crawford, 1989, 1992; Leibowitz, 1971; Macías & Wiley, 1998). The primary goal of foreign language instruction is the proficiency of a monolingual native speaker of the language in question, as the widely accepted proficiency guidelines developed by the American Council on the Teaching of Foreign Languages (ACTFL, 1986) indicate. For instance, in the training manual for the oral proficiency interview (OPI), interviewers are advised to look for vocabulary, discourse strategies, and command of language that are "native-like" in superior speakers (Buck, 1989, pp. 2-3). This monolingual orientation to language use, which views English at one end and a target foreign language at the other, ignores a host of linguistic characteristics, sociopsychological factors, and verbal strategies, such as codeswitching, that are typical of individuals who speak more than one language (see, for example, Bailey, 2000; Blom & Gumperz, 1972; Rampton, 1995; Zentella, 1997).

If we add heritage language speakers to discussions of bilingual and foreign language education, we should be able to come up with broader and more inclusive language policies that allow room for multiple language varieties, cultures, literacies, and discourses (Gee, 1996; McKay & Wong, 1996; New London Group, 1996; Street, 1995). The gains for the nation will be immeasurable in terms of our economic and political competitiveness around the world and our social and cultural diversity at home. For these reasons, government, private agencies, and businesses also have a stake (along with schools) in the development of these policies.

Heritage language groups themselves, of course, are also stakeholders in this process. Language maintenance is critically important to any group concerned with the transmission of its language and culture from one generation to the next. The goals of this group may be different from those of the government and business sectors of society, but by maintaining their languages, heritage language speakers contribute to the public good and help the nation meet its economic and political needs by building a strong language capacity.

Heritage language groups must empower themselves and take control of the language education of their own communities. While they continue to seek ways to collaborate and partner with the educational system, they need to engage in their own language planning as well. There are ample examples of this approach to language maintenance, both among immigrant languages, such as Chinese, Hebrew, Japanese, Korean, Polish, and Russian (Fishman, 1991; Fishman, Gertner, Lowy, & Milán, 1985; Fishman, Nahirny, Hofman, & Hayden, 1966/1978; S. Wang, 1996, 1999b; X. Wang, 1996) and among indigenous languages, such as Hawaiian and Navajo (e.g., McCarty & Zepeda, 1995; Tharp & Gallimore, 1990). Hornberger (1997) also provides examples of language maintenance activities from North, Meso, and South America.

For What Ends Under What Conditions

Needs of Heritage Language Students

The immediate linguistic and educational needs of heritage language students vary tremendously depending on background circumstances and experiences. Newly arrived students may come from rural or urban areas. Their educational and socioeconomic backgrounds vary widely, as do their linguistic and academic abilities. They may be well-educated speakers, readers, and writers of the heritage language, or they may speak a colloquial or even stigmatized variety of the language and have little or no formal education in their own countries. Although most of these students need assistance in learning the English language and academic content in English, their paths and pace in reaching these goals may be very different.

Those students who were born in the United States to immigrant or indigenous parents who speak languages other than English may have been exposed to the heritage language in childhood, but most have been educated exclusively in English (Campbell, 1998). As a result, while they may or may not be able to speak the heritage language, their literacy skills in the language are usually limited. Only those who have had the opportunity (usually in community-based programs) to receive formal instruction in their ancestral language will have developed a degree of literacy. In other words, this group's linguistic skills in the heritage language are generally very uneven, and may fall anywhere on the continuum from receptive at one end to fully productive at the other. Schools need to be flexible and culturally responsive in their educational approaches in order to meet the needs of this varied population of students (see below; see also Heath, 1983; McCarty & Zepeda, 1995; Philips, 1983; Tharp & Gallimore, 1990; Vygotsky, 1978).

Language education has undergone a number of changes in recent years, and language learners have been in and out of an array of programs, including sheltered English, newcomer, ESL pull-out, transitional bilingual, developmental bilingual, two-way dual language, and immersion. (For details about these programs, see Genesee, 1999; see also the discussion on acquisition planning below.) Although many English language learners have transitioned successfully to mainstream English classes, many others have fallen through the cracks of the system and are limited in English, the heritage language, and academic content knowledge. Educators who wonder why the dropout rate for certain student groups is so high might consider the possibility that they have been "pushed out" (Tyack, 1996) by ineffective educational programs.

As for those students who have been successfully mainstreamed, the price they often pay is a loss of proficiency in their heritage language. In other words, they suffer subtractive bilingualism (Lambert, 1975) and have evolved from bilingualism to English monolingualism. It is worth considering whether, in light of our understanding of language ability as a resource and our knowledge of our nation's language needs, English monolingualism is a desirable outcome for our students, our schools, and our country.

For both U.S.- and foreign-born heritage language speakers, language, race, ethnicity, culture, and socioeconomic status can become boundaries that prevent them from crossing from one group to another (Erickson, 1996b, p. 38; Erickson & Shultz, 1982). These factors may also create "sites of struggle" between the heritage and mainstream cultures or between different heritage groups (Ogbu, 1996, pp. 93-94). Attitudes of peer groups, ethnic groups, and the wider community help or hinder language development in the heritage language as well as in English. When heritage language students feel that others value their language and culture, they will be more likely to claim them as their own and want to learn about them. They will also be more likely to learn English and participate in the mainstream culture. When they feel that their language and culture are stigmatized and ridiculed, heritage language speakers are more likely to distance themselves from other groups or their own groups. Education professionals need to give these learners tools to build a healthy identity and to negotiate membership in their own heritage group and in other language and social groups (Bucholtz, 1995; Erickson, 1996a, 1996b; Erickson & Schultz, 1982; Gumperz & Hymes, 1964, 1972; Ogbu, 1996; Rampton, 1995).

This point is particularly poignant for U.S.-born heritage language speakers. Many have a strong desire to be seen as "American," especially if their physical features differ from the two major racial groups in the United States, Blacks and Whites. Their badge of identity is often their linguistic ability in English, and they may take pains to sound "American." Many have adopted society's negative attitudes toward their own heritage group and refuse to be identified as members of it, even when others have identified them as such (González Pino & Pino, 2000; Tuan, 1998). School staff need to help these students affirm their membership in the mainstream society while maintaining affinity to their cultural roots. Helping these students develop strategies to negotiate different languages, cultures, and group memberships is a critical issue for educators.

Educators must also attend to complex sociolinguistic issues faced by heritage language speakers. Some students, for example, may speak a dialect that happens to be stigmatized in relation to the standard variety. They may need to expand the domains of their language use from those of the family, playground, and street to those of school and the workplace (Fishman, 1972). They need to know "when," "what," and "how" to speak "to whom" in "what" situations (Hymes, 1974) and to upgrade their language proficiency from that of a child in a social situation to a more mature and age-appropriate academic level (see Cummins, 1981; Valdés & Geoffrion-Vinci, 1998). Some may have stopped developing proficiency in the heritage language (fossilization) or lost proficiency (attrition) as a result of the exclusive use of English (Celce-Murcia, 1991, p. 462; Ellis, 1994, pp. 353-355; Hyltenstam, 1988, p. 68; Selinker, 1972, p. 215).

Needs of the Education System

Schools need to help their heritage language students learn in three broad skill areas: English, content knowledge, and a foreign language (which, in some instances, will be the home or heritage language). In foreign language and English as second language education, recently established standards have set expected educational outcomes aimed at enabling students to function successfully in the classroom and in the workplace (National Standards in Foreign Language Education Project,

1999; Teachers of English to Speakers of Other Languages, 1997).

These are daunting tasks, made all the more so by an education system that traditionally views the languages and cultures that students bring to school not as skills and resources to be nurtured and developed, but as obstacles to be overcome. In an education system that promotes assimilation, heritage language students have the added burden of dealing with two languages and cultures while trying to achieve academically in their school subjects.

A complex host of social, historical, and cultural factors affect language development and identity formation. When educators design programs for heritage language speakers, they must pay attention to numerous factors: where learners were born; how they came to the United States; how long they have lived here; how old they were when they came or, if U.S. born, how many generations their families have been here; and their families' socioeconomic and educational backgrounds.

One effective educational strategy is to view students' backgrounds as an instructional starting point and to engage in culturally responsive teaching (Vygotsky, 1978). Because language socialization is a culturally specific practice, children from different cultural backgrounds usually have been socialized into different language practices. For example, in her seminal work that explored language socialization patterns in three North Carolina communities (White working class, Black working class, and Black and White middle class), Heath (1983) found that the ways that children learned to talk at home and in their communities made a difference in how well they learned the literacy practices of their schools. Philips's (1983) study of schooling with Native American children on a Warm Spring Indian reservation in central Oregon; Tharp and Gallimore's (1990) study of the Hawaiian Kamehameha Early Education Program (KEEP) program; and Jordan's (1995) study of the KEEP/Rough Rock Project on a Navajo reservation in northeastern Arizona (see also McCarty & Zepeda, 1995) showed that instruction is more effective when it is culturally compatible with and responsive to the interactional styles and social norms of the children in the program. Likewise, teachers of heritage language speakers need to practice culturally responsive teaching so that students have equal opportunities for success in school.

Needs of the Heritage Language Community

Heritage language groups that wish to maintain their language and culture must work alongside professionals in the education system. In discussing how indigenous groups may preserve their language and culture while learning English, Ruíz (1995, pp. 71-81) points out that the approach they take must be geared toward strengthening both the instrumental and sentimental functions of the language in the community. "Since languages live in communities, the activities of the community must be the targets of language policies" (Ruíz, 1995, p. 78). Toward this end, community media, social service agencies, recreation centers, and other local organizations can all implement strategies that support the use of the heritage language in the community's daily life.

Similarly, Fishman emphasizes that language maintenance efforts need to be an integral part of family, neighborhood, and community life (1991, p. 398). He cautions that although schools are able to help learners gain proficiency in the heritage language and deepen their commitment to its preservation, what schools are able to provide is usually "too little and too late" to effect language maintenance (p. 379).

Schools also appear to play a limited role in identity formation (Erickson & Shultz, 1982; Wang, 1998, 1999b). This does not mean that school staff should not pay attention to children's identity issues. Rather, it means that the major responsibility lies with families and the heritage language groups themselves, who must mobilize the community to provide a network of home and community support for heritage language and cultural activities that take place outside of school (Fishman, 1991, pp. 368-380).

By What Means
Through What Decision-Making Process

What can schools and communities do to help heritage language speakers develop their language proficiencies and build the language capacity of the nation? This question may be answered with reference to three aspects of language planning—status planning, corpus planning, and acquisition planning (Cooper, 1989; Hornberger, 1994, 1997). Status planning refers to deliberate efforts to influence the use and study of a language within a community. Selecting a language as the medium of instruction is an example of a status planning activity. Corpus planning focuses on the language itself and attempts to maintain or change the language system—creating new linguistic forms, modifying old ones, or making choices among alternative forms. Acquisition planning refers to users of the language and efforts to increase the number of users. It includes, but is not limited to, language teaching activities. Establishing local or national language education policies are acquisition planning activities. In what follows we propose implementation strategies in these three categories.

Status Planning

In status planning, language goals may differ according to the sectors involved. For example, at the national level, one goal in status planning is to promote the study of a foreign language in order to meet the country's social, economic, and political needs. These needs may be quite different from those of the K–12 school system, which must concern itself with its own goals and needs—the study and mastery of English and of academic content, and the offering of foreign languages based on community interest and local capacity. Heritage language communities may have still different goals, which could include passing down the heritage language, culture, and religion, and encouraging the younger generations to maintain or acquire their own language and culture while developing English language skills and an American identity.

Although each sector has its own goals and needs, all three share common interests and issues. For instance, all sectors expect students to achieve academically. All sectors must deal with issues related specifically to language study, such as how to elevate the status of foreign language study, how to provide all students with opportunities and incentives to study another language, and how to make instruction more effective. These are areas of discussion to which all sectors can contribute and from which all can learn.

A host of factors determines whether or not a school system will decide to offer a particular language as a course of study. The most important factors relate to local interest, funding, scheduling, staffing, materials, perceived economic utility of the language, and the political relationship between the United States and the country where the language is spoken. While some might view these factors as obstacles to the development of language programs, they may also be viewed as opportunities for collaboration between ethnic communities and the school system. For example, if community members would like the local school system to teach their language or to give credit for community language classes, they will need to convince the school system of the value of heritage language education and then work together with the system to make their wishes a reality.

Corpus Planning

The focus of corpus planning includes the contexts and uses of various languages and language varieties, pronunciations, writing systems, and lexical items, to give a few examples. Because corpus planning decisions vary from language to language and group to group, we do not explore them in depth in this chapter. However, one aspect of corpus planning is important in heritage language education—the issue of stigmatized language varieties versus the standard variety, vernacular discourses versus the school discourse, and different types of literacies versus the narrowly defined reading and writing literacy of school (Hornberger & Skilton-Sylvester, 2000).

Schools *should* teach the standard variety of a language. However, instruction should begin with the students and what they know. If the language variety that students speak is a nonstandard (and stigmatized) one, they should be made aware of the differences between their variety and the standard variety and learn when to use which variety, with whom, in what situations. Likewise, if students' discourse or literacy styles are different from those of the classroom, teachers should build on students' personal or home knowledge and show them how to bridge the gap between what they know and what the school expects.

In bridging this gap, Hymes's notion of the Ethnography of SPEAKING (1974) is useful. Incorporating linguistics, anthropology, and sociology, Hymes proposes an ethnography of communication as a means to study "ways of speaking" (pp. 45-46) in a community. He has developed a grid that includes the following components:

S Setting—time, place, physical circumstances of interaction
P Participants—roles, social relations, and distance
E Ends—goals and purpose, outcomes of interaction
A Act sequence—message form and content
K Keys—tones, manners of speaking
I Instrumentalities—channels, oral versus written (verbal and nonverbal) communication, styles, registers
N Norms of interaction and interpretation
G Genres—lectures, poems, songs, conversations, etc.

This typology addresses the who, what, when, where, why, and how of language use. S(etting) is the "where" and "when" that set the stage of the interaction. P(articipants) is the "who" that shows the actors in a social act, the speakers, the hearers, and their relationships. E(nds) is the "why" that explains the purposes, goals, motivations, and intentions of certain acts and behaviors. A(ct) is the "what" that is being said and done. K(eys), I(nstrumentalities), N(orms), and G(enres) are the "how" of things being said and done in a speech community. Students who have acquired this tool and learned how to use it to analyze language and their own interactions with the mainstream culture will better understand their own positions on the continuum from their own "ways with words" (Heath, 1983) to those of the standard and schooled type, and decide how they may proceed from one end to the other.

Acquisition Planning

Heritage language acquisition planning concerns itself with the teaching of heritage languages and pedagogical and administrative issues that programs must address.

Initial Decisions

The following basic questions must be addressed first. Is there a need for heritage language classes? When and where will the classes take place? Will families teach their children at home, or will they pool their resources and set up a community school? Should families decide to establish a school, they need to think about how they are going to fund and maintain it.

How a school is funded depends on local conditions, needs, and desires. Some schools receive funding from the U.S. government (e.g., Amerindian schools; see McCarty & Zepeda, 1995); some receive funding from other countries (e.g., some Japanese language schools serving the children of expatriates); some are supported by tuition (e.g., Hebrew schools; see Fishman, 1991); and some depend on a combination of sources (e.g., Chinese or Taiwanese language schools; see X. Wang, 1996).

While many programs begin as grassroots initiatives, others evolve from efforts by government, business, and education systems. For example, a heritage language education program might be launched after a school system investigates the use of heritage languages in the local community and decides to establish the program in collaboration with members of the heritage community.

Community–school collaboration can take different forms, depending on local conditions and interest. A school district may work closely with the community to set up heritage language classes that offer instruction to both heritage language speakers and other students interested in studying the language. Alternatively, the school may grant credit for language classes offered in the community (Chen, 1996; Liu, 1996). When language classes are offered to all students in the community, there are at least two advantages. Students from different language and cultural backgrounds have opportunities to interact with and learn from one another, and the presence of mainstream students in the heritage language classes may heighten the heritage speakers' pride in their own language and culture. (For more detail about heritage communities and schools, see Compton, this volume.)

Program Models

School programs with heritage language speakers take a variety of forms. In recent years, research has described developmental bilingual education (Genesee, 1999; Ramírez, Yuen, & Ramey, 1991), foreign language immersion (Center for Applied Linguistics, 1999; Cincinnati Public Schools, 1988; Gouin, 1998; Lambert & Macnamara, 1969; Lambert & Tucker, 1972), and two-way or dual language immersion programs (e.g., Cazabon, Nicoladis, & Lambert, 1998; Christian, Montone, Lindholm, & Carranza, 1997; Lindholm-Leary, in press). Although the end goal of most bilingual education programs is proficiency in English, in some programs academic content is taught in students' native languages and in English (Genesee, 1999, pp. 19-24). Originally designed for English-speaking children, foreign language immersion programs provide instruction in non-English languages. Research shows that this type of program can be effective for heritage language speakers of the language who would like to reacquire or develop literacy in it (Genesee, 1999, pp. 24-30). As the name suggests, two-way immersion or dual language programs involve both English and heritage language speakers. Academic subjects are taught in two languages, so that students develop oral and literacy skills in both languages while learning content knowledge (Genesee, 1999, pp. 31-35; see also Met, 1998).

Some school systems are attempting to meet the needs of heritage language students in foreign language classes, often with separate classes for these students (see, for example, resources in Roca & Marcos, 2001). Webb and Miller (2000), Valdés (this volume), and Schwartz (this volume) make the point that instruction and teaching materials need to be adapted to the particular needs of heritage language speakers. In addition, educators need to be sensitive to issues of identity when recruiting and working with heritage language speakers, who often do not wish to be seen as "different."

Assessment

At present, assessment instruments designed specifically for heritage students do not exist, and it is unclear whether standards and guidelines developed for foreign language students (ACTFL Performance Guidelines for K–12 Learners Task Force, 1998; National Standards in Foreign Language Education Project, 1996, 1999) can be applied to heritage language students without modification. As we learn more about the characteristics and learning needs of heritage language speakers, assessment instruments that meet their special needs should be developed.

Foreign language programs that reach out to heritage language students need to assess learners for proper placement. In some cases, it may be necessary to award credit for language skills already mastered. Assessment also enables programs to establish course sequences and curricula that build on skills and knowledge students already possess.

In order to build the best possible program, a host of questions related to student assessment and program evaluation should be addressed: What are program goals and instructional objectives? What are expected outcomes? How can learners' strengths and needs in the heritage language be identified? What evaluation and assessment criteria and policy for student placement, promotion, and exit should be used? What qualitative and quantitative measurements can be gathered and used? Are there other social and psychological considerations to be included in the evaluation? Heritage language speakers with limited English will also need to be assessed in English language proficiency and in academic content knowledge.

Articulation

Ideally, decision-makers from K–12 schools, the heritage community, and institutions of higher education will work together to design a well-articulated package of course offerings in logical sequence (Wang, 2000). In designing such a program, decision-makers need to address the following:

- Needs and characteristics of students
- Alignment of proficiency levels across institutions
- Placement and promotion policies and criteria; performance benchmarks
- Curriculum design
- Materials development and textbook selection
- Instructional strategies

- Assessment
- Teacher education and certification
- Program accreditation
- Funding support for collaborative efforts

Curriculum and Materials Development

Of the many curriculum issues that heritage language educators must address, three in particular are important: Curriculum developers need to align program standards with students' proficiency levels; take into account students' diverse cultural backgrounds, learning styles, and abilities; and promote a balanced view of both the heritage and mainstream cultures. In materials development, the sensitive issue of language varieties in pronunciation, vocabulary, and syntax emerges.

One approach to curriculum and materials development for this population of learners is to focus on the heritage culture. For example, important figures from the heritage language group, particularly those who have contributed to both the mainstream society and the heritage culture, may serve as the foundation on which to build an appreciation for the heritage culture. Another approach is to treat language awareness as a curriculum subject, as suggested by Rampton (1995, pp. 331-336). Through learner-centered, discovery-oriented activities that raise awareness of language use and interethnic/interracial relationships, schools can offer diversity education that is beneficial to all students.

Teacher Development

Heritage language programs have the choice of recruiting native speakers of the languages taught or foreign language teachers who may not be native speakers. There are several advantages to having native speakers as teachers or paraprofessionals, particularly in the case of the less commonly taught languages (see Gambhir, this volume). In addition to their language and cultural knowledge and ability to provide excellent language input for all students, native speakers can also serve as role models for heritage language students.

While native speakers can make important contributions to heritage language education, they also have professional needs. In addition to needing training in general education, pedagogy, and applied linguistics, native speakers often need to better understand American culture and the American educational system. They need to understand that the heritage language student is neither a traditional foreign language learner nor a typical first language learner. As a result, the field of heritage language education draws knowledge and strategies from the fields of both first and second language acquisition. To become effective, teachers need to understand the linguistic and cultural needs of their students as well as their sociopsychological orientations (see Schwartz, this volume).

Shuhan Wang (one of the authors of this chapter) is an example of a native speaker of a language other than English who has made the journey from heritage language teacher in a community setting to certified K–12 teacher to educational administrator. Working with the University of Pennsylvania to develop a special teacher training program for Chinese heritage language teachers in schools in Delaware, New Jersey, New York, and Pennsylvania, she is now helping others make the same journey. The Chinese Teachers' Summer Institute, one component of the program, offers heritage Chinese teachers a wide range of teacher education courses relevant to their work. (For more details on the teacher training needs of heritage language teachers, see Wang, 1999a.)

Conclusion: With What Effect

In this chapter, we have discussed the topic of heritage language students in the K–12 educational system in the context of Cooper's language planning framework: "What actors attempt to influence what behaviors, of which people, for what ends, under what conditions, by what means, through what decision-making process, with what effect?"(Cooper, 1989, p. 98). In answering the question of "what behaviors of which people," we defined heritage languages and heritage language students. In answering "what actors attempt to influence," we identified key players in this arena—heritage language students; foreign language, bilingual, and ESL educators; the school system as a whole; government and business leaders; policymakers; and the heritage language communities themselves.

In answering "for what ends under what conditions," we analyzed the needs of heritage language students, the school system, and the heritage community. In answering "by what means through what decision-making process," we suggested various programmatic approaches in the areas of status planning, corpus planning, and acquisition planning. In status planning, we suggested that different sectors have both different and common interests and goals. In corpus planning, we suggested that attention be paid to the value of multiple language varieties, literacies, and discourses as a first step in helping students bridge the gap between what they already know and what they still need to know. In acquisition planning, we discussed specific administrative and pedagogical issues that heritage language programs face.

We conclude by returning to Ruíz (1981), quoted at the beginning of this chapter. It is through underuse, not overuse, that we exhaust our linguistic resources. It is heartening, therefore, that more and more educators in this country support heritage language development. In a nation of diverse languages and cultures, we must do what we can to ensure that our linguistic wealth and cultural heritage are passed down to the next generation.

Identity: A Sensitive Issue

Heritage language speakers are often reluctant to be identified as such in school. As a result, many students resist enrolling in classes created specifically for them.

This observation is supported by a series of studies conducted by González Pino & Pino (2000) at the University of Texas at San Antonio. Students whom the university identified as heritage language speakers did not so identify themselves and instead signed up for beginning-level foreign language courses. While one reason for this was the desire for lower placement and higher grades, there were other reasons as well. The researchers found that these students often did not see themselves as heritage language speakers. They lacked confidence in their heritage language abilities and skills, had little understanding of their linguistic and curricular needs, had internalized negative societal attitudes toward their language and culture, and did not want to be segregated into the heritage language track (González Pino & Pino, 2000, pp. 29-32). Similar attitudes have been reported among Chinese American college students (Chao, 1997; M. Dietrich, personal communication, May 20, 1999).

While more research with various language groups is needed to analyze the issues in depth, we feel that they can be partially addressed by deconstructing the notion of a "native speaker," as Rampton (1995, p. 336) has suggested. Analyzing how adolescent groups of Afro-Caribbean, Anglo, and Panjabi descent in Ashmead and South London use languages and language varieties, such as Panjabi, Creole, and stylized Asian English, to cross ethnic and racial lines and "live with difference," Rampton calls into question the widely accepted notions of native speaker and mother tongue. He suggests that we look at native language in terms of a speaker's "expertise" (ability to operate a language) and "allegiance" (identification with a language and the values, meanings, and identities that it stands for)

(p. 340). He emphasizes that these two terms refer to the linguistic identities of an individual, serving as "cultural reinterpretations of a person's relationship to a language" (p. 340).

Rampton further divides *allegiance* into *affiliation* and *inheritance*. Although both refer to the attitudes of a speaker toward a certain language, affiliation refers to "a connection between people and groups that are considered to be separate or different," while inheritance is concerned with "the continuity between people and groups who are felt to be closely linked." That is, affiliation takes place *across* social or ethnic groups, and inheritance occurs *within* the group (p. 342). Thus, a nonnative speaker of a language may develop a social identity linked to the language if the individual feels an affiliation to the group that speaks the language.

Rampton's notion of looking at native language in terms of "expertise, affiliation, and inheritance" is worthwhile to consider, particularly in the case of heritage language students. As Wang (2001) has argued, it is problematic to "assign" the heritage language as the mother tongue to many heritage language youths, particularly to those who were born in the United States. Although many of them indeed grew up with the language at home, they may not feel comfortable or confident enough to identify themselves as native speakers of the heritage language.

Given the ambivalent attitudes that students often have toward their home languages, educators, community leaders, and parents need to be more sensitive in how they categorize or try to motivate these students. We need to take into account their language proficiency in the heritage language; their attitudes toward English, the heritage language, and the speakers of these languages; and how they feel about themselves. In short, we cannot assume that heritage language students automatically belong to a heritage language group, but we can carefully encourage them to search for connections with the language and its speakers.

References

ACTFL Performance Guidelines for K–12 Learners Task Force. (1998). *ACTFL performance guidelines for K–12 learners.* Yonkers, NY: American Council on the Teaching of Foreign Languages.

American Council on the Teaching of Foreign Languages. (1986). *Proficiency guidelines.* Yonkers, NY: Author.

Bailey, B. (2000). Language and negotiation of ethnic/racial identity among Dominican Americans. *Language in Society, 29,* 555-582.

Blom, J., & Gumperz, J. (1972). Social meaning in linguistic structure: Code switching in Norway. In J. Gumperz & D.H. Hymes (Eds.), *Directions in sociolinguistics* (pp. 407-434). New York: Holt, Rinehart and Winston.

Brecht, R.D., & Ingold, C.W. (1998). *Tapping a national resource: Heritage languages in the United States. ERIC Digest.* Washington, DC: ERIC Clearinghouse on Languages and Linguistics. Retrieved from http://www.cal.org/ericcll/digest/brecht01.html

Bucholtz, M. (1995). From mulatta to mestiza: Passing and the linguistic reshaping of ethnic identity. In K. Hall & M. Bucholtz (Eds.), *Gender articulated: Language and the socially constructed self* (pp. 351-373). New York: Routledge.

Buck, K. (Ed.). (1989). *The ACTFL Oral Proficiency Interview: Tester training manual.* Yonkers, NY: American Council on the Teaching of Foreign Languages.

Campbell, R.N. (1998). Conserving national language resources: How we can build on the bilingual students. In M. Met (Ed.), *Critical issues in early second language learning* (pp. 84-88). Glenview, IL: Scott Foresman–Addison Wesley.

Cazabon, M., Nicoladis, E., & Lambert, W. (1998). *Becoming bilingual in the Amigos two-way immersion program* (Research Report No. 3). Washington, DC, and Santa Cruz, CA: Center for Research on Education, Diversity & Excellence.

Celce-Murcia, M. (1991). Grammar pedagogy in second and foreign language teaching. *TESOL Quarterly, 25,* 459-480.

Center for Applied Linguistics. (1999). *Directory of total and partial immersion language programs in U.S. schools.* Washington, DC: Author. Retrieved from http://www.cal.org/ericcll/immersion

Chao, D.L. (1997). Chinese for Chinese-Americans: A case study. *Journal of the Chinese Language Teachers Association, 32*(2), 1-13.

Chen, R.S. (1996). Obtaining credit from local school districts. In X. Wang (Ed.), *A view from within: A case study of chinese heritage community language schools in the United States* (pp. 51-57). Washington, DC: National Foreign Language Center.

Christian, D., Montone, C., Lindholm, K., & Carranza, I. (1997). *Profiles in two-way immersion education.* McHenry, IL, and Washington, DC: Delta Systems and Center for Applied Linguistics.

Cincinnati Public Schools. (1988). *The future is happening in the Cincinnati Public Schools.* Cincinnati, OH: Author.

Cooper, R. (1989). *Language planning and social change.* Cambridge, UK: Cambridge University Press.

Crawford, J. (1989). *Bilingual education: History, politics, theory, and practice.* Trenton, NJ: Crane.

Crawford, J. (1992). *Hold your tongue: Bilingualism and the politics of "English only".* Reading, MA: Addison-Wesley.

Cummins, J. (1981). Four misconceptions about language proficiency in bilingual education. *NABE Journal, 5*(3), 31-45.

Ellis, R. (1994). *The study of second language acquisition.* Oxford, UK: Oxford University Press.

Erickson, F. (1996a). Ethnographic microanalysis. In S.L. McKay & N.H. Hornberger (Eds.), *Sociolinguistics and language teaching* (pp. 283-306). New York: Cambridge University Press.

Erickson, F. (1996b). Transformation and school success: The politics and culture of educational achievement. In E. Jacob & C. Jordan (Eds.), *Minority education: Anthropological perspectives* (pp. 27-51). Norwood, NJ: Ablex.

Erickson, F., & Shultz, J. (1982). *The counselor as gatekeeper: Social interaction in interviews.* New York: Academic Press.

Fishman, J.A. (1972). Domains and the relationship between micro- and macro-sociolinguistics. In J. Gumperz & D. H. Hymes (Eds.), *Directions in sociolinguistics* (pp. 435-453). New York: Holt, Rinehart and Winston.

Fishman, J.A. (1991). *Reversing language shift: Theoretical and empirical foundations of assistance to threatened languages.* Clevedon, UK: Multilingual Matters.

Fishman, J.A., Gertner, M.H., Lowy, E.G., & Milán, W.C. (1985). *Ethnicity in action.* Binghamton, NY: Bilingual Press/Editorial Bilingüe.

Fishman, J.A., Nahirny, V., Hofman, J.E., & Hayden, R.G. (1978). *Language loyalty in the United States.* New York: Arno Press. (Original work published 1966)

Gee, J.P. (1996). *Social linguistics and literacies: Ideology in discourses.* Bristol, PA: Taylor & Francis.

Genesee, F. (1999). (Ed.). *Program alternatives for linguistically diverse students* (Educational Practice Report No. 1). Washington, DC, and Santa Cruz, CA: Center for Research on Education, Diversity & Excellence.

González Pino, B., & Pino, F. (2000). Serving the heritage speaker across a five-year program. *ADFL Bulletin, 32*(1), 27-35.

Gouin, D. (1998). Report on current practice: Immersion program in Montgomery County, Maryland. In M. Met (Ed.), *Critical issues in early second language learning* (pp. 62-64). Glenview, IL: Scott Foresman–Addison Wesley.

Gumperz, J., & Hymes, D.H. (1964). The Ethnography of communication. *American Anthropologist, 66*(2), 137-164.

Gumperz, J., & Hymes, D.H. (Eds.). (1972). *Directions in sociolinguistics.* New York: Holt, Rinehart and Winston.

Heath, S.B. (1983). *Ways with words.* New York: Cambridge University Press.

Hornberger, N.H. (1994). Literacy and language planning. *Language and Education, 8*(1 & 2), 75-86.

Hornberger, N.H. (1997). Indigenous literacies in the Americas. In N.H. Hornberger (Ed.), *Indigenous literacies in the Americas: Language planning from the bottom up* (pp. 3-16). Berlin: Mouton de Gruyter.

Hornberger, N.H., & Skilton-Sylvester, E. (2000). Revisiting the continua of biliteracy: International and critical perspectives. *Language and Education, 14*(2), 96-122.

Hyltenstam, K. (1988). Lexical characteristics of near-native second language learners of Swedish. *Journal of Multilingual and Multicultural Development, 9*(1 & 2), 7-84.

Hymes, D. (1974). *Foundations in sociolinguistics: An ethnographic approach.* Philadelphia: University of Pennsylvania Press.

Jordan, C. (1995). Creating cultures of schooling: Historical and conceptual background of the KEEP/Rough Collaboration. *Bilingual Research Journal, 19*(1), 83-100.

Kloss, H. (1998). *The American bilingual tradition.* McHenry, IL, and Washington, DC: Delta Systems and Center for Applied Linguistics. (Original work published 1977)

Lambert, W.E. (1975). Culture and language as factors in learning and education. In A. Wolfgang (Ed.), *Education of immigrant students* (pp. 55-83). Toronto, Ontario, Canada: Ontario Institute for Studies in Education.

Lambert, W., & Macnamara, J. (1969). *Some intellectual consequences of following first-grade curriculum in a foreign language.* Unpublished manuscript, McGill University, Montreal, Quebec, Canada.

Lambert, W., & Tucker, G.R. (1972). *Bilingual education of children.* Rowley, MA: Newbury House.

Leibowitz, A.H. (1971). *Educational policy and political acceptance: The imposition of English as the language of instruction in American schools.* (ERIC Document Reproduction Service No. ED 047 321)

Lindholm-Leary, K. (in press). *Dual language education.* Avon, UK: Multilingual Matters.

Liu, J. (1996). Awarding credit through testing: The case of the San Francisco Unified School District. In X. Wang (Ed.), *A view from within: A case study of Chinese heritage community language schools in the United States* (pp. 59-67). Washington, DC: National Foreign Language Center.

Macías, R.F., & Wiley, T.G. (1998). Introduction to the second edition. In H. Kloss, *The American bilingual tradition* (pp. vii-xix). McHenry, IL, and Washington, DC: Delta Systems and Center for Applied Linguistics.

McCarty, T.L., & Zepeda, O. (Eds.). (1995). Indigenous language education and literacy [Special issue]. *Bilingual Research Journal, 19*(1).

McKay, S.L., & Wong, S.C. (1996). Multiple discourses, multiple identities: Investment and agency in second-language learning among Chinese adolescent immigrant students. *Harvard Educational Review, 66*(3), 577-608.

Met, M. (Ed.). (1998). *Critical issues in early second language learning.* Glenview, IL: Scott Foresman–Addison Wesley.

National Council of State Supervisors of Foreign Languages. (1977). *Bilingual education: A position paper.* See http://www.ncssfl.org

National Standards in Foreign Language Education Project (1996). *Standards for foreign language learning: Preparing for the 21st century.* Yonkers, NY: Author.

National Standards in Foreign Language Education Project. (1999). *Standards for foreign language learning in the 21st century.* Yonkers, NY: Author.

New London Group. (1996). A pedagogy of multiliteracies: Designing social futures. *Harvard Educational Review, 66*(1), 60-92.

Ogbu, J.U. (1996). Variability in minority school performance: A problem in search of an explanation. In E. Jacob & C. Jordan (Eds.), *Minority education: Anthropological perspectives* (pp. 83-111). Norwood, NJ: Ablex.

Philips, S. (1983). *The invisible culture: Communication in classroom and community on the Warm Springs Indian Reservation.* New York: Teachers College Press.

Ramírez, J.D., Yuen, S.D., & Ramey, D.R. (1991). *Longitudinal study of structured immersion strategy, early-exit, and late-exit transitional bilingual education programs for language-minority children* (Final report to the U.S. Department of Education. Executive Summary and Vols. I and II). San Mateo, CA: Aguirre International.

Rampton, B. (1995). *Crossing language and ethnicity among adolescents.* New York: Longman.

Roca, A., & Marcos, K. (2001). *Teaching Spanish to Spanish speakers* (ERIC/CLL Resource Guide Online). Washington, DC: ERIC Clearinghouse on Languages and Linguistics. Retrieved from http://www.cal.org/ericcll/faqs/rgos/sns.html

Ruíz, R. (1981). *Ethnic group interest and the social good: Law and language in education.* Unpublished manuscript, University of Wisconsin—Madison.

Ruíz, R. (1984). Orientations in language planning. *NABE Journal, 8*(2), 15-34.

Ruíz, R. (1995). Language planning considerations in indigenous communities. In T.L. McCarty & O. Zepeda (Eds.), Indigenous language education and literacy [Special issue]. *Bilingual Research Journal, 19*(1), 71-81.

Selinker, L. (1972). Interlanguage. *International Review of Applied Linguistics, 10,* 209-231.

Street, B. (1995). *Social literacies: Critical approaches to literacy in development, ethnography and education.* New York: Longman.

Teachers of English to Speakers of Other Languages, Inc. (1997). *ESL standards for pre-K–12 students.* Alexandria, VA: Author.

Tharp, R., & Gallimore, R. (1990). *Rousing minds to life: Teaching, learning, and schooling in social context.* Cambridge, UK: Cambridge University Press.

Tuan, M. (1998). *Forever foreigners or honorary whites? The Asian ethnic experience today.* New Brunswick, NJ: Rutgers University Press.

Tyack, D.B. (1996). *The one best system: A history of American urban education.* Cambridge, MA: Harvard University Press.

Valdés, G., & Geoffrion-Vinci, M. (1998). Chicano Spanish: The problem of the "underdeveloped" code in bilingual repertoires. *Modern Language Journal, 82*(4), 473-501.

Van Deusen-Scholl, N. (2000, March). *Toward a definition of "heritage language": Pedagogical and sociopolitical considerations.* Paper presented at the meeting of the American Association of Applied Linguistics, Vancouver, British Columbia, Canada.

Vygotsky, L. (1978). *Mind in society: The development of higher psychological processes.* Cambridge, MA: Harvard University Press.

Wang, S.C. (1996). Improving Chinese language schools: Issues and recommendations. In X. Wang (Ed.), *A view from within: A case study of Chinese heritage community language schools in the United States* (pp. 63-67). Washington, DC: National Foreign Language Center.

Wang, S.C. (1998). *Language and ethnic identity from post-structural gender and ethnic perspectives: A case study of Chinese-American children.* Unpublished manuscript.

Wang, S.C. (1999a). Teacher training: Meeting the needs of the field. In M. Chu (Ed.), *Mapping the course of the Chinese language field* (Chinese Language Teachers Association Monograph Series, Vol. III, pp. 25-36). Kalamazoo, MI: Chinese Language Teachers Association.

Wang, S.C. (1999b). Crossing the bridge: A Chinese case from mother tongue maintenance to foreign language education. In M. Chu (Ed.), *Mapping the course of the Chinese language field* (Chinese Language Teachers Association Monograph Series, Vol. III, pp. 271-312). Kalamazoo, MI: Chinese Language Teachers Association.

Wang, S.C. (2000, March). *Articulation among pre K–12, colleges, and heritage schools.* Paper presented at the meeting of the American Association of Applied Linguistics, Vancouver, British Columbia, Canada.

Wang, S.C. (2001). *A story of a tug-of-war: Heritage language mainte-nance of a Chinese immigrant community in the United States.* Unpub-lished dissertation research proposal, University of Pennsylvania.

Wang, S.C., & García, I. (in press). *Heritage language learners* (Position paper of the National Council of State Supervisors of Foreign Lan-guages). To be available at http://www.ncssfl.org/position.htm

Wang, X. (Ed.). (1996). *A view from within: A case study of Chinese heri-tage community language schools in the United States.* Washington, DC: National Foreign Language Center.

Webb, J.B., & Miller, B.L. (Eds.). (2000). *Teaching heritage language learners: Voices from the classroom.* Yonkers, NY: American Council on the Teaching of Foreign Languages.

Zentella, A.C. (1997). *Growing up bilingual: Puerto Rican children in New York.* Malden, MA: Blackwell.

Useful Resources

American Council on the Teaching of Foreign Languages (ACTFL)
www.actfl.org

Center for Applied Linguistics (CAL)
www.cal.org

ERIC Clearinghouse on Languages and Linguistics (ERIC/CLL)
www.cal.org/ericcll

National Clearinghouse for Bilingual Education (NCBE)
www.ncbe.gwu.edu

National Foreign Language Center (NFLC)
www.nflc.org

National Language Resource Centers
www.lll.hawaii.edu/nflrc/othernflrcs.html

9
Heritage Languages and Higher Education:
Challenges, Issues, and Needs

Nariyo Kono, University of Arizona
Scott McGinnis, National Foreign Language Center

Despite the increasing need for language competence in international trade, business, and education, heritage languages have not been recognized as valuable national resources in the United States (Roca, 1999). Many researchers attribute this lack of recognition to the "power and international status of English in the media and economy" (University of California, Los Angeles, 2001, p. 3) and to national policies, both overt and covert, that support English at the expense of other, less powerful languages.

Within higher education in the United States, the study of languages other than English is seen as a "luxury" (Kramsch, 1989, p. 2) rather than an important contribution to individual self-fulfillment and national development. Given this neglect, it is not surprising that heritage language study has received little attention in higher education. This situation has begun to change in the past few years, however, in response to a growing interest in these languages among students with a home background in them, and a number of fledgling heritage language programs now exist in colleges and universities around the country. While Spanish is the most commonly taught heritage language, other languages are being taught as well.

This chapter describes the current situation of heritage language education at the college and university level. It discusses the challenges and issues faced by postsecondary language educators and administrators and outlines some of the steps that they need to take to establish the field as a legitimate course of study in higher education.

Challenges

Heritage languages present new challenges to post-secondary language educators and administrators. Some of these challenges stem from the low status and lack of recognition that these languages face in higher education and the society at large. Other challenges arise from the fact that heritage language education is a new field that we are just beginning to understand.

To begin with, there is the question of definition: Who is a heritage language learner? How is such a learner different from a foreign language learner? What criteria will we use to distinguish between the two? Specifically, what level of proficiency and how much previous exposure to the language are required in order to enroll a student in a heritage language class? This is not only a pedagogical issue but an administrative one as well, because each institution needs to consider enrollment targets and budget constraints. With the less commonly taught languages (LCTLs), financial constraints are a central issue, given the typically low enrollment in these languages at the postsecondary level.

The low status of heritage languages in higher education is a central administrative and pedagogical issue. At the administrative level, heritage languages receive little or no recognition and support. Pedagogically, the distinction between high and low prestige—or standard and nonstandard—language varieties is a pivotal factor since it affects both student and teacher attitudes toward the language. How do students feel about the distinction and what are their expectations in learning heritage languages? What about teachers? What attitudes and beliefs do *they* bring to the classroom? How do they deal with dialects and language variations in the classroom? What language variety is needed in a particular community?

How to treat language variation is an important factor in assessment as well. How do teachers assess heritage language proficiency and learning outcomes when not all students speak the standard language variety?

The motivation of heritage language learners in postsecondary programs is often quite different from that of traditional foreign language learners. Many are dealing with deeply felt issues of identity, struggling to understand their relationship to their home culture and language, mainstream "American" society, and perhaps other groups as well. How should teachers treat these issues? Should they be part of the curriculum? How does the curriculum meet the requirements of the educational institution at the same time that it meets the needs of the students?

Behind these questions lie many teacher training issues. How different are heritage language courses from nonheritage language courses? How much nonheritage language teaching methodology can heritage language teachers apply in their classes? What training is needed to prepare teachers for the postsecondary heritage language classroom?

Successful First Steps

Although the field of heritage language education is new, developers of higher education programs do not need to start from the beginning. Interesting work is being done, and some of it has been documented. The American Association of Teachers of Spanish and Portuguese (AATSP) has recently published a volume on teaching heritage speakers of Spanish (Anderson, 2000). A successful teacher development program, jointly conducted by the American Council on the Teaching of Foreign Languages and Hunter College (City University of New York), with support from the Fund for the Improvement of

Postsecondary Education, is described in a recent report (Webb & Miller, 2000).

Since Spanish is the most commonly taught heritage language, it has received the most attention and development, although one should note that the American Indian Language Development Institute (AILDI) has been offering graduate and undergraduate courses for credit in indigenous language teaching since 1978 (McCarty, Watahomigie, Yamamoto, & Zepeda, 1997). Some of the Spanish heritage language programs take into account local language variations. For example, some programs on the West Coast and in the Southwest build instruction on local varieties of Spanish—that is, Mexican and South American varieties. These programs combine classroom teaching with a tutoring system and offer small scholarships as incentives.

While these programs, as well as the joint ACTFL–Hunter College project, have most directly benefited heritage students at the precollegiate level, aspects of these instructional models may well be applicable at the college and university level. For example, the Framework for Learning About Your Students, developed for K–12 use by the ACTFL–Hunter College Project Development Team (Webb & Miller, 2000, pp. 47-54), can be used just as effectively with college and university students.

For most college and university programs with significant heritage populations, the key has been the development of "tracks" to meet the specific needs of heritage learners, in particular their need for developing greater literacy skills. McGinnis (1996) has described one such model implemented by the University of Maryland Chinese language program. Similar successes have been noted for South Asian programs at the University of Texas (Moag, 1995) and the University of Pennsylvania (Gambhir, 1995, this volume), and for Thai at the University of California, Los Angeles (Meepoe, 1998). When an institution lacks the human resources necessary to set up a special heritage language track or course, as is often the case in smaller colleges, self-instructional models, such as the Five Colleges Program (Mazzocco, 1995; see also Gambhir, this volume) have proven to be effective.

Higher Education and Heritage Language Learners: A Mismatch

While these developments are heartening, it is clear that much work remains to be done. With the exception of Spanish and, to a lesser extent, Chinese, college and university heritage language education is in need of significant development. Underlying any such development is a fundamental issue: University and college language education is frequently at direct odds with the goals of many heritage language learners. For heritage language learners, fulfilling an academic requirement is generally not the primary purpose for language study. They may be studying the language to enhance career opportunities or simply to gain a greater understanding of their own linguistic and cultural heritage. Whatever their goals, their interests are often at odds with the traditional focus on literature and linguistics found in most foreign language departments in American colleges and universities. Higher education needs to recognize heritage language education not as a discrete academic course of study but as part of a learner's lifelong educational career. This entails a reexamination of how higher education fits into the total American educational infrastructure, and how transition from secondary to higher education can be better facilitated.

For heritage language learners of the LCTLs, the present structure of higher education programs is fundamentally inadequate. While in the commonly taught languages—French, German, and Spanish—most precollegiate settings provide at least elementary levels of instruction, such instructional opportunities are the exception rather than the rule for the LCTLs. For the truly less commonly taught languages (TLCTLs), such as Arabic, Hindi, and Thai, the opportunities for precollegiate study are virtually nonexistent. As a result, college and university instruction in LCTLs tends to focus on the lower levels, while in the TLCTLs it rarely ventures beyond the elementary level. University program staff assume that the learners of these languages will arrive on campus with little or no proficiency in all four modalities (listening, speaking, reading, and writing). Since many heritage language learners come to college with high, often near-native oral proficiency, the curricular structure is often at odds with their needs.

What Needs to Be Done

As Romero (2000) points out, there is a need for "a paradigm for instruction that differentiates foreign language instruction from effective heritage language instruction" (p. 129). This paradigm would take into account the special nature of heritage languages and heritage language learners. We have organized the key issues that need to be addressed into five general categories: administration, pedagogy, articulation and collaboration, teacher training, and research.

Administration

First and foremost, college and university administrators need to recognize that heritage languages are legitimate and worthy areas of study in higher education. Administrators need to be convinced that responding to the needs of heritage language learners is not simply a drain on institutional resources, but rather a demonstration of the institution's commitment to overall academic quality and service to society. Administrators then need to understand how heritage language education is similar to and different from other fields of language education—bilingual and dual language, second language, foreign language, and heritage language education.

Pedagogy

Teachers of heritage language courses at the college and university level have many issues to address. They need to identify student populations and construct student profiles, and use this information to design curricula and materials that respect and build on what learners know. Teaching materials should be developed based on how the languages are actually used in the communities (Kono, 2001). Assessment instruments and procedures that take into account heritage language use also need to be developed.

Articulation and Collaboration

Heritage language education takes place in a variety of settings—K–12, community-based schools, and colleges and universities. Institutions of higher education need to understand their position within the broader American educational structure so that well-articulated programs that move students smoothly from one educational setting to another can be developed. Colleges and universities need to seek ways to collaborate with the various other institutions that are also involved in heritage language education.

Teacher Training

Outside of Spanish, little teacher training in heritage language education has taken place. Above all, heritage language educators need to understand that their learners' home and community heritage languages are worthy of our respect and interest. Teachers need to learn how to build on the skills and knowledge that learners bring to the classroom. They need to understand that most of their learners are not studying the language for academic purposes but for deeply personal reasons.

Research

As Valdés (this volume) points out, for the most part heritage language instruction has not been based on research, because little research in this field has been conducted. We need to understand more about heritage language learners and their communities. We need to know more about how learners use their languages outside the classroom in order to create curricula and materials that build on their background knowledge and actual language use. Codeswitching, for example, has been much discussed in bilingual education (see, for example, Milroy & Mysken, 1995; Myers-Scotton, 1988, 1993) but not in the traditional foreign or heritage language classroom (Valdés, 2000).

Conclusion

Many potential heritage language learners remain invisible in the higher education system. Some of them are sitting quietly in foreign language classrooms, where their special strengths and needs are often overlooked. Others are unable to study their language at all because it is not taught at the college or university level. There are many challenges that higher education needs to address in the area of heritage language education, but they all begin with the understanding that heritage language learners and the languages that they speak are worth our respect, our recognition, and our resources.

References

Anderson, N. (Ed.) (2000). *Spanish for Native Speakers: A handbook for teachers* (American Association of Teachers of Spanish and Portuguese (AATSP) Professional Development Handbook Series for Teachers K–16, Vol. 1). Orlando, FL: Harcourt College.

Gambhir, V. (1995). Developing reading proficiency in modern South Asian languages. In V. Gambhir (Ed.), *The teaching and acquisition of South Asian languages* (pp. 108-135). Philadelphia: University of Pennsylvania Press.

Kono, N. (2001). *Language orientations: Case study of a Japanese-as-a-foreign-language classroom.* Unpublished doctoral dissertation, University of Arizona, Tucson.

Kramsch, C.J. (1989). *New directions in the teaching of language and culture* (NFLC Occasional Papers). Washington, DC: National Foreign Language Center.

Mazzocco, E.H.D. (1995). A consortium discovers NASILP: The five college self-instructional language program. NASILP Journal 23, 13-19.

McCarty, T.L., Watahomigie, L.J., Yamamoto, A.Y., & Zepeda, O. (1997). School–community–university collaborations: The American Indian Language Development Institute. In J. Reyhner (Ed.), *Teaching indigenous languages* (pp. 85-104). Flagstaff, AZ: Northern Arizona University Center for Excellence in Education.

McGinnis, S. (1996). Teaching Chinese to the Chinese: The development of an assessment and instructional model. In J. Liskin-Gasparro (Ed.), *Patterns and policies: The changing demographics of foreign language instruction* (pp. 107-121). Boston: Heinle & Heinle.

Meepoe, A. (1998). Reading materials for heritage language learners of Thai. *Journal of Southeast Language Teaching 7,* 33-59.

Milroy, L., & Muysken, P. (Eds.) (1995). *One speaker two languages: Cross-disciplinary perspectives on code-switching.* Cambridge, UK: Cambridge University Press.

Moag, G. (1995). Semi-native speakers: How to hold and mold them. In V. Gambhir (Ed.), *The teaching and acquisition of South Asian languages* (pp. 168-181). Philadelphia: University of Pennsylvania Press.

Myers-Scotton, C. (1988). Code-switching as indexical of social negotiations. In M. Heller (Ed.), *Codeswitching* (pp. 151-186). Berlin: Mouton de Gruyter.

Myers-Scotton, C. (1993). *Social motivation for code-switching: Evidence from Africa.* Oxford, UK: Oxford University Press.

Roca, A. (1999). Foreign language policy and planning in higher education: The case of the state of Florida. In T. Huebner & K. Davis (Eds.), *Studies in bilingualism (SiBil): Vol. 16. Sociopolitical perspectives on language policy and planning in the USA* (pp. 297-311). Philadelphia: John Benjamins.

Romero, M. (2000). Heritage language classrooms in action—Three case studies: An introduction to the research. In J.B.Webb & B.L. Miller (Eds.), *Teaching heritage language learners: Voices from the classroom* (pp. 129-134).Yonkers, NY: American Council on the Teaching of Foreign Languages.

University of California, Los Angeles. (2001). *Heritage language research priorities conference report.* Los Angeles, CA: Author. Retrieved from http://www.cal.org/heritage

Valdés, G. (2000). Introduction. In N. Anderson (Ed.), *Spanish for Native Speakers: A handbook for teachers* (American Association of Teachers of Spanish and Portuguese Professional Development Handbook Series for Teachers K–16, Vol. 1). Orlando, FL: Harcourt College.

Webb, J.B., & Miller, B.L. (Eds.). (2000). *Teaching heritage language learners: Voices from the classroom.* Yonkers, NY: American Council on the Teaching of Foreign Languages.

10
Truly Less Commonly Taught Languages and Heritage Language Learners in the United States

Surendra Gambhir
University of Pennsylvania

Over the last four decades, enrollments in foreign language courses in institutions of higher learning in the United States have been growing steadily. Most of this growth, however, reflects a gradual rise of interest in the study of a single language—Spanish. According to a 1998 survey (Brod & Welles, 2000), Spanish attracts 55% of total registrations for foreign languages in the United States, up from 32.4% in 1968 (p. 26, Table 5). Enrollment in four other commonly taught languages—French, German, Latin, and Russian—declined significantly during this period. French, for example, declined from 34.4% to 16.7% and German from 19.2% to 7.5%.

During this period, enrollments in less commonly taught languages (LCTLS) have risen. Japanese (0.4% to 3.6%), and Chinese (0.4% to 2.4), have enjoyed significant growth (p. 26, Table 5). Increases have also been seen for American Sign Language (0.1% to 1%), Arabic (0.1% to 0.5%), Hebrew (0.9% to 1.3%), Italian (2.7% to 4.1%), Korean (0.01% to 0.4%), and Portuguese (0.4% to 0.6%).

As a group, the LCTLs span a broad range in terms of numbers of learners. At one end of the spectrum is Japanese, with more than 43,000 learners in 1998; at the other end are languages such as Sinhala, which had one student in the whole country in 1998 (Brod & Welles, 2000, p. 27, Table 6). Some, such as Bengali, Hindi, Indonesian, and Turkish, are significant languages that represent politically, culturally, and economically important nations and constitute a large segment of the population of the world. For example, Hindi, which, in spite of being the second most commonly spoken language in the world, attracted only 1,279 college and university students in 1998, representing 0.1% of all foreign language learners in the United States (Janus, 1998). Undoubtedly these lopsided figures reflect to some extent America's conventional view of the world.

For LCTLs with the fewest number of learners, the term *truly less commonly taught language* (TLCTL) has come into use. In their survey, Brod and Welles identified 138 TLCTLs; together these languages attracted 1.5% of the total number of foreign language learners in 1998 (Table 6, p. 27).

The TLCTL subclassification is necessary, as these languages face special pedagogic and administrative issues and challenges. The changing demograhics of the foreign language classroom has had a greater impact on LCTLs and TLCTLs than it has had on commonly taught languages. In contrast to previous generations of students, many foreign language learners are heritage language learners—that is, learners with a home background in the target language. While all foreign languages have felt the impact of this shift, TLCTLs have been particularly affected; in some university programs, heritage language learners greatly outnumber traditional foreign language learners. The presence of these heritage language speakers presents new challenges to educational institutions unused to dealing with students who already have an intimate, if unevenly developed, knowledge of the language being taught. These challenges are compounded when the languages attract only a small number of learners.

This chapter examines the situation of the TLCTL learner and the challenges that this new learner presents to educational institutions. While much of the discussion explores the issue in the context of the university, other educational settings are discussed as well.

Background: History and Nomenclature

U.S. interest in LCTLs can be traced back to 1958, when the federal government passed the National Defense Education Act (NDEA). The goal of this act was to address the national security needs of the United States through education at all levels, with a focus on the study of modern foreign languages, particularly less commonly taught languages (Brecht & Rivers, 2000). In 1965, Title VI of the Higher Education Act (popularly known as Title VI/Fulbright-Hays), created to provide resources for establishing teaching programs and learning opportunities in these languages, first described such less commonly taught languages as "low density languages." Spurred by a perceived foreign language crisis, especially after the Russians' launching of Sputnik in 1957 (Lambert, 1992), this act focused on the study of the world's languages even more than its 1958 predecessor had.

In 1985, the U.S. Department of Education published a list of 169 "critical" foreign languages (referred to as "strategic" in the MLA literature) that were spoken in different parts of the world. Knowledge of these languages, according to the government, was important for scientific research and national security (Crystal, 1987). This list included many languages (e.g., Chinese, French, German, Italian, Japanese, Russian, and Spanish) that were already well represented in U.S. schools and colleges, but it also included those that were seldom taught (e.g., Modern Greek, Modern Hebrew, Hindi, Hungarian, and Portuguese), and others (e.g., Burmese, Hmong, and Pushto) that were not being taught at all. This list served to raise awareness in higher education of the importance of underrepresented languages, prompting more support for those LCTLs that were considered "critical." The National Security Education Act of

1991 further reinforced the foreign language study objective "to equip Americans with an understanding of less commonly taught languages and cultures and enable the nation to remain integrally involved in global issues related to U.S. National Security" (http://www.ndu.edu/nsep).

Today, the designation *critical* survives in some sectors of government and higher education. The U.S. National Security Agency, for example, distinguishes between LCTLs that are critical (e.g., Chinese, Hindi, and Portuguese) and those that are not (e.g., Bhojpuri and Icelandic), and some academic institutions apply the word to underrepresented languages. Increasingly, however, researchers use the term *less commonly taught languages*, modifying this term to create further subcategories.

The Foreign Service Institute (FSI) at the U.S. Department of State developed a useful classification for the languages it teaches based on linguistic distance from English. Such a classification gave rise to four categories of languages: Afrikaans, French, and Spanish, which are linguistically close to English, were included in Category 1; Hindi and Persian, among others, were included in Category 2; languages such as Burmese, Hebrew, and Russian made up Category 3; Category 4 included Chinese, Japanese, and Korean. A higher number category represents greater linguistic distance from English, implying the need for more time to achieve comparable results (Hadley, 1993).

Focusing on LCTLs, Walton (1992) simplified the FSI categorization, dividing LCTLs into European and non-European less commonly taught languages as a measure of their linguistic distance from American English. Such a classification clearly has pedagogically useful implications, but its disadvantage is that Europe continues to be the reference point. It preserves the European bias that scholars and educators are struggling to shed in order to understand the non-European languages on their own terms.

More recently, Brecht and Walton (1994) have come up with a classification based on numbers of learners in LCTLs. By this classification, Chinese, Italian, Japanese, and Russian are principal LCTLs. Many Asian, African, and East European languages, such as Czech, Hausa, Hebrew, Hindi, Hungarian, Korean, Portuguese, and Thai, are classified as *much less commonly taught languages*. Their third category consists of *least commonly taught languages*, such as Bengali, Punjabi, Sinhala, and Zulu. Their fourth category includes languages that have rarely or never been taught, such as Hmong, Kashmiri, and Pashto.

There have been attempts to define these categories more precisely by attaching a numerical bar to each one. Such a number-based taxonomy means, of course, that languages can shift categories over time as demand for them changes. Chinese and Japanese, for example, are LCTLs, but their rising numbers may put them in the future on a par with other commonly taught languages. It is very likely that other LCTLs will become more important in the coming decades as the countries to which these languages belong expand their economies.*

The TLCTL Learner

In U.S. schools and colleges, heritage language learners make up a growing proportion of enrollees in TLCTL courses. In the university, their predominance is the result of two simultaneous developments that may or may not be linked by cause and effect: At the same time that the number of heritage language students has risen, the number of nonheritage language students has dropped significantly.

Thus, increasingly, the two terms—*heritage language* and *TLCTL*—are inseparably connected. Few learners of South Asian languages at the University of Pennsylvania were heritage language speakers 20 years ago. Today, I would estimate

---

*These nations include Brazil, India, Indonesia, Korea, Poland, and Turkey (Campbell, 1998).

that about 80% of the students enrolled in these courses have a South Asian family background.

Who are these learners? What are their reasons for studying the heritage language? What are their strengths? These are some of the questions that I address below.

Reasons for Studying

Students' reasons for learning TLCTLs vary. Young learners in community-based schools may be in class because of their parents, or they may be there by their own choice, often because they want to be able to communicate better with relatives (especially grandparents) who do not speak English.

Some high school and college students may see a heritage language course as a relatively easy way to fulfill a language requirement or credit. Other learners see a career advantage in knowing the heritage language, believing that "being bilingual will increase their future academic and/or professional opportunities" (Rosenthal, 2000, p. 168). At the graduate level, some heritage language speakers are studying these languages in order to conduct research in areas where these languages are spoken, and their numbers are growing gradually.

For undergraduate-level heritage language speakers, the reasons for learning heritage languages are usually more cultural and personal than academic. For these learners, the home language and culture are part of their identity. The language allows them to access their ethnic literature and maintain connections with their extended families. On campus, the language provides a strong communicative link with ethnic student organizations and a way to publicly celebrate their ethnic identity in cultural shows.

Learner Strengths

Many heritage language speakers bring to the TLCTL class a firsthand knowledge of the language and its social uses. Linguistically, these learners bring with them knowledge of the phonology, lexicon, and syntax that varies in interesting ways from the way the language is spoken in the home country. On the communicative level, they often have a native-like, though limited, appreciation for intonation and for linguistic collocations that defy a straightforward connection between word and meaning. They are often quick to understand humor and sarcasm.

In an informal test I carried out in one of my classes, I once presented the following scenario to my beginning-level Hindi students: An Indian woman calls a friend and invites her for dinner. When the second woman finds out that it is the caller's wedding anniversary that day, she congratulates her, telling her that she would be delighted to accept her invitation for dinner. She then remarks that she would like to bring all her neighbors to the dinner as well, if it would be all right with the caller. For her, it is a humorous way to show excitement for a well-deserved big celebration. Interestingly, nearly all of the heritage language speakers in the class understood the humorous intent behind the invited friend's remarks, but all of the nonheritage students thought that the friend really meant to take her neighbors along to the dinner.

As the above example shows, heritage language learners have acquired some of the aspects of a communicative system that are often difficult to impart in the formal setting of a classroom. Well-rooted in the home language and culture, most heritage language learners have the potential to achieve native proficiency.

Different Learner Groups

Despite similar backgrounds, heritage language learners are not a completely homogenous group. Some come from homes where the target language was spoken, while others grew up using a closely related variety of the language, but not the language itself. Thus, students have been exposed to a wide range of linguistic input and cultural experiences.

In terms of their language proficiency, most heritage language learners can be placed in one of two groups. Variations of these groupings can be found in all educational contexts. To these two groups, I have added a third that is found only on college campuses.

The first group consists of *true beginners*. These are students who have had little or no prior contact with the target language. This group may also include learners from speech communities that are genetically or geographically related to the target language. Linguistically, these learners may be neophytes, but they are likely to have some fuzzy notions and intuitions about the language. For example, at the University of Pennsylvania, we often see students from a "non-cognate" (see Gambhir, 2000) Dravidian language background registering in the beginning-level Hindi course. Similarly, in the context of African languages, a true beginners class may include African Americans whose family connections with the target language and culture have been virtually nonexistent for centuries, but they have recently renewed their interest in the ancestral language and culture for ethnic and religious reasons (A. Schleicher, personal communication, October 15, 1999).

The second group consists of *learners who are not true beginners*; they come to the classroom with some knowledge of the target language and culture. Often, they can get a general sense of what is being said, but they have limited speaking competence, indicating that their parents and others often spoke to them at home in the native language but that they responded in English. Typically, they have little or no ability to read and write the language. While there are variations among learners in terms of what and how much they know about the target language, teachers across languages seem to agree that the pace of language acquisition for heritage learners is often much faster than it is for their counterparts in the nonheritage group. Some of these students will continue their studies at advanced levels of instruction.

A third group of heritage language learners are *graduate students*. This group, which has very specific needs for research in social sciences and area studies, used to be made up of only nonheritage students but now includes more and more heritage students. The materials for graduate students are often customized, and in some cases instruction is individualized. It is at this level of research and professional interest that heritage learners come closer to nonheritage learners and that the proficiency levels of the two groups begin to converge.

The TLCTL Classroom: Issues, Concerns, and Needs

Although the field of language teaching has finally begun to pay attention to heritage languages and heritage language learners, to date most of the attention has focused on the commonly taught languages. Very little attention has been paid to the LCTLs and TLCTLs. As a result, as Campbell (1998) has pointed out, "we presently lack the expertise base to design, implement, and evaluate quality instruction for most of these languages" (p. 173). Developing the needed expertise base will take a concerted and coordinated effort on the part of those who are involved in the heritage languages initiative.

Teaching LCTLs and TLCTLs is a new undertaking, with many issues, concerns, and needs. The following highlights the most critical.

Mixed-Level Classes

At the beginning and intermediate levels, the language proficiencies of TLCTL learners is so varied and their placement in appropriate groups so challenging that mixed-level classes are often the result. Experienced teachers can elicit information during placement tests that can help minimize heterogeneity within a class, but it can seldom be eliminated. Because of low enrollments in TLCTLs, programs are often unable to afford two separate tracks, one for heritage learners and the other for true beginners. The result is heterogeneous classes that present the teacher with the daunting task of dealing with two very different kinds of students in the same classroom. The heritage learner's quicker pace of learning intimidates the true beginner, but a slower pace to accommodate the beginner frustrates the heritage student. Even the heritage learner who has been exposed to a different but related heritage language at home (for example, a Gujarati or Tamil speaker learning Hindi) tends to learn the target language at a faster rate than does the nonheritage beginner.

Teachers have devised different strategies for accommodating groups with different abilities in the same class. Teachers may find it difficult to find a pace that will satisfy all learners, but an experienced teacher makes the best of the situation by turning a mixed-level class to everyone's advantage through smart strategies. For example, an instructor might allay the fears of true beginners by making it clear to them that their progress will be judged against their own starting point and not against the progress of others in the class. Group work is another useful strategy that can be used to alleviate pressures and insecurities that nonheritage learners might feel. Such an approach can be used to turn the classroom into a cooperative environment in which all learners, including nonheritage learners (who usually have a better grasp of the analytical aspects of the language), have something to contribute.

Nevertheless, it is undeniable that most heritage learners are able to learn the target language at a greatly accelerated speed, and organizing them in a separate group is unquestionably a pedagogically sound idea. Recognizing crucial differences in the two populations, some programs have instituted a two-track system despite the added cost.

The South Asia program at the University of Pennsylvania was the first among South Asian language programs to institute two separate tracks—one track for true beginners and an "accelerated" track for heritage learners. In accelerated classes, learners build on previous knowledge and are able to develop their language proficiency with astonishing speed. Although there has been no systematic assessment of how quickly these students learn, it appears that they are able to activate their passive knowledge of the language and construct and fix the missing and misconstrued pieces of their structure in a short period of time. By and large, they are able to restore basic knowledge of the structure of the language in one semester and expand their vocabulary into domains of academic discourse in the following semester. In the second year of study, where they may be grouped with advanced-level students from the conventional track, such heritage learners work on their formal vocabulary and oral fluency, enhance their appreciation of different genres of literature, and delve into the subtleties and idiom of the target language.

Heritage Learners and Nonheritage Instructors

The presence of heritage learners in the classroom is a new challenge for instructors who themselves have learned the language as a foreign language and therefore may not be highly proficient in some of its subtler uses and colloquial variations. Moreover, their knowledge of the culture in which the language is spoken may be somewhat superficial. Today, when classroom instruction is not grammar driven and is organized around the principle of communicative competence, the language is more likely to go into those areas of communication in which the teacher is less proficient. Students who find their teachers' analyses of the target language puzzling, their nonnative errors amusing, and their discourse unnatural and slow, may have a less-than-satisfying classroom experience. For their part, teachers may find it uncomfortable to have in their class students who in some respects are more proficient in the language than they are.

One possible strategy is a team approach in which one professionally trained instructor takes care of the "fact" part of language instruction, explaining the language and culture; while the other, a native speaker, takes care of the "act" part of the language classroom—communication (Jorden & Walton, 1987). This approach, however, is not ideal. The division of labor between fact and act in language learning is highly artificial, and the danger of hierarchy in such a team presents its own problems. Today's language classrooms focus heavily on communication, with the target language brought to learners in a variety of creative ways. Language fact plays a relatively minor role. Long, involved discussions about structure are avoided in favor of brief explanations in the context of a language-related activity. If the two members of a teaching team stay together in the classroom with the "fact" member tight-lipped most of the time, it becomes embarrassing for the teacher and disconcerting for learners.

Instructional Materials

The lack of appropriate instructional materials is a major problem for LCTLs and needs to be addressed. This is particularly the case with TLCTLs. In general, the less commonly taught the language, the more urgent the need, since no publisher wants to invest money in a book that will not sell in large enough numbers to cover the cost of printing. In many languages, beginning-level materials exist, but there is little available at the higher proficiency levels. Some programs use materials that have been prepared for native speakers. Since they are primarily geared toward elementary and middle school students in the home country, these materials are not appropriate, in either language or content, for adult learners in the United States. For example, adult learners often require facility in the formal domains of language, but few such materials address this need.

Writing about the LCTLs, Morahg (1998) persuasively argues for materials that integrate culture into language instruction. "There is a good reason to believe that an effectively designed, culturally oriented curriculum for a less commonly taught language is likely to add significantly to the appeal of a program and thus add to its enrollments at every level of instruction" (p. 6). I can only add that this statement applies even more to TLCTL learners, whose primary motivation for language study is to stay connected to the home culture.

Given the shortage of materials for TLCTLs, many instructors have created their own. A productive next step might be for these instructors to work together on material development projects. Such cooperative endeavors will not only bring different perspectives to a much-needed undertaking but will also help ensure a favorable reception for the materials on different campuses.

Some institutions have collected information about available materials for LCTLs. The University of California, Los Angeles and the Center for Applied Linguistics have collected information on the resources available for hundreds of different languages (http://www.lmp.ucla.edu). For South Asian languages, the Columbia University web site provides an Inventory of Language Materials (ILM), with a list of all available materials for South Asian languages (www.columbia.edu/~fp7/ilm/hindi.htm). The LangNet web site, sponsored by National Foreign Language Center in Washington, D.C., will provide an extensive collection of materials for the study of the TLCTLs (www.nflc.org).

Professional Training for Teachers

There is an urgent need, particularly in higher education, for teachers and supervisors who not only have superior proficiency in TLCTLs but who also have been professionally trained in the theory and practice of language teaching. Only experienced, professionally educated teachers can make informed decisions about curriculum design, teaching methodology, learning tools, methods of assessment and evaluation, and material selection. Thus far, there are no programs that prepare university-level heritage language teachers for their jobs. There are workshops for new language teachers and teaching assistants that provide quick overviews of important teaching concepts, but there is no systematic program of coursework on the theory and practice of second language acquisition and teaching focused on the TLCTLs. Often instructors without any professional training are hired inexpensively from local communities, and students' needs are not met.

Two complementary models are available to provide teachers with professional training: inservice training in the form of periodic workshops and seminars, and summer institutes where teachers can attend a series of workshops before the commencement of classes. Given the small number of teachers of TLCTLs, it may be a good idea to combine different but related languages at summer institutes.

Teaching Methodology

An effective teacher builds on learner strengths while addressing areas that need further development. For heritage learners of TLCTLs, effective instruction combines a bottom-up (analytical) approach to help students repair structural gaps in their knowledge of language structure and with a top-down (content-based) approach that helps them expand and enrich their exposure to and uses of the language. Students typically enter class with vague notions of word boundaries, lack of formal vocabulary, and regional influences on the standard language. A bottom-up approach addresses these lacunas. In a top-down approach, heritage learners who are exposed to lengthy texts are often able to figure out the essence of the content even though they may not understand each word. Materials based in their native culture have better potential of stimulating their interest and their involvement in class activities.

The Student as Independent and Informed Language Learner

TLCTL teachers need to prepare learners to take charge of their own learning outside the classroom. Classroom instruction alone is seldom enough for students to reach meaningful levels of proficiency in the target language. This is particularly the case with TLCTLs, given the absence of qualified teachers. Self-management of learning enables learners to ask questions that address their needs and encourages teachers to maintain a learner-centered environment. Furthermore, language learning is a lifelong undertaking, and it is important for learners to be aware of effective and efficient ways to learn.

TLCTLs and the University

If TLCTLs are to get the attention they need, they will need the recognition and support of educational administrators. Others in this book discuss the need for administrative support from the K–12 educational systems. Here I focus my remarks on the educational setting I know best—the university.

Low enrollments in TLCTLs and the subsequent administrative reluctance to commit resources for these languages has been a major stumbling block in improving the status of TLCTLs on college campuses. Judging from the low-level and poorly paid appointments of instructors for TLCTLs, many administrators on educational campuses do not look upon the learning of TLCTLs as a serious academic undertaking. In general, administrators seem to regard European languages more favorably than they do the non-European languages.

The lack of institutional support for TLCTLs threatens the professional stature and sometimes the very existence of many minor languages in educational institutions. The need to view immigrant languages as a national resource has been widely discussed in the literature and at conferences, but the discussion does not appear to have filtered down to the level of university administrations. Most of the TLCTL programs would not have survived over the years without federal Title VI funding (Brecht & Rivers, 2000). It is not clear why colleges and universities should be absolved from their responsibility for promoting the study of these languages.

Despite this general climate of administrative indifference toward TLCTLs, there have been some interesting and successful initiatives in higher education. One in particular is noteworthy. Back in the 1970s, an American scholar with a vision, Professor John Means of Temple University, took the giant step of establishing the National Association of Self-Instructional Language Programs (NASILP). At minimal cost, NASILP helped universities set up self-instructional programs, providing information on strategies for effective self-instruction, suitable textbooks, audio and videotapes, and native language tutors. NASLIP also provided the services of a professional external examiner once a semester for quality control. Programs that wanted to offer particular languages but did not have the resources welcomed NASILP with great enthusiasm. Recent developments, such as a consortium of neighboring institutions (Mazzocco, 1995) and the use of the Internet and video-conferencing, have helped self-instructional programs grow. At present, more than 100 such programs exist across the nation, providing self-instruction to approximately 13,000 students every year. (For more information on NASILP, see Rosenthal, 2000.)

TLCTLs and the Nation

More than 20 years ago, a presidential report (President's Commission on Foreign Languages & International Studies, 1979) called on planners and educators to "make provisions for the less commonly taught languages that are spoken by 80 percent of the world's population" and recommended that special attention should be given to encouraging ethnic and other minority group members to enter linguistic and international studies, and to build on their existing linguistic resources so they may contribute more to American education, diplomacy and international business. (pp. 29-30)

The resources we need already exist in our own backyard—in the 32 million recent immigrants with knowledge of dozens of languages. However, given the negative attitudes that immigrant children often have toward their own languages and the strong pull of the English language, most of these languages are not likely to survive in these families for more than a generation or two. If no incentives are given and if no efforts are made at the national level, most will disappear. (For further details about the process and pace of the disappearance of immigrant languages, see Gambhir, 1988.) Does it make sense that while we are spending millions of dollars to train our college graduates, putting them through the painful process of learning a foreign language as adults, we are letting the rich linguistic resources in our communities die a quiet and unmourned death?

We need to figure out ways to preserve what we have. We need a national policy on heritage language conservation that provides incentives for language maintenance. It is not difficult to imagine how such a system might work: Incentives could be easily factored into college and university admissions and into applications for jobs at schools and colleges, the armed forces, the foreign service, international business corporations, hospitals, and law enforcement establishments.

TLCTLs and Community Organizations

While TLCTLs are resources that can be used to both national and international advantage, preserving them is not an effortless experience. Communities need to make a concerted effort to keep their languages alive in a context in which the pull of English and "Americanism" is strong and constant.

Different communities deal with language preservation differently. For example, the East Indian immigrant community generally has not given much attention to language maintenance. Despite the existence of many weekend community-run schools where community volunteers teach students with great enthusiasm, many in the community seem to think it is necessary, as a part of their assimilation into the all-powerful American culture, to get rid of the more visible aspects of their ethnic baggage, including their language. Such an attitude promotes English as a more natural choice, even in culturally significant events. One sees English dominating everywhere and people of all generations using it. The use of the heritage language is often limited to those whose proficiency in English is insufficient.

In many other immigrant communities, however, there is a great deal of enthusiasm for teaching and maintaining the heritage languages. Chinese, Korean, and Vietnamese afterschool and weekend language programs are thriving in California. It is interesting, but not unexpected, that many of the community schools are church based. Many are taught by parent volunteers.

I bring my discussion to a close with profiles of two communities that have managed on their own initiative to preserve their heritage languages. One hopes that such success stories will become increasingly common as more and more communities understand the value, to themselves and to the nation, of keeping their languages alive.

Rose and Alex Pilibos Armenian School, Los Angeles, California

The Rose and Alex Pilibos Armenian School is one of the most ambitious community-based heritage language schools in the country—a full-fledged pre-K–12 school, with 5000 students, an annual budget of $2.5 million, and a per-student, per-year cost of $3,200. Fully accredited by the state, the school offers a complete K–12 curriculum taught by both credentialed and noncredentialed teachers. All subjects except Armenian History, Religion, and Language are taught in English. Students, 90% of whom are Armenian, are exposed to 2 hours of Armenian language each day.

The school offers a balanced curriculum that fully prepares students for life in the society at large while anchoring them in the heritage language and culture. An agreement with the University of California system giving high school students 4 years of college language credit provides a practical incentive—and real-world confirmation to the community of the worth of their language.

The success of this school is firmly rooted in the community that it serves. Under the energetic leadership of the school's principal, the school raises $500,000 each year. The PTA alone raises $100,000 a year.

Khmer Language Classes, Long Beach, California

In contrast to the Armenian school, the Khmer initiative in Long Beach is a modest project, but in some ways its success is even more impressive.

Several years ago, when a volunteer ESL teacher decided to start a Khmer language class for children in his Long Beach, California, community, few people would have predicted success. Even the California Association of Bilingual Education (CABE) didn't see the need for teaching Khmer in local schools. English had become the primary language of communication for most of the children in the community. Most parents were nonliterate, with little or no experience of schooling themselves. For most, the first priority was to work hard to provide for their families. Preservation of Khmer did not seem to be a widespread concern.

There was, however, one clear area of Khmer language need—communication between children and their monolingual Khmer-speaking grandparents. When the volunteer teacher set up an afterschool Khmer speakers club for school children, the response was immediately positive. By the second week, enrollment rose from a handful of students to 30. Soon there were three classes and a waiting list.

Impressed by the success of the school, principals of local schools started showing interest in Khmer. Eventually, with the help of school administrators, the language was introduced into the local school system. Today the former community volunteer teaches 3 hours of Khmer a day in the Long Beach school system while studying to obtain his teaching credentials.

Conclusion

The key difference between TLCTLs and LCTLs is in numbers. This, in turn, leads to other problems: When numbers of learners are small, it is difficult to convince school administrators to hire qualified faculty. It is also difficult to expect publishers to invest money in publishing books that will have a limited market. In these circumstances, we need to think of other ways and means to promote the languages. The community success stories above point to the importance of committed, insightful leadership at the community level, but such efforts are only part of the solution and should not replace the obligations that educational administrators have to their students and the nation has to its citizens.

Acknowledgments

This chapter is based on discussions that took place during two sessions on TLCTLs at the 1999 Heritage Languages Conference in Long Beach, California. The heritage languages represented in these sessions were American Indian, Amharic,

Armenian, Chinese, Filipino, Greek, Hawaiian, Hindi, Khmer, and Vietnamese. Representatives from state departments of education and bilingual education were also present. Among those who contributed to the discussion in the two sessions were Vijay Gambhir (first session chair), Surendra Gambhir (second session chair), Elizabeth Hartung-Cole, Betty Lau, Antonia Schleicher, Janne Underriner, Darith Ung, and Viken Yacoubian. This chapter has also benefited from comments from Vijay Gambhir, Scott McGinnis, Joy Kreeft Peyton, and Donald Ranard.

References

Brecht, R.D., & Rivers, W. (2000). *Language and national security in the 21st century.* Dubuque, IA: Kendall/Hunt.

Brecht, R.D., & Walton, A.R. (1994). *National strategic planning in the less commonly taught languages* (NFLC Occasional Papers). Washington, DC: National Foreign Language Center.

Brod, R., & Welles, E.B. (2000). Foreign language enrollments in United States institutions of higher education, Fall 1998. *Association of Departments of Foreign Languages Bulletin, 31*(2), 22-29.

Campbell, R.N. (1998). Less commonly taught languages of emerging importance: Major issues, cost problems, and their national implications in international education in the global era. In J.N. Hawkins, C.M. Haro, M.A. Kazanjian, G.W. Merkx, & D. Wiley (Eds.), *International education in the new global era: Proceedings of a national policy conference on the Higher Education Act, Title VI, and Fulbright-Hays programs* (pp. 172-174). Los Angeles: University of California, International Studies and Overseas Programs.

Crystal, D. (Ed.). (1987). *The Cambridge encyclopedia of language.* Cambridge, UK: Cambridge University Press.

Gambhir, S. (1988). The modern Indian diaspora and language in countries of South Asia. In P. Gaeffke & D. Utz (Eds.), *The countries of South Asia: Boundaries, extensions, and interrelations* (pp. 147-157). Philadelphia: University of Pennsylvania, Department of South Asia Regional Studies.

Gambhir, V. (2000). *Background, needs, motivation and attitudes of heritage and non-heritage learners of Hindi.* Unpublished manuscript.

Hadley, A.C. (1993). *Teaching language in context.* Boston: Heinle & Heinle.

Janus, L. (1998). Less commonly taught languages of emerging importance: Major issues, cost problems, and their national implications In J.N. Hawkins, C.M. Haro, M.A. Kazanjian, G.W. Merkx, & D.Wiley (Eds.), *International education in the new global era: Proceedings of a national policy conference on the Higher Education Act, Title VI, and Fulbright-Hays programs* (pp.165-171). Los Angeles: University of California, International Studies and Overseas Programs.

Jorden, E.H., & Walton, A.R. (1987). Truly foreign languages: Instructional challenges. *Annals of the American Academy of Social and Political Science, 490,* 110-124

Lambert, R. (1992). *Foreign language planning in the United States* (NFLC Occasional Papers). Washington, DC: National Foreign Language Center.

Mazzocco, E. (1995). A consortium discovers NASILP: The five college self-instructional language program. *NASILP Journal, 25,* 37-46.

Morahg, G. (1998). Promoting and protecting the LCTLs. In N.J. Stenson, L.E. Janus, & A.E. Mulkern (Eds.), *Report of the less commonly taught languages summit* (Carla Working Paper Series No. 9, pp. 5-6). Minneapolis, MN: Center for Advanced Research on Language Acquisition.

President's Commission on Foreign Languages & International Studies. (1979). *Strength through wisdom: A critique of U.S. capability* (Document No. HE 19.102:F76). Washington, DC: U.S. Government Printing Office.

Rosenthal, J.W. (2000). *Handbook of undergraduate second language education.* Mahwah, NJ: Lawrence Erlbaum.

Walton, R. (1992). *Expanding the vision of foreign language education: Enter the less commonly taught languages* (NFLC Occasional Papers). Washington, DC: The National Foreign Language Center.

II
Preparing Teachers to Work With Heritage Language Learners

Ana María Schwartz
University of Maryland Baltimore County

The percentage of students with a language other than English in their home background has risen dramatically in recent years. Nearly 18% of U.S. residents age 5 and older speak a language other than English at home, according to the 2000 census (U.S. Census Bureau, 2000). Although the availability of language classes specifically designed for heritage language speakers is still very limited—by one 1997 estimate, 7% of secondary schools offer such classes (Brecht & Ingold, 1998)—it stands to reason that as the population of speakers of languages other than English grows, the demand for specialized programs to develop these language proficiencies will increase as well. Most social groups view language maintenance or revival as crucial to the preservation of their cultural identity, and some see school as the best place for this to be done (Schecter & Bayley, 1997). If our schools are going to be responsive to this need, a readily available pool of language teachers who have been specifically trained to work with heritage language speakers is crucial.

Is the language teaching community ready to accommodate an increased demand for heritage language classes? It doesn't appear to be. Few teacher preparation programs include training in heritage language issues, and those that do find little to guide them in the development of instructional methods and curricula.

To a large extent, existing heritage language programs (for both commonly and less commonly taught languages) are still patterned after foreign language models. For example, in a review of undergraduate Native American language instruction, Reyhner, Lockard, and Rosenthal (2000) found that the methods currently used to teach indigenous languages "are often adaptations of those used for the instruction of modern foreign languages . . . and English as a second language" (p. 152). Most teachers of heritage language classes are trained as foreign language teachers, or they are native speakers of the language taught with little or no training in language instruction. Those who are certified are trained to teach monolingual English speakers, and their training takes place in university teacher preparation programs where the instructors typically have little or no exposure to the realities of today's classrooms. That reality includes growing numbers of heritage language speakers in foreign language classes.

How should we teach language learners who are already familiar with the target language? What are their needs? How are they different from traditional foreign language learners? What existing foreign language instructional strategies, materials, and assessments can be adopted or adapted? Which must be disregarded?

Valdés (2000, this volume) has expressed concern that the "multiple practices and pedagogies currently being used to teach heritage speakers are not directly supported by a set of coherent theories about the role of instruction in the development of language proficiencies in bilingual language learners" (p. 241). Several shortcomings hamper the development of professional preparation programs for heritage language teachers in Grades K–16, as well as in afterschool and weekend programs. These include the lack of a theoretical foundation in the field of heritage language education as a whole; the lack of knowledge about effective curricula, materials, and instructional strategies; the lack of public and institutional support for heritage language programs; and the nationwide shortage of language teachers. How can we prepare teachers to teach heritage language learners in a variety of contexts?

In order to further the dialogue on this most important topic, this chapter addresses three areas regarded as critical in the preparation of heritage language teachers:

- The understandings, theories, assumptions, and beliefs that teachers must bring to their professional preparation as heritage language professionals
- The content knowledge that underlies effective teaching of heritage language learners
- The pedagogical skills that teachers need to have to be effective heritage language teachers

In the discussion below, I outline the challenges in each of these areas and make recommendations for action in this new and growing field of heritage language teacher preparation. Strategies for addressing the serious teacher shortage that we face are discussed at the end of the chapter.

Understandings, Beliefs, and Assumptions

The question of who is a heritage language learner is, perhaps, the first question that heritage language teachers must address. The answers are sure to reflect the diversity of learners in the population. Heritage language learners may be children, adolescents, or young adults. They may have recently immigrated to the United States, or they may be second- and third-generation bilinguals. They include individuals from other countries and Native Americans. They may live in homes where the heritage language is spoken or they may have picked up the language through interactions with family members and friends. Heritage language learners generally, though not always, have some functional proficiency in the language they are learning. They may have had some formal education in the language, or they may not. Although they have a wide range of literacy skills in the language, their oral skills are usually stronger.

Heritage language learners are different from traditional foreign language learners in a number of ways. The table on the facing page, compiled from Campbell and Rosenthal's (2000) comparisons of the competencies and knowledge of "typical" university-level heritage language learners and traditional foreign language learners who have completed 2 years of language instruction in university foreign language programs, illustrates the differences between the two groups.

Campbell and Rosenthal conclude that given the disparity in the competencies displayed by each group of students, university programs designed for foreign language learners cannot meet the instructional and other needs of heritage language speakers.

We must also understand who the heritage language teachers are, as both teachers and teaching environments fit many descriptions. Some teachers may be native speakers of the language taught; others may not. Some may be certified to teach foreign languages or ESL; others may be certified, but in other academic subjects; still others may not be certified at all. Teachers may or may not be part of a foreign language department, or they may be the sole language teacher in the school and have no models, mentors, or other sources of professional support in the school. Finally, they may teach traditional foreign language classes in which heritage language speakers have been placed because no specific classes for them are available.

With such a wide spectrum of learners, and variety in teachers' backgrounds and teaching situations, it is particularly important that teachers of heritage language learners get to know their students and understand their language varieties, cultural identities, and their communities. We can gain much information on how to approach these tasks from the insights of the ACTFL–Hunter College FIPSE Project (Webb & Miller,

Comparison of Heritage Language and Traditional Foreign Language Learners

Knowledge and competencies	Typical heritage language learners	Traditional foreign language learners
Phonology	Pronunciation, stress, and intonation conform to educated native speaker level.	Have acquired 75-85% of the phonological system of a prestige dialect; pronunciation is accented.
Grammatical rules	80-90% of their grammatical competence is consistent with the rules of a prestige dialect.	Are aware of many grammatical rules, but cannot use them fluently nor comprehend them fully in real-life communication.
Vocabulary	Have acquired extensive vocabulary, but range is limited to home, community, and religious institutions; a large number of "borrowings" from the majority language are noted.	Vocabulary is extremely limited, but consistent with the prestige dialect.
Sociolinguistic rules	Control registers relating to verbal interactions with family and community members; competence is limited by range of social interactions.	Have very limited knowledge and control of sociolinguistic rules except for those appropriate to the classroom.
Culture	Have learned and adopted the culture of their ethnolinguistic communities, but the customs, values, and traditions may be hybridized with those of the majority culture.	Have superficial understanding and sensitivity to the target culture; have few opportunities to interact in the target culture communities.
Literacy skills	Have not developed literacy skills beyond elementary levels.	Have a good to very good foundation for development of literacy; will depend on the writing system of the target language.
Motivation	Have wide range of motivations for studying the heritage language	Have pragmatic, instrumental motivation for learning the language.

2000), whose goal was to develop a preparation program for teachers of heritage language learners. One outcome of the project is an extensive series of questions focusing on the backgrounds and experiences that students bring to the heritage language classroom. This provides teachers with a holistic understanding of their students and with the insights necessary to tailor curricula, teaching strategies, and materials to their needs. The framework consists of questions in six categories (p. 47):

- *Linguistic proficiency*, providing a view of the strengths that the learners bring to class with them and the areas in which they need further language instruction
- *Motivation*, investigating learners' identification with the heritage language and their reasons for studying the language in school
- *Academic preparedness*, focusing on the types of prior educational experiences the students have had and the academic areas in which they need further development
- *Cultural connectedness*, providing insights into the relationship that the learners have with their culture, the extent of their involvement with the culture at home and in the community, and their attitudes about that relationship
- *Emotional factors*, helping teachers to understand how the learners feel about themselves as people and as students within the context of the classroom and the school
- *Societal factors*, yielding information about the place of the students and their families in the larger community

While it is important for teachers to know their students, it is just as important for them to understand the assumptions and beliefs *they* hold in relation to their own language varieties and cultural backgrounds. The beliefs that teachers bring to the classroom will shape how they work with their students and what they expect of them. Thus, it is critically important for teachers to explore and clearly understand issues such as the value of the standard or prestige dialect of the language taught, the value of the often stigmatized dialects that teachers encounter in the classroom, and the status of those dialects in the students' communities. Such understanding will foster respect for their students' views of and uses of language.

The ACTFL–Hunter College Project also addressed teachers' assumptions and beliefs. The "Statement of Shared Goals and Fundamental Beliefs" lists the beliefs that guided staff in their development of the project. This statement can guide teachers as they reflect upon their beliefs in four areas: who they should strive to be as teachers of heritage languages, the goals they should hold for their students, what successful heritage language learning environments are like, and what constitutes effective heritage language instruction (Webb & Miller, 2000, pp. 83-85).

Content Knowledge

A well-grounded content foundation is essential in the preparation of all teachers. In the case of heritage language teachers, professional preparation programs must include concepts from an array of related disciplines, such as linguistics, psycholinguistics, sociolinguistics, applied linguistics, and psychology (Fillmore & Snow, 2000; González & Darling-Hammond, 1997). Crandall (2000) argues that *all* teachers should receive preservice coursework or inservice training to prepare them to better meet the needs of linguistically and culturally diverse students. She recommends that the following topics be included in such courses: "First and second language acquisition and development; cross-cultural communication and strategies for linking instruction with language and literacy activities in the home and community; strategies for adapting materials and instruction . . . [and] appropriate assessment strategies" (p. 285).

Teachers of heritage language learners must have a high level of proficiency in the language taught, a great deal of knowledge about and personal experience with the learners' cultures, and a strong background in linguistic principles and language acquisition processes. Basic principles of first and second language and second dialect acquisition—especially the acquisition of a standard dialect by speakers of nonprestige varieties—and of language development in different contexts and at different ages, must also be included in the curriculum. In particular, teachers must understand how social factors such as age, gender, social class, and ethnic identity (Ellis, 1994) interact with language acquisition and maintenance; have a notion of the range and characteristics of language registers and the relationship between register and social status (Valdés & Geoffrion-Vinci, 1998); understand the concepts of additive versus subtractive bilingualism and how languages in contact develop (Ellis, 1994); know about the different components that make up language competence, recognizing that heritage speakers' competencies develop unevenly; and understand what can be done to help learners expand their bilingual range so that they may be able to meet more of their communicative needs in the heritage language (Valdés, 1997).

Heritage language teachers must also understand the differences between spoken and written language and between social and academic language, how literacy skills transfer across languages, and the ways that non-Western writing systems affect the teaching of reading and writing. Knowledge of diverse cultures, of historical and current immigration issues and language policy, and of the challenges of diversity and multiculturalism in the United States are also essential to a well-rounded heritage teacher preparation curriculum.

Pedagogical Skills

Strong preparation in effective pedagogy is also key to a successful teacher-preparation program. As mentioned above, the research and knowledge base in the heritage languages field is scant, and in no other area is this lack of knowledge more evident that in pedagogy—what teachers need to be able to do to teach heritage language learners effectively.

Instructional Strategies

Heritage language learners not only speak many different languages, but they also represent many dialects and nationalities. They may be immigrants or children of immigrants. They may come from well-established families or from families struggling to enter the social and economic mainstream. It is common to find a wide range of language levels, educational backgrounds, and cognitive abilities in a class of heritage language learners. Heterogeneity is generally the norm in these classes. As a result, the advice most often heard in regard to teaching heritage language students is to "start where the student is and move forward" (Draper & Hicks, 2000, p. 27). This is, in a sense, a statement of philosophy as well as a practical guide for instructional practice. This regard for the individual sets the direction for classroom organization, instructional strategies and materials, and assessment procedures. The pedagogical suggestions that follow are based on the emerging knowledge of who heritage language learners are and their strengths and needs. They flow from the experiences of heritage language educators, including the teachers, program administrators, and university faculty who participated in the teacher preparation sessions at the 1999 Heritage Languages in America Conference in Long Beach, California.

- The heritage language curriculum should be student centered and literacy based, with many reading, writing, and speaking activities focused on formal, academic language. It should include, as Valdés and Geoffrion-Vinci (1998) suggest, written and oral activities that model the high-level registers of authentic academic contexts.

- While the curriculum should be structured and systematic, every opportunity should be taken to learn about and build on students' interests, prior knowledge, experiences, and learning styles. This may be accomplished in part by involving parents, community leaders, and other community resources in the instructional program; by using authentic language data such as student-conducted interviews and presentations by heritage language speakers; and by incorporating artistic, cultural, and historical information into instruction.

- Often one finds different national and cultural groups together in a class or program. Where this is the case, the teacher must take care to include multiple perspectives from literature, language, and culture that represent all of the students in the class.

- Given the linguistic diversity found in the heritage language classroom, the most valuable instructional strategies are those that include small-group and individualized instruction. Thematically organized and content-based curricula, designed in modules that can be adapted to different language needs, interests, and proficiency levels, are particularly appropriate for this population.

- Roca (1992) recommends several techniques appropriate to various levels of instruction. These include individual writing logs in which students record comments or reflections on topics of special interest; dialogue journals with the teacher; vocabulary expansion assignments; translation of literature and other materials; interpreting practice; individual, peer, and group editing of written work; and oral presentations.

- Also important in the design of curriculum is the integration of television (including international satellite television), film, video, and technology (CD-ROM and the Internet), which provide opportunities for direct contact with the learners' languages and cultures (Roca, 1992).

- The strategies listed below were gleaned from classroom observations of exemplary heritage language teachers in the ACTFL–Hunter College Project (Webb & Miller, 2000).

— Create a language-rich environment in which the teacher exclusively uses the heritage language but allows the students to answer in English while encouraging them to use the heritage language.
— Accept only the heritage language for written assignments; compile and publish the students' best work.
— Acknowledge and use the dialect varieties of the students; validate their knowledge of the language by asking them to share and explain idiomatic expressions or vocabulary.
— Create opportunities for students to share the dances, music, recipes, and other cultural products and practices of their heritage communities.
— Weave cultural information into classes; provide examples and make analogies using this information to help the students make personal connections to the assigned readings.

As important as methods and techniques are, teachers of heritage language learners must go beyond only teaching to also being their students' mentors and advocates. They must use their own knowledge and understandings to help their students develop confidence in their abilities as language learners. They must make judicious decisions about when and how to use the heritage language or English in class and how to ease students into greater and more sophisticated uses of the heritage language in an environment free of intimidation. By fostering a feeling of acceptance in the classroom, the successful teacher will guide students toward developing fluency and proficiency in the standard dialect, while also knowing where and when to use their home dialects.

Instructional Materials and Resources

The last few years have seen an increase in the number of textbooks and other published materials for heritage language instruction. Many of these materials—for example, the AATSP's handbook, *Spanish for Native Speakers* (American Association of Teachers of Spanish and Portuguese, 2000)—are for Spanish-for-native-speakers courses (e.g., see www.cal.org/ericcll/faqs/rgos/sns.html) and for the secondary and high school levels. This is hardly surprising, given that Spanish is the second most widely spoken language in the United States. Yet teachers of *all* heritage languages must develop skills in designing and adapting materials for different age groups and language proficiency levels. This may involve adapting successful curricula from one heritage language to another, adapting textbooks and materials published in the home countries to make them more relevant to the U.S. heritage language population, or even adapting the heritage materials and textbooks used in a class or program to better fit the levels of proficiency within a particular class.

The National Foreign Language Standards, with its interrelated goals of communication, cultures, connections, comparisons, and communities, can also provide some guidance in the development of heritage language curricula. For example, the communication goal reformulates the traditional view of the four language skills into three communicative modes:

interpersonal, interpretive, and presentational. By defining the communicative modes in terms of different functional abilities (Valdés, 1997), the standards recognize the heritage language learners' strengths in interpersonal skills and present "a mechanism for focusing on the [presentational] skills that need further work" (Draper & Hicks, 2000, p. 28).

The most recent publication by the National Standards in Foreign Language Education Project (1999) describes language-specific standards for nine languages. The writers recognize the presence of heritage learners in language classes and suggest that the standards may need to be modified when applied to heritage learners. Recommendations for working with heritage language students are made for different languages. For example, the Chinese standards include special 12th-grade sample progress indicators, "to keep advanced-level students and Chinese heritage learners challenged and performing at their maximum level of ability" (p. 116). The Russian standards document discusses the needs of heritage Russian learners at length, especially within the context of a "blended" classroom, and describe the positive contributions that heritage learners can make in a class as well as their different needs. The Spanish standards document also discusses working with heritage language speakers, in particular within the communication and cultures standards, and includes a heritage Spanish class scenario.

Online resources provide information and support to the heritage language teacher. The ERIC/CLL Online Resource Guide, *Teaching Spanish to Spanish Speakers* (www.cal.org/ericcll/faqs/rgos/sns.html) lists an extensive bibliography of resources ranging from articles, books, and reports to listservs, conferences, and web sites. The Heritage Languages Listserv, housed at the National Foreign Language Center (NFLC), acts as a clearinghouse for all kinds of information relating to heritage languages (to subscribe, e-mail heritage-on@lists.nflc.org.) Several ERIC Digests (www.cal.org/ericcll/digest/) focus on heritage language issues. Titles include *African Languages at the K–12 Level; Chinese Heritage Community Language Schools in the United States; Instructional Conversations in Native American Classrooms; Involuntary Language Loss Among Immigrants: Asian-American Linguistic Autobiographies; Spanish for Spanish Speakers: Developing Dual Language Proficiency;* and *Tapping a National Resource: Heritage Languages in the United States.* LangNet (www.nflc.org/projects/information.asp) is a web-based system designed to provide for language learners materials customized to their language learning needs and goals. These materials include information on assessment and testing, lesson plans, recommendations for starting a course, and teaching methods. The UCLA Language Materials Project provides Web-based learning resources for the less commonly taught languages (www.lmp.ucla.edu).

Information about resources for heritage language learners of specific languages is available from the individual language organizations and from other organizations, such as the Group of Universities for the Advancement of Vietnamese Abroad (GUAVA) at www.public.asu.edu/~ickpl/guava.html. Centers such as the Heritage Languages and Cultures Institute at California State University, Long Beach (www.csulb.edu/colleges/cla/heritage-languages-program/home.html) and the Heritage Languages Initiative, a joint project of the Center for Applied Linguistics and the National Foreign Language Center, act as clearinghouses for information, materials, and professional opportunities for heritage language teachers (www.cal.org/heritage).

Assessment

The issue of assessment is particularly difficult for the heritage languages profession and an area in which there has not been much work, either in the design of new instruments or in the validation of existing instruments with the heritage language population. Still, heritage language teachers must be able to effectively place students within a program and assess their progress.

Placement strategies must identify the strengths that students bring to the program or class as well as the skills that need to be developed. On the whole, placement instruments tend to be locally designed and may consist of written tests, interviews, language use questionnaires, or a combination of these. In addition, at the university level students may also take special tests to identify a heritage language background, take generic placement tests, take course-specific tests, or self-place in heritage language courses (González-Pino & Pino, 2000).

The oral interview, one of the most widely used assessment tools in foreign language programs, may not be as effective in programs for heritage language speakers. Draper & Hicks (2000) argue that use of the ACTFL Oral Proficiency Interview (OPI) (Buck, Byrnes, & Thompson, 1989) and the ACTFL Proficiency Guidelines (American Council on the Teaching of Foreign Languages, 1986) with heritage speakers is questionable on the grounds that they were developed for a different population and may not provide a valid description of heritage speakers' competencies. Another area of concern is ACTFL's "educated native-speaker" standard, which is controversial in itself (e.g., Salaberry, 2000), and may be inadequate as a standard for heritage speakers. Campbell and Rosenthal (2000) note that an oral proficiency interview will only provide information on speaking and comprehension, heritage language learners' strongest skills, and give no data on reading and writing, their least developed skills. Moreover, González-Pino & Pino (2000) observe that heritage language speakers often score at the high-intermediate and advanced proficiency levels, and as a result are placed in foreign language upper-level classes for which they have insufficient literacy skills.

Alternative assessments are particularly well suited to assess progress in the heritage language class (Baker, 1990; Herman, Aschbacher, & Winters, 1992). They emphasize that the processes and products of learning are ongoing and individualized. Alternative assessments, such as portfolios, contextualized individual performance tasks, peer and self-assessments, rubrics, assessment of the products of real-life activities, debriefings of what has been learned, portfolio conferences, personal narratives, self-reports, and self-ratings are effective assessment instruments for this population (Mercado, 2000).

As heritage language teachers assess students' linguistic competencies for placement and for assigning a grade, they must also assess students' needs beyond knowledge of the language. In this vein, the ACTFL–Hunter College Project has developed a model for monitoring student progress that has three dimensions: sociolinguistic, usage, and behavioral. According to Mercado (2000), the model

> seeks to go beyond examining students' grammatical competence to include other dimensions such as students' attitudes and learning strategies. Second, it acknowledges the important role that students and their homes and communities play in heritage language learning. Third, it reflects a system of values and beliefs premised on the view that the best way to support heritage language learners is by accepting socioemotional influences that impede successful learning as an integral part of the language learning experience and by attending to those influences in some significant way. (p. 221)

Mercado describes four major strategies for assessing the students' competence within the model: "(1) self-reports, (2) classroom observations, (3) analysis of student written work over time, and (4) contacts with the home" (p. 221).

Teacher Shortage

According to Recruiting New Teachers (RNT) (www.rnt .org), a nonprofit organization formed to improve teacher recruitment and development policies and practices, the United States will have to hire two million teachers between the years 2000 and 2010 to replace retiring teachers and meet rising enrollments. The shortage of qualified teachers affects all K–12 education systems and is most acute in the foreign and second language education fields. We face not only a general shortage of foreign language teachers, but a particular shortage of teachers who have the understandings, knowledge, and skills described above (Joint National Commission on Languages, 1999). This section summarizes national and local strategies to improve teacher recruitment as well as mentoring programs and other strategies to foster teacher retention.

The population of heritage language speakers in our schools and universities could, in principle, provide a large pool of heritage language teachers. The following programs are but a few of many designed to acquaint students with teaching as a profession and to ensure that speakers of languages other than English get a college education.

- The Heritage Language Literacy Club in Falls Church, Virginia, attempts to "grow teachers from the grass roots" (R. Armengol, personal communication, September 30, 1999) by recruiting fifth- and sixth-grade bilingual students to assist teachers with younger heritage speakers who are learning to read in Spanish and paying them with savings bonds for college.
- At the university level, tutoring programs like the EBLO program at the Shriver Center of the University of Maryland Baltimore County (UMBC), recruit college students who are heritage Spanish speakers to tutor low-income Spanish-speaking children in Baltimore, Maryland, on weekdays after

school and on Saturdays. Students may receive internship credits for participating in the program.

- At the national level, the RNT organization, in collaboration with the Council of the Great City Schools and the Council of the Great City Schools of Education, operates the Urban Teacher Academy Project (UTAP), academic teaching career academies located within high schools and designed to encourage students to consider careers in teaching.
- The University of Texas, El Paso (UTEP) offers electives related to teaching, learning, and children; pre-collegiate internships at local elementary, middle, and high schools; and partnerships with colleges and universities that provide a "pathway or corridor into college and teacher education" (Urban Teacher Academy Project, 2000, p. 3).

Outreach programs to students at risk of not attending college can be effective in providing professional bilingual models and college student mentors. The following are two examples.

- The Early Identification Program (www.gmu.edu/departments/unilife/eip) at George Mason University in Fairfax, Virginia. This program is a partnership between the university and middle or junior high schools in low-income communities. Its purpose is to increase the number of minority students who enter college. The program selects minority students with academic potential and provides year-round tutoring and other support throughout high school, a mandatory Summer Academy prior to ninth grade on the GMU campus, and afterschool tutorial sessions by GMU students at local high schools and at the university.
- The Para Educator Pathways into Teaching, at the University of Southern California Rossier School of Education Latino and Language Minority Teacher Projects (www.bcf.usc.edu/~cmmr/LTP.html). The goal of this program is to increase the

number of language minority teachers by providing financial, social, and academic support and assistance to bilingual paraeducators (teachers' aides) who work in Los Angeles schools and attend classes full time at USC and several other area universities.

Although a growing number of concerned university professors integrate heritage language topics into their pedagogy, language acquisition and learning, language planning, and linguistics courses, few university teacher training programs provide specific coursework in heritage languages education. The exception is Hunter College. As a result of the 3-year ACTFL–Hunter College FIPSE grant, Hunter College has developed a methods course on teaching heritage language learners. This course, together with a general foreign language methods course, will be required for New York state certification through Hunter College. In addition to methods courses, teacher preparation programs can acquaint preservice teachers with heritage language teaching issues by providing fieldwork experiences that include classroom observations, student teaching placements in heritage language classrooms, and opportunities to work with mentor teachers who are heritage language speakers. At the very least, foreign language methods courses can include basic information about what heritage languages are and how teaching heritage speakers is different from teaching students who have no previous experience with the language.

Summer language institutes, such as the National Endowment for the Humanities summer institute for middle and high school teachers of Spanish to Spanish speakers, co-sponsored by the Center for Applied Linguistics (CAL) and UCLA and funded by the NEH (www.cal.org/heritage/sns.html) provide opportunities for teachers to share knowledge and experiences and develop curricula, assessments, and instructional strategies that add to the pool of heritage languages teaching resources. National and local conferences also provide opportunities to develop professionally and to share materials and classroom insights and experiences.

At the state and national levels, education agencies must designate grants and scholarships to encourage teachers to specialize in heritage language teaching and to encourage local school systems to put in place innovative programs to attract potential teachers. The heritage community must maintain a high profile in national and local foreign language associations and be actively involved in national projects such as the ACTFL-sponsored New Visions 2000 project. Dealing with a number of issues, this project focuses on teacher recruitment and retention, and teacher development and mentoring in the foreign language profession. Other programs and resources involved in innovative approaches to teacher recruitment, induction, and mentoring are

- The California Foreign Language Teacher Recruitment Program, a collaborative project of the California Language Teachers Association (CLTA), the California Foreign Language Project (CFLP), and the California State University Foreign Language Council (CSUFLC) (www.stanford.edu/group/CFLP)
- The Clearinghouse for Beginning Teacher Support and Assessment Resources (www.usc.edu/dept/education/CMMR/CMMR_BTSA_home.html), a database of programs, full-text resources, web sites, books, and other resources for beginning teachers, maintained by the Center for Multilingual Multicultural Research at the University of Southern California
- The National Education Association's (NEA) publication *Creating a Teacher Mentoring Program* (www.nfie.org/publications/mentoring.htm)

Finally, local systems must petition their state departments of education to revise credentialing requirements for heritage language teachers and investigate alternative certification programs.

Conclusion

The field of heritage language teaching has come far in a very few years, but it still has a very long way to go. One of the most difficult tasks as the field grows and develops will be to collect and disseminate information about the developments and initiatives in all of the heritage languages and in all of the instructional contexts. We have much to learn from each other.

We must also aggressively pursue small grants as well as multiyear funding for large projects like the ACTFL–Hunter College FIPSE Project (Webb & Miller, 2000) that will enable us to devote the time, effort, and creativity needed to continue learning how to best do our jobs and serve our students. We must advocate not only for our students but also for our profession. We must encourage research in all areas that affect the teaching and learning of heritage languages, for it is this knowledge that informs our practice.

In "The Role of the University in Preparing Teachers for a Linguistically Diverse Society," Crandall (2000) describes three excellent approaches to teacher development that are generally found in combination: "the applied science model (providing courses that link theory to practice), the apprenticeship or skill-building model (where teachers observe and receive support from more experienced colleagues), and the reflective practice model, including classroom-based research and teacher inquiry groups (where teachers learn by researching and reflecting on their own teaching)" (p. 289). We can look at professional growth as coming from the outside (teacher preparation) or coming from the inside (professional development). Regardless of where we teach, what languages we teach, what resources are available, or the extent of our training, professional development starts with teachers, and we are those teachers.

References

American Association of Teachers of Spanish and Portuguese. (2000). *Handbook for teachers K–16: Spanish for native speakers* (AATSP Professional Development Series, Vol. 1). Orlando, FL: Harcourt College.

American Council on the Teaching of Foreign Languages (ACTFL). (1986). *Proficiency guidelines.* Yonkers, NY: Author.

Anstrom, K. (1996). Defining the limited-English proficient student population (*Directions in language and education, 1).* Retrieved May 15, 2001, from http://www.ncbe.gwu.edu/ncbepubs/directions/09.htm

Baker, E.L. (1990). *What probably works in alternative assessment.* Los Angeles: National Center for Research and Evaluation, Standards, and Student Testing.

Brecht, R.D., & Ingold, C.W. (1998). *Tapping a national resource: Heritage languages in the United States. ERIC Digest.* Washington, DC: *ERIC Clearinghouse on Languages and Linguistics.* Retrieved May 16, 2001, from http://*www.cal.org/ericcll/digests/brecht01.html*

Buck, K., Byrnes, H., & Thompson, I. (Eds.). (1989). *The ACTFL Oral Proficiency Interview: Tester training manual.* Yonkers, NY: American Council on the Teaching of Foreign Languages.

Campbell, R.N., & Rosenthal, J.W. (2000). Heritage languages. In J.W. Rosenthal (Ed.), *Handbook of undergraduate second language education* (pp. 165-184). Mahwah, NJ: Lawrence Erlbaum.

Crandall, J. (2000). The role of the university in preparing teachers for a linguistically diverse society. In J.W. Rosenthal (Ed.), *Handbook of undergraduate second language education* (pp. 279-299). Mahwah, NJ: Lawrence Erlbaum.

Draper, J.B., & Hicks, J.H. (2000). Where we've been; what we've learned. In J.B. Webb & B.L. Miller (Eds.), *Teaching heritage language learners: Voices from the classroom* (pp. 15-35). Yonkers, NY: American Council on the Teaching of Foreign Languages.

Ellis, R. (1994). *The study of second language acquisition.* Oxford, UK: Oxford University Press.

Fillmore, L.W., & Snow, C. (2000). *What teachers need to know about language.* Washington, DC: Center for Applied Linguistics. Retrieved May 15, 2001, from http:// www.cal.org/ericcll/teachers/teachers.pdf

González, J.M., & Darling-Hammond, L. (1997). *New concepts for new challenges: Professional development for teachers of immigrant youth.* McHenry, IL, and Washington, DC: Delta Systems and Center for Applied Linguistics.

González-Pino, B., & Pino, F. (2000). Serving the heritage speaker across a five-year program. *ADFL Bulletin, 32,* 26-35.

Herman, J.L., Aschbacher, P.R., & Winters, L. (1992). *A practical guide to alternative assessment.* Alexandria, VA: Association for Supervision and Curriculum Development.

Joint National Commission on Languages & National Council for Languages and International Studies. (1999). *Professional development for language teachers: 1998 state survey.* Washington, DC: Authors.

Mercado, C.I. (2000). Monitoring the progress of heritage language learners: Assessment trends and emerging practices. In J.B. Webb & B.L. Miller (Eds.), *Teaching heritage language learners: Voices from the classroom* (pp. 209-230). Yonkers, NY: American Council on the Teaching of Foreign Languages.

National Standards in Foreign Language Education Project. (1996). *Standards for foreign language learning: Preparing for the 21st century.* Yonkers, NY: Author.

Reyhner, J., Lockard, L., & Rosenthal, J.W. (2000). Native-American languages. In J.W. Rosenthal (Ed.), *Handbook of undergraduate second language education* (pp. 141-163). Mahwah, NJ: Lawrence Erlbaum.

Roca, A. (1992). *Spanish for U.S. Hispanic bilinguals in higher education. ERIC Digest.* Washington, DC: ERIC Clearinghouse on Languages and Linguistics.

Salaberry, R. (2000). Revising the revised format of the ACTFL Oral Proficiency Interview. *Language Testing, 17,* 289-310.

Schecter, S.R., & Bayley, R. (1997). Language socialization practices and cultural identity: Case students of Mexican-descent families in California and Texas. *TESOL Quarterly, 31,* 513-541.

Urban Teacher Academy Project. (2000). *The UTAP toolkit.* Belmont, MA, and Washington, DC: Recruiting New Teachers, Inc., and Council of the Great City Schools. Retrieved May 15, 2001, from http:// www.rnt.org/utap/toolkit.pdf

U.S. Census Bureau. (2000). *Census 2000 supplementary survey: Profile of selected social characteristics.* Retrieved from http://factfinder .census.gov/home/en/c2ss.html

Valdés, G. (1997). The teaching of Spanish to bilingual Spanish-speaking students: Outstanding issues and unanswered questions. In M.C. Colombi & F.X. Alarcón (Eds.), *La enseñanza del español a hispanohablantes: Praxis y teoría* (pp. 8-44). Boston: Houghton Mifflin.

Valdés, G. (2000). The ACTFL–Hunter College FIPSE Project and its contributions to the profession. In J.B. Webb & B.L. Miller (Eds.), *Teaching heritage language learners: Voices from the classroom* (pp. 235-251). Yonkers, NY: American Council on the Teaching of Foreign Languages.

Valdés, G., & Geoffrion-Vinci, M. (1998). Chicano Spanish: The problem of the "underdeveloped" code in bilingual repertoires. *The Modern Language Journal, 82*(4), 473-501.

Webb, J.B., & Miller, B.L. (Eds.). (2000). *Teaching heritage language learners: Voices from the classroom.* Yonkers, NY: American Council on the Teaching of Foreign Languages.

Research and
Practice

12
Heritage Language Education: Needed Research

Russell N. Campbell, UCLA
Donna Christian, Center for Applied Linguistics

The field of heritage language education is growing and will continue to grow, as is evident from the discussions throughout this book. The numbers of individuals living in the United States who speak a language other than English or who come from homes where a language other than English is spoken (and therefore may have passive competence in the language and extensive knowledge of another culture) continue to increase. The foreign born constitute the fastest-growing segment of our population, reaching over 30 million in 2000, more than 10% of the U.S. population (U.S. Census Bureau, 2001). More than 150 non-English languages are used in the United States, and many of them are taught in our colleges and universities (Brecht & Ingold, 1998).

The language proficiencies and cultural knowledge of the foreign-born and indigenous populations in the United States who speak languages other than English represent a valuable national resource that can promote this country's social, economic, and political well-being domestically and around the world. Fortunately, these individuals are beginning to recognize the importance of their knowledge and skills in their personal lives, their careers, and their roles in society in general. Many are seeking ways to develop their own knowledge and skills as well as those of their children and grandchildren.

However, as Brecht and Ingold (1998) point out, we as a nation have placed little value on the development of skills in languages other than English for either personal or professional purposes. There is very little research on heritage language speakers, communities, or programs that might serve them. A considerable amount of research has been conducted on language programs and instructional strategies in foreign language development among English language speakers (see, for example, Campbell, Gray, Rhodes, & Snow, 1985; Met, 1998); English language development among speakers of other languages (e.g., August & Hakuta, 1997; Collier, 1992; García, 2000; Lucas, Henze, & Donato,1990); and second language development in general (Ellis, 1999; Grabe, 1998). Little research, however, has been conducted on the development of proficiency in languages other than English among speakers of those languages. The primary goal of many "bilingual" programs is transition to English language proficiency (see, for example, Genesee, 1999; Ramírez, Yuen, & Ramey, 1991). The exception is dual language programs, in which the goal is to develop proficiency in English and another language. There is a small but growing body of research on this topic (e.g., Cazabon, Nicoladis, & Lambert, 1998; Christian, Montone, Lindholm, & Carranza, 1997; Lindholm-Leary, in press).

The research cited above represents a rich body of knowledge about language use and development that will inform a research program focused on heritage language proficiencies and knowledge. However, research focused specifically on this area is sorely needed so that we know what policies, programs, and instructional approaches exist now; what are most effective; and what need to be created or developed further. The purpose of this chapter is to outline the areas in which existing research needs to be synthesized and the areas in which new research needs to be carried out. It is our hope that this information will stimulate and provide direction for future research into listed here. For more detailed discussion of the issues and questions to be addressed in these and additional areas, see Heritage Language Research Priorities Conference Report (University of California, Los Angeles, 2001).

Research needs in the area of heritage language education can be organized into the following broad categories:

- Heritage Language Populations
- Heritage Language Communities
- Opportunities for Heritage Language Speakers
- Heritage Language Learning
- Heritage Language Education Systems and Strategies
- Language Policies
- Resources

Each of these categories covers a wide array of topics for research. A sample of important topics follows.

Heritage Language Populations

First and foremost, we need to know more about heritage language speakers.

- Where are the communities with significant heritage language populations located?
- What languages and varieties of languages are spoken?
- How many speakers of these languages are there?
- What are the background characteristics and experiences of heritage language learners in terms of age, gender, socioeconomic status, educational experience, levels of proficiency in the heritage language and in English, language attitudes, and motivation to learn?

Heritage Language Communities

Over time, heritage languages and cultures are either maintained or lost. We need to know more about the role the community plays in the processes of language maintenance and loss.

- How do communities of heritage language speakers support or hinder heritage language development?
- What is the role of the community in establishing goals and aspirations for heritage language learning and in intergenerational transmission of heritage languages?
- How do the belief systems of parents and other community members concerning heritage language maintenance and growth contribute to program development?
- What are the community structures and organizations that have helped and could help heritage language community members become active and successful in establishing heritage education programs? How could we build on these structures?

Opportunities for Heritage Language Speakers

Increasing globalization and the dramatic growth of the immigrant population in the United States have created a need for individuals with proficiency in languages other than English. We need to know what opportunities have been created by those needs.

- What are the academic, occupational, and professional opportunities available to heritage language speakers?
- How can instruction be linked to these opportunities to prepare learners for them?

Heritage Language Learning

We need to know more about heritage languages, in terms of both their linguistic features and their sociolinguistic status in the community and the processes by which they may be learned, relearned, maintained, and developed.

- What are the features of the languages (and language varieties) spoken and written by heritage language speakers, and how are these languages and varieties developed?
- What are the linguistic features of heritage language varieties that students bring to school (pre-K–12) and college and university?
- How do heritage language varieties spoken in the community vary linguistically from the "prestige" dialects that are valued and used in school and the workplace?
- How is second dialect acquisition similar to and different from first language acquisition and second language acquisition?
- What factors promote and inhibit heritage language learning?
- What strategies promote heritage language relearning for speakers who have experienced attrition in their proficiency?

Heritage Language Education Systems and Strategies

There are many kinds of heritage language classes taking place in a wide range of public, private, and community-based settings. We need to know more about these programs, and what makes them effective, and we need to know more about efforts in the area of teacher professional development.

Programs

- What are the factors that motivate parents, school staff, and community members to establish programs?
- What are the program goals?

- Which languages are being taught? Why these? What functions do they serve in the community, the nation, and the world at large?
- What skills are being taught?
- Who are the learners? What are their ages, grade levels, gender, heritage language backgrounds, and heritage language proficiency levels?
- What are the sponsoring institutions (e.g., public schools, private schools, churches, community organizations)?
- What are the program structures? How are programs structured in terms of number and level of courses, frequency and length of courses, and articulation of courses within and across programs and with K–12 and higher education systems?
- What curricula and instructional materials are being used?
- What are the instructional methods and strategies?
- What assessments and accountability systems are being used?
- What is being done in the areas of teacher qualifications and preparation?
- What are parental expectations? To what extent do parents support and become involved in these programs?
- How effective are the programs, as evidenced by student proficiency levels in the heritage language, student motivation to succeed in school, levels of success in school, and career accomplishments?
- What is the extent of postprogram follow-up and support?
- How do programs vary by location and student population? For example, are programs for indigenous populations different from those that serve immigrant populations? How do programs for Cuban students in Miami, Dominicans in New York City, Salvadorans in Northern Virginia, Puerto Ricans in Pennsylvania, and Chicanos in the Southwest differ from one another?

- What are the most effective practices? What programs show evidence of academic excellence and cost effectiveness? How have these programs addressed challenges?

Teacher Professional Development

We need to know what is being done in the area of teacher professional development and how those efforts could be more effective.

- What are the sources of heritage language teachers in our schools and communities?
- What state and institutional standards for preparation and certification of heritage language teachers exist?
- What knowledge and skills do heritage language teachers need? What materials are needed to develop that knowledge and those skills?
- What makes for effective heritage language teachers? What do effective teachers know? What are they able to do?
- What preservice and inservice professional development programs for heritage language teachers exist?
- Where are they located?
- How many teachers are involved?
- What are the program goals?
- What are the core curricula?
- What are the assumptions on which curriculum is built?
- How effective are these programs?

Language Policies

Language policies at all levels—national, state, local, and school—affect heritage language communities and learners. We need to know more about these policies and better understand their impact.

- What policies are in place around the country, and what are their effects on heritage language speakers and programs?
- What are the policies of secondary schools and higher education institutions concerning acceptance of heritage language proficiencies toward fulfillment of high school and college foreign language requirements and credits, and how do these policies help and hinder heritage language education?
- What policies are there in place in other countries that promote heritage language development and that support heritage language instructional programs?
- What roles do governments (or other external agencies) in other countries play in establishing and maintaining heritage language programs?

Resources

Over the years, there have been efforts by many people to promote heritage languages and cultures in this country. The work is scattered; much of it is unheralded; some of it is largely unknown. We need to compile collections of resources that provide comprehensive, up-to-date information in three areas.

Individual Accomplishments

This annotated compilation would provide information on scholars, educators, and policymakers who have made significant contributions to heritage language education and research. It would include a biography of each individual's personal and academic background and a summary of accomplishments in the field.

Documents

This annotated bibliography would list books, articles, dissertations, monographs, and other publications on history, current practices, research findings, assessment instruments, and public policy regarding heritage language education.

Instructional Materials and Assessments

This annotated bibliography would list available instructional materials (curricula, student materials, and teacher guides) and assessment instruments and procedures for learner diagnosis, placement, and achievement.

Conclusion

As evidenced by the outcomes of the Heritage Languages Conference in 1999 and its subsequent research meeting in 2000, we have begun to articulate the needs for research. We now need to develop policies and seek funding that will support and promote research in the areas identified and develop systems to support researchers and students to carry it out.

References

August, D., & Hakuta, K. (1997). *Improving schooling for language-minority children: A research agenda*. Washington, DC: National Academy Press.

Brecht, R.D., & Ingold, C.W. (1998). *Tapping a national resource: Heritage languages in the United States. ERIC Digest*. Washington, DC: ERIC Clearinghouse on Languages and Linguistics. Retrieved from http://www.cal.org/ericcll/digest/brecht01.html

Campbell, R.N., Gray, T.C., Rhodes, N.C., & Snow, M.A. (1985). Foreign language learning in the elementary schools: A comparison of three language programs. *Modern Language Journal, 69*(1), 25-37.

Cazabon, M., Nicoladis, E., & Lambert, W. (1998). *Becoming bilingual in the Amigos two-way immersion program* (Research Report No. 3). Washington, DC, and Santa Cruz, CA: Center for Research on Education, Diversity & Excellence.

Christian, D., Montone, C., Lindholm, K., & Carranza, I. (1997). *Profiles in two-way immersion education*. McHenry, IL, and Washington, DC: Delta Systems and Center for Applied Linguistics.

Collier, V.P. (1992). A synthesis of studies examining long-term language minority student data on academic achievement. *Bilingual Research Journal, 16,* 187-212.

Ellis, R. (1999). Input-based approaches to teaching grammar: A review of classroom-oriented research. *Annual Review of Applied Linguistics, 19,* 64-80.

García, G.N. (2000). *Lessons from research: What is the length of time it takes LEP students to acquire English and succeed in an all-English classroom?* (Issue Brief No. 5). Washington, DC: National Clearinghouse for Bilingual Education. Retrieved from http://www.ncbe.gwu.edu/ncbepubs/issuebriefs/ib5.pdf

Genesee, F. (Ed.). (1999). *Program alternatives for linguistically diverse students.* (Educational Practice Report No. 1). Washington, DC, and Santa Cruz, CA: Center for Research on Education, Diversity & Excellence.

Grabe, W. (Ed.). (1998). Foundations of second language teaching. *Annual Review of Applied Linguistics, 18.* New York: Cambridge University Press.

Lindholm-Leary, K. (in press). *Dual language education.* Avon, UK: Multilingual Matters.

Lucas, T., Henze, R., & Donato, R. (1990). Promoting the success of Latino language minority students: An exploratory study of six high schools. *Harvard Educational Review, 60*(1), 315-340.

Met, M. (Ed.). (1998). *Critical issues in early second language learning.* New York: Scott Foresman-Addison Wesley.

Ramírez, J.D., Yuen, S.D., & Ramey, D.R. (1991). *Final report: Longitudinal study of structured immersion strategy, early-exit, and late-exit transitional bilingual education programs for language-minority children.* San Mateo, CA: Aguirre International.

University of California, Los Angeles. (2001). *Heritage language research priorities conference report.* Los Angeles: Author. Retrieved from http://www.cal.org/heritage

U.S. Census Bureau. (2001). *Census 2000 supplementary survey: Profile of selected social characteristics.* Retrieved from http://factfinder.census.gov/home/en/c2ss.html

Related Efforts

The following research agenda development efforts, currently underway, can inform the development of a research agenda in the heritage language field.

The American Council of Teachers of Foreign Languages (ACTFL), as part of its New Visions initiative, is developing a research agenda for the field of foreign language teaching. [www.actfl.org/public/articles]

The National Center for ESL Literacy Education has developed a Research Agenda for Adult ESL (1998) focused on needs for research on the population of adult English learners in the United States and effective programs and instructional practices for working with this population. [www.cal.org/ncle/agenda]

Teachers of English to Speakers of Other Languages (TESOL) has developed a research agenda related to the field of English language acquisition. [www.tesol.org/assoc/bd/0006researchagenda01]

Westat is developing a research agenda to improve the educational achievement and academic progress of American Indian and Alaska Native students, in response to Executive Order 13096 (American Indian and Alaska Native Education, August, 1998). One of the goals is to evaluate the role of native language and culture in the development of educational strategies. [www.ed.gov/nativeamericanresearch]

Acknowledgments

We are grateful to Ana Roca (Florida International University), Thom Huebner (San José State University), and a number of other researchers interested in heritage languages and cultures for their valuable contributions to this summary of needed research. These researchers worked together before and during the 1999 Heritage Languages Conference in Long

Beach, California, to note issues, problems, and questions that need to be addressed. The research areas outlined in this article reflect the group's informal collection, recording, and classification of general and specific research domains.

13
Heritage Language Education: Summaries of Research and Practice

This chapter contains summaries of research and practice underway in the field of heritage language education. Based on presentation abstracts from the 1999 Heritage Languages Conference in Los Angeles, the summaries are organized into five categories, which match those in the previous chapter on needed research (Campbell & Christian, this volume).*

* Heritage Language Communities
* Heritage Language Learning
* Heritage Language Education Systems and Strategies
* Language Policies
* Heritage Language Resources

Heritage Language Communities

The Aftereffects of Relocation

Maria E. Trillo, Texas Woman's University, Denton, TX
E-mail: mtrillo@unm.edu

Being a native speaker of Spanish in the United States is a devalued commodity in the national educational and political arenas. This paper focuses on research on successful strategies used to produce fluent bilingual/bicultural individuals. In a now defunct border community known as Rio Linda (El Chamizal) in El Paso, 32 of 50 families were interviewed on the aftereffects of relocation. A composite profile of the community, based on a preliminary study of 9 subjects, is provided. It

*There were no presentations on heritage language populations or on professional opportunities for heritage language speakers.

was discovered that a high percentage of professionals, most of whom are fluent bilinguals, survived the forced displacement period. Their survival strategies included speaking Spanish in the home and English at school; reading Spanish out loud to their elders and younger siblings; listening to Spanish radio and TV programs; writing and performing their own miniplays in Spanish; and living in a community where Spanish was the expected mode of communication even though the school physically repressed use of Spanish. These strategies are compared with those of two other minority Spanish-speaking diaspora communities—the Salvadorean and Chilean communities in Winnipeg, Manitoba, Canada. The paper also explores implications for further research into successful strategies for maintaining linguistic skills in the first language while subsequent languages are learned.

A Community-Based Effort to Institutionalize a Vietnamese Heritage Language Program

Kim-Oanh Nguyen-Lam, Center for Language Minority Education and Research, California State University, Long Beach
E-mail: kclam@csulb.edu

This presentation described the collaborative effort of a community-based group, made up of community members, parents, heritage language teachers, and a university bilingual education specialist, to establish a Vietnamese language program at a local high school with a high percentage of Vietnamese heritage speakers. The process involved a series of meetings between the community-based group and school staff. Community resources included a bilingual Vietnamese lawyer, community civic leaders, and the president of the Vietnamese Heritage Language Schools and Centers, Southern California Association. The group also made use of the heritage language media (radio stations and newspapers) to garner community-wide support. Despite challenges and barriers, such as institutional resistance and discrimination, lack of state-licensed teachers in the target language, and no representation of the heritage language community on the school district governing board, the group managed to integrate their heritage language into the mainstream educational system.

Language Awareness, Exploration, and Appreciation in a South Texas Border Community

Kati Pletsch de Garcia, Texas A&M International University, Laredo
E-mail: kdegarcia@tamiu.edu
Web site: http://www.TAMIU.EDU/~KDEGARCIA/TEXMEX

Laredo, Texas, is noted for its conservative nature, and for guarding and maintaining its Hispanic customs and Spanish language in spite of its location within the United States and its increased contact with the Anglo American population. The linguistic situation of this border community is unique since 93% of Laredo's 172,000 residents are of Hispanic descent.

An investigation of language attitudes in this bilingual community is important because a positive attitude toward a language has been linked to language maintenance, while a negative attitude may play a key role in language shift. Attitude surveys provide social indicators of changing beliefs and the chances of success in policy implementation.

Codeswitching (often referred to in this community as Spanglish or TexMex) is an important characteristic of the dynamics of linguistic interaction in this Texas border community. This presentation summarizes research that examines the ambiguous attitudes toward the Spanish variety used in this community, and presents a web that explores language usage in Laredo. The results of the attitude survey suggest that Laredoans have ambivalent attitudes toward language mixing, Spanish proficiency, societal identity, bilingualism, and the viability of Spanish in the Laredo community. For example, while 60% of the subjects agreed or strongly agreed that mixing Spanish and English in the same sentence should be avoided, 72% of the subjects agreed that codeswitching is a symbol of belonging to the community.

The Laredo web site gives examples of the TexMex language used in the community as well as examples of materials developed for the Internet to increase awareness and appreciation of the language varieties spoken in this Spanish heritage language community. Material development has focused primarily on making the language link between the three codes spoken—Spanish, English, and TexMex.

Language Contact Among Heritage Speakers of Romanian in the United States
Domnita Dumitrescu, California State University, Los Angeles
E-mail: ddumitr@calstatela.edu

Jon Amastae (1989) observed that "investigators of bilingualism and language contact face three principal tasks. One is to understand the nature of bilingual societies; a second is to understand the nature of bilingual individuals; the third is to understand what happens to grammatical systems when they are in prolonged contact with other systems" (p. 810).

In the United States, contact between English and other languages that are widely spoken in North America—especially Romance languages, such as Spanish and French—has been a topic of interest. This paper sheds light on certain effects of the contact between English and another much-less-studied Romance language, Romanian. These effects manifest themselves at the lexicogrammatical level in the speech of Romanian Americans living in the United States. As Alexandra Roceric (1982) has pointed out, "This community has been little studied as a distinct group within the larger context of the American nation and culture. It is, however, a clearly identifiable minority, which has exhibited . . . a surprising capability to preserve its cultural identity and attachment to ethnic roots, while integrating itself increasingly into the American society" (p. 2). The study of its language variety "contributes directly to the observations provided in recent years by studies of the bilingualism of several American groups of European origin whose social and linguistic histories are similar to those of Romanian immigrants" (p. 3).

This paper focuses on single-word loans, single-word calques, multiple-word calques, and syntactic deviations, as well as codeswitching and codemixing phenomena in speech samples of Romanian Americans living in California (mainly in the Los Angeles basin) with whom the researcher, a Romanian American, has had the opportunity to interact on a regular basis. (California has the second highest number of Romanian immigrants in the Unites States, according to the 1990 census.) The researcher also uses examples from data collected by Roceric (1982) in Cleveland, Detroit, New York, and St. Paul (which include speakers of all four generations); data collected by Hartular (1996) from elderly first-generation speakers living in Cleveland, Detroit, Gary, East Chicago, and Philadelphia in the 1970s; and writing samples from the Romanian press published in the United States.

This paper expands on previous work on the parallel effects of English contact on Spanish and Romanian in the United States (Dumitrescu, 1993, 1998).

Teaching Heritage Languages in Quebec: Integration or Enrichment?

Michel Laurier and Khatoune Temisjian, Heritage Language Centre, University of Montreal
E-mail: laurierm@SCEDU.Umontreal.ca;
khatoune.temisjian@Umontreal.ca

Since 1977, heritage languages have been taught in the public schools in Quebec, Canada. Depending on the year, 15 to 17 languages are taught. While half of the students are learning Italian, others are learning less commonly taught languages, such as Tamil and Cambodian. The original objectives of Quebec's heritage language program were drawn from research results that showed the positive impact of heritage language learning on the development of additive bilingualism and integration into a new learning and social environment (Cummins, 1981). With the evolution of these programs, more emphasis has been placed on the importance of preserving the cultural and linguistic characteristics of language minorities in Canada. This presentation traces the evolution of heritage language programs in Quebec in relation to approaches in the United States and Europe, focusing on the linguistic situation in Quebec, where mastering a heritage language often means developing trilingualism.

Heritage Language Learning

Cross-Cultural Discourse Analysis in Spanish for Native Speakers (SNS) Classes

Rebeca Acevedo, Loyola Marymount University, Los Angeles
E-mail: racevedo@lmumail.lmu.edu

By becoming sensitive to cross-cultural similarities and differences and by taking into consideration difficulties that heritage language speakers are likely to encounter in understanding and writing texts, we can better design materials for teaching Spanish in SNS classrooms. This presentation provides an overview of cross-cultural discourse studies, with specific emphasis on one particular study (Pak, 1996) of Spanish newspaper editorials in three cultural contexts (United States, Mexico, and Spain). Additional data examine adjectival word order from Mexican American editorials.

Preposed adjectives—adjectives that precede nouns—are regularly used in newspaper editorials. From the data analyzed in this study, it is clear that the writers of Mexican editorials employ significantly more preposed adjectives than do the writers of the Spanish editorials. The results also indicate U.S. Spanish editorials employ slightly more preposed adjectives than Mexican editorials. However, the difference between U.S.

Spanish and Peninsular Spanish editorials is even more significant. This study confirms the close relation between Mexican and Southwestern U.S. Spanish norms. It also confirms that preposed adjectives in Spanish are a common tendency that is no longer confined to literary language. Finally, there is no clear evidence of English language interference in U.S. Spanish.

The presentation discusses the application of cross-cultural discourse analysis to enhance students' critical reading and writing skills, and includes a sample teaching technique, as outlined below.

Material: Newspaper editorials from U.S. Spanish newspapers and other samples from The Hispanic World.

Goal: To expose students to the variability of Spanish word order, specifically the position of adjectives, and their communicative functions.

Step 1. Explain the regular NP structure: (Adj.) N (Adj.).

Step 2. Ask students to identify all the adjectives in the editorials and to underline the ones that are preposed.

Step 3. Ask students to describe the functions of the preposed adjectives.

Step 4. Ask students to comment on alternative orders and their communicative functions.

Optional expansion: Ask students how the editorial tone will change if the preposed adjectives are postposed. Are there any differences among the dialectal varieties?

Function Word Blends in Spanish L1 Writing
Raul Aranovich, University of California, Davis
E-mail: aranovch@sprynet.com

Error analysis (James, 1998) can give insights into the development of advanced skills in adult native speakers of a language. This paper classifies some writing errors typically made by native speakers of U.S. Spanish. Taken from advanced compositions written by undergraduate students at the University of Texas, San Antonio, the errors involve, as in example (a), replacing some sequences of words (a ser, 'to be') with a single homophonous word (hacer, 'to do or to make'); or, alternatively, as in example (b), replacing single words (hacer, 'to do or to make') with a homophonous sequence (a ser, 'to be').

(a) Pensó que iba *hacer una cena romántica con velas y vino.
([He] thought it was going to be a romantic dinner, with candles and wine.)
(b) Robar es una cosa que no necesita educación para *a serlo.
(Stealing is something you don't need an education to do.)

These blends affect function words. Blends arise when the speaker has an option between two well-defined targets (Baars, 1992; Dechert & Lennon,1989). In the case of (a) and (b), the error forms are not misspellings, but rather well-formed expressions in the target language. The blends affect verbs often used as auxiliaries together with a preposition used in verbal periphrases. The common membership in the class of function words makes the alternative forms in (a) and (b) a potentially well-defined target, causing the blend. This type of mistake presupposes nonexplicit knowledge of the language, and is therefore expected in heritage language learners.

Is Heritage Language Maintenance Necessary? A Response from Second Generation Korean American Adults

Grace Cho, California State University, Fullerton
E-mail: gcho@fullerton.edu

The purpose of this study was to examine the effects of having or not having heritage language (HL) competence among 98 Korean American college students enrolled in Korean language classes. Specifically, this study examined the ways in which HL competence affects individuals, their social interactions, and their relationships with parents and other HL speakers.

The findings show that heritage language proficiency provides many advantages. Strong HL competence was found to positively affect relationships with parents, the HL community, and HL speakers from the country of origin, as well as enhance personal well being. Moreover, HL competence plays an important part in the personal, social, and intellectual life of those who are proficient in the language.

Language and Literacy Development of Bilingual Japanese Children

Masahiko Minami, San Francisco State University
E-mail: mminami@sfsu.edu

The researcher assessed the bilingual language and literacy development of a group of Japanese American schoolchildren. To measure each child's bilingual verbal ability, the Bilingual Verbal Ability Tests (BVAT) (Muñoz-Sandoval, Cummins, Alvarado, & Ruef, 1998) were administered. Interviews with the children's mothers were also conducted.

The interviews indicate that, despite the mothers' desperate efforts to maintain Japanese, the children prefer to speak English in all situations. The language shift to English is so entrenched that it is the language of choice for even informal intergenerational interactions at home. The children's preference for speaking English is further illustrated by the results of the BVAT, which reveal that many of the children demonstrate "fluent to advanced" English proficiency. That is, these children find the English language demands of age-level tasks easy. The results of the BVAT also suggest that the children's bilingual verbal and cognitive abilities in English and Japanese combined are not significantly higher than they are in English alone. Implications of these findings are significant in terms of promoting bilingualism and multiculturalism.

Putting a Gloss on Your Irish: A Particular Case of Language Learning

Sharon Toomey Clark, California State University, San Bernadino
E-mail: Sharon.Clark@cgu.edu

This study presents results of research exploring learner motivation conducted at an Irish language immersion program for teenage students in western Ireland, in July and August 1999.

For approximately 500 years, English has been the lingua franca of Ireland, drowning out the original Irish (Gaelic). This century has seen increased efforts to reinstate use of the Irish language. Currently, Irish remains a subject of instruction in classrooms in Ireland. Those students who wish to "put a gloss on" their language skills participate in supplemental language programs in the western part of the country, where the use of the Irish language is more prevalent. This situation constitutes a unique language learning case.

Motivation for learning a language figures prominently as a factor affecting success in language learning. Prior research (Gardner & Lambert, 1972) has identified two kinds of motivation for language learning—instrumental motivation and integrative motivation. Instrumental motivation is concerned with learning a language to fulfill a secondary goal—for example, to do business in a particular location. Integrative motivation is concerned with learning a language to be able to participate in the social life of a community. However, the Irish language learning situation fits neither category. Rather, motivation for Irish language proficiency seems to derive from the pride of heritage.

Rainbow Children: How We Teach About Maintaining Our Heritage Languages

Daniel Villa, New Mexico State University, Las Cruces
Millie Smallcanyon, Crownpoint Institute of Technology, Crownpoint, New Mexico
E-mail: dvilla@crl.NMSU.edu

The title of this paper comes from the writing of Millie Smallcanyon, from Kayenta, Arizona, and a member of the Navajo Saltwater Clan. She and Daniel Villa, a *surumato* (Mexicano from southern New Mexico), were brought together through a Kellogg Foundation grant to work on a grassroots approach to preserving and maintaining their native languages. Rainbow children (Smallcanyon's term for children of mixed ethnic and racial backgrounds) often do not possess the prototypical physical characteristics associated with their language group and may have a special motivation to reacquire their mother tongue. The study of this motivation may help identify individuals who are open to reacquiring their heritage language.

Both researchers in this project are of mixed ethnic and racial backgrounds, have experienced the loss of their native languages, and have been successful in relearning those languages. Both have created a strong bond with their heritage communities through the reacquisition of their families' native tongue.

Villa and Smallcanyon researched their individual efforts to relearn their mother tongues in order to find out if there are certain shared experiences, regardless of linguistic group, that lead to the reacquisition of an ancestral language. While one speaks Navajo and the other Spanish, they found many similarities in their separate quests to reconnect with their non-English linguistic communities. Both were exposed to their mother tongues from the first moments of their lives. While these languages played a fairly major role in their early communicative environments, even if in a mostly receptive manner, both researchers later experienced a rupture in their contact with the mother tongue that accelerated the process of language loss. Between the ages of 11 and 15, during what is considered the critical period for language acquisition, they rarely spoke their heritage languages. They also experienced a distancing from the mother culture as well. Subsequently, they experienced a key event, which they cannot precisely specify, that motivated them to relearn the language. In the process, they participated in the language community in general, but at the same time formed a special bond with a particular member of the community—in each case, an elder from their grandparents' generation. They looked to these elders as teachers, not in the traditional sense of the word, but rather as guides or mentors who provided them with a model of the linguistic patterns they sought to reacquire. Finally, they found that reacquiring the mother tongue went hand in hand with reentering the heritage culture.

Sociolinguistic Attitudes and Language Maintenance Patterns of Heritage Language Students

David Cruz de Jesus, Baruch College, New York City
Luz Lenis, Fordham University, New York City
Eva Mendieta, Indiana University Northwest, Gary
E-mail (David Cruz de Jesus): dc36@cornell.edu

This paper describes a comparative study of Spanish language maintenance and patterns of language use in a sample of bilingual students from New York City and from a region in northwest Indiana. All are enrolled in Spanish for heritage speaker classes at the university level. As a framework to determine patterns of linguistic maintenance and change, the study combines the evaluation of maintenance indices from sociolinguistic surveys with the notion of social networks. Special attention is also devoted to students' linguistic attitudes in an effort to draw conclusions that will help educators better meet the needs of Spanish heritage language learners.

Heritage Language Education Systems and Strategies

Programs

Bilingual Program Design, Grades 6–12: Creating a Support Network for Developing Bilingualism in the Upper Grades

Mike Croghan, California State University, San Marcos
E-mail: mcroghan@csusm.edu

As two-way immersion programs develop more balanced bilinguals in the earlier grades and as bilingualism becomes more valued, secondary schools are called upon to respond to the needs and resources of language learners. A few programs are leading the way, but they are not yet well known. This presentation provides program sketches and characteristics of successful programs serving Grades 6–12. The presentation also describes a network for upper-grade educators who want to share theory, thoughts, and practices for the development and improvement of bilingualism in upper-grade students through an interactive web site and a listserv.

Creating a Heritage Language Curriculum: Lessons from Tagalog

Irma Pena Gosalvez, University of California, Berkeley
Nelleke Van Deusen-Scholl, University of Pennsylvania, Philadelphia
E-mail: gngg@uclink4.berkeley.edu; pldeusen@ccat.sas.upenn.edu

Foreign language classes at the university level are experiencing a gradual shift in emphasis and constituency. The traditional foreign—often European—language classroom is being replaced by a very different model that favors non-Western languages and attracts students who may already be familiar with the language and culture that is being taught. At UC Berkeley, the foreign language programs are in the midst of this transformation, as many of the less commonly taught languages (e.g., Chinese, Hindi, Korean, Tagalog, and Vietnamese) draw large numbers of heritage language learners. Yet existing curricula and textbooks are geared toward the traditional foreign language learner and not the heritage language learner. In this presentation, we provide a brief overview of the pedagogical and curricular issues that the university language program staff face. These issues include the wide range in oral proficiency levels that heritage learners bring to the classroom; the learners' need to acquire academic literacy (both formal registers and academic writing skills); dialect differences, as for many heritage learners the standard that is being taught may not be the variety that they grew up with; and the need for learners to acquire a knowledge of grammar and orthography.

Using a model curriculum for Tagalog as an example, we show how language lessons can be adapted to better address the needs of the heritage learner and how new teaching strategies can benefit both heritage and foreign language students. Suggested strategies include undertaking ethnographic projects in the heritage language; utilizing community resources (e.g., local publications and cultural centers); and using native speakers to act as cultural and linguistic resources. Recommendations for designing a heritage language curriculum include incorporating reading and writing activities that take into account the students' home language background and interests; teaching reading and writing on varied topics related to the heritage culture; and structuring classroom activities that help learners develop a positive attitude toward the language, culture, and themselves.

Creating Balanced Curricula in Navajo Language Teaching

Evangeline Parzons-Yazzie and Joe Kee, Northern Arizona University, Flagstaff
E-mail: yazzie@nau.edu

Concern has been growing among Navajo Christian parents since the Navajo Nation mandated that all reservation schools include Navajo language teaching in the curriculum. These parents are apprehensive that their children will be exposed to

Navajo religion, since many Navajo language teachers incorporate philosophy and traditional beliefs into their teachings.

Most Navajo language curricula endorsed by the Navajo Nation acknowledge that the language is embedded in culture, which is embedded in traditional beliefs. Christian parents, however, perceive much of traditional culture as Navajo religion. This controversy has been ongoing since the turn of the century. While Navajo people do not draw the line between culture and Navajo religion, religious leaders, school and Indian agency administrators, teachers, and missionaries do. Lack of knowledge of Navajo culture and tradition and loyalty to their own faith have caused Christian parents to adhere to the lines drawn between culture and religion by non-Navajos. Because Navajo language teaching does not reflect the wishes of Christian parents, children are being excluded from Navajo classes.

This presentation demonstrates the beauty of the Navajo languages; explains the shift away from Navajo language teaching by Christian parents; presents aspects of the differences in beliefs; and offers an inclusive, balanced curriculum.

Curriculum Design and Materials Development in a Korean Heritage Program at UCLA

Sung-Ock Shin Sohn, University of California, Los Angeles
E-mail: Sohn@humnet.ucla.edu

The teaching of Korean language at the college level in the United States poses a unique challenge since most of the students in Korean classes have a Korean heritage background. For instance, at UCLA, where there are approximately 3,300 Korean-American undergraduate students, 80% of the students who take Korea-related courses are heritage speakers. These courses pose special problems for Korean language educators who face the dilemma of dealing with both heritage and nonheritage learners in the same classroom.

While heritage speakers display a wide range of skills, they lack the opportunity to develop their reading and writing skills, and a huge disparity exists between their oral and literacy skills. In order to provide heritage students with optimal learning opportunities, UCLA has initiated a two-track curriculum in the Korean program. In this system, heritage and nonheritage learners are placed in separate classes during the first 2 years of Korean language study but in combined classes for Year 3. Traditional foreign language instructional methods are employed with nonheritage learners, while literacy skills and cultural enhancement are emphasized for heritage speakers. For advanced heritage speakers, special courses such as Reading Korean Academic Texts and Advanced Korean Conversation have been developed.

Both heritage and nonheritage learners have benefited immensely from the dual track program. Nonheritage learners no longer feel intimidated by the presence of heritage speakers, and heritage learners find that these courses are tailored to their special needs. The greatest imperative is to develop instructional materials and multimedia resources for heritage speakers.

Curriculum Design for Heritage Learners in a Kindergarten Saturday Japanese School

Masako O. Douglas, University of California, Los Angeles
Tamayo Harada, California State University, Los Angeles
E-mail: masakoUCLA@aol.com

Weekend Japanese language schools play an important role in the instruction of children with a Japanese heritage background. However, two challenges are commonly observed in these schools: a traditional focus on grammar and writing and a difficulty meeting the individual needs of children, who differ in their cognitive development and language proficiency.

This presentation describes a pilot study of curriculum design and an actual curriculum for heritage learners at the kindergarten level in a Saturday Japanese language school. The attempt was made to design a curriculum that integrates language education into early childhood education and takes into consideration the developmental needs of young children. In order to accommodate the children's cognitively and linguistically divergent needs, opportunities were included to individualize learning experiences.

The presentation includes a demographic and environmental description of the school and discusses curriculum issues, sample teaching plans, instructional activities and materials, and the results of an assessment of orthographic knowledge (from a case study of two children from Japanese/English bilingual families).

Dual Language Design
Ganzhi Di, Eugenio Maria de Hostos Community College, New York City

Eugenio Maria de Hostos Community College is undergoing a renaissance that will enable students to profit from innovative approaches to language teaching and learning. A cornerstone of the college's mission is to offer dual language educational opportunities in a multicultural environment that fosters appreciation, understanding, and respect for cultural diversity, second language acquisition, and intellectual growth. To this end, a new department, Language and Cognition, was created, with four academic Language Corridors—Dual Language, Spanish Immersion, Linked Courses, and English Critical Thinking.

Corridor I is a dual language program for English language learners that offers ESL linked with content courses in Spanish. Corridor II is a Spanish language immersion program with English content for students who are English dominant but who want to acquire Spanish language skills to enhance their employability in the careers of their choice. Corridor III links an ESL course for intermediate and advanced students with a content course, to improve students' English language proficiency while helping them to succeed in their content courses. Corridor IV is a critical thinking program to develop thinking and writing skills in the English language.

English Dominant Chicanos in Spanish/English Dual Language Programs

Sheila M. Shannon and Heather Riley-Bernal, University of Colorado at Denver
Jorge García, Project ACCESS, Greeley, CO
E-mail: sshannon@ceo.cudenver.edu

This presentation describes three Spanish/English dual language programs in Colorado and Arizona. English-dominant Mexican Americans comprise the majority of the English-speaking students in each program. This feature makes these programs unique and gives them the potential to improve not only linguistic outcomes for these students but academic and personal ones as well. The theoretical implications are complex, however. Therefore, we present three programs that are distinct because of their settings and student populations. One program in Colorado is rural, the other is urban, and the program in Arizona is on the border. The Spanish-dominant students in each of these programs are from Mexican immigrant families; some in the Arizona program are Mexican nationals. Thus, each program brings together Mexicans and Mexican Americans.

Nothing in dual language programs can be left to chance. If language status and distribution are not carefully structured, English tends to dominate. If social status and racial tensions are not attended to and understood, English speakers and nonimmigrants take on tacit positions of power. Each of the three programs represents a different facet of the same puzzle. With careful attention to linguistic and social issues, these programs can accomplish three things: create a meaningful bond between Mexicans and Mexican Americans around Spanish as a heritage language, develop bilingualism and biliteracy in both groups, and improve the sense of identity and self-worth of both groups.

Filipino as a Heritage Language: The Hawai'i Model

Teresita V. Ramos, University of Hawaii, Manoa
E-mail: teresita@hawaii.edu

The teaching of Filipino to heritage students at the University of Hawai'i at Manoa is founded on the philosophy of developing a heritage language as a tool for learning the heritage culture, establishing identity, and promoting community efforts for social and political empowerment. Heritage language learning, therefore, is not just a means to learning a language, but is also a means to learning the history of the homeland and understanding the community where the learners belong so that they can be active participants in shaping its goals and guiding its direction.

This presentation introduces the curriculum, activities, and strategies undertaken by the University of Hawai'i Filipino and Philippine Literature Program, so that it may serve as a model for heritage language learning in the United States. Program components include the philosophical foundation of a community language (including curriculum goals for each level); activities and strategies that include promotion and preservation of the culture; building or expanding community-based "language laboratories," and academic and external evaluation of language production (oral and written) through culturally measurable means.

French Immersion in Louisiana: A Way to Safeguard "Notre Heritage"

Michelle Haj-Broussard, Louisiana State University, Baton Rouge
E-mail: mhajbr1@lsu.edu

This presentation describes French Immersion programs in Louisiana. It sketches the history of French in Louisiana from 1699 to the present day. Using video clips and pictures, it provides information on successful strategies that the state has used to preserve French as a heritage language. These strategies include the immensely popular Histoire et Chansons program in which students adopt a nursing home resident who is a native speaker of Louisiana French; the use of parent support groups, Action Cadienne and Codofil (The Council for the Development of French in Louisiana); and the development of a French-language children's book based on Louisiana folktales.

The Hawaiian Language Immersion Program
Puanani Wilhelm, State of Hawaii Department of Education
E-mail: Puanani_Wilhelm@notes.k12.hi.us

The Papahana Kaiapuni Hawaiʻi (the Hawaiian Language Immersion Program) is a full-time immersion program in the Hawaiʻi public school system. The program began in 1987 at two schools and is currently in 16 schools with approximately 1,600 students. The first class of students educated entirely in Hawaiian language in the Papahana Kaiapuni graduated in June of 1999. However, the implementation of this 12-year-old program is ongoing. There are still many concerns regarding English language introduction, curriculum focus, and academic achievement. While there has been progress in the development of the components necessary to successfully implement such a program, there is still much more to do.

This presentation addresses the following areas of concern: the development of appropriate curricula and materials; teacher preparation and inservice training of teachers; and culturally appropriate pedagogy. Examples of materials are provided, and the issue of the use of translated English materials is discussed. Current efforts to develop teachers' proficiency in the Hawaiian language are described. A short video highlights some of the unique qualities of the Kaiapuni program.

Heritage Schools and Public School Partnerships for Early Language Education

Betty Lau, Chong Wa Benevolent Association School, Seattle
Larry Strickland, Office of the State Superintendent of Public Instruction, State of Washington, Olympia
E-mail: laubet_59@netzero.net; lstrickland@ospi.wednet.edu

This presentation describes a partnership among the state of Washington, local school districts, and community-based language schools to launch a highly popular summer language program that featured several less commonly taught languages—Chinese, Japanese, Korean, Arabic, and Russian. More than 300 students and 40 instructors and staff members participated in the project. Major project components included

- University training in language teaching methodology for native speakers recruited from community-based language schools
- Guidance provided by certified staff who could speak the target languages with varying degrees of fluency
- High school and college-age native speakers and students of the target languages who served as teacher aides
- Enough practicum experience to allow participants to qualify for Washington state conditional teaching certificates.

Heritage Students in Asian Language Classes: Student Motivation and Proficiency and Teacher Challenges

Amado M. Padilla and Hyekyung Sung, Stanford University, Palo Alto
E-mail: apadilla@leland.Stanford.edu; sung@stanford.edu

This presentation discusses a study that examined students' motivation to enroll in Asian language classes, factors influencing their oral language development, and challenges faced by teachers of Asian languages. The sample consisted of students enrolled in Asian language programs in elementary and secondary schools and parents who volunteered to complete a questionnaire. The survey asked about attitudes toward language learning, motivation for studying an Asian language, parental involvement in language study, and strategies used by students to learn the language. Students' language proficiency correlated significantly with motivation to learn the language, the amount of time dedicated to using the language outside of class, and parents' interest and encouragement.

Interviews with teachers of Asian languages identified numerous challenges: a scarcity of instructional materials and assessment instruments; a lack of support from the foreign language department; limited opportunities for professional development; and difficulty in teaching a mixed group of ethnic and nonethnic heritage students in the same class.

Findings from this study have implications for how teachers plan language instruction for Asian ethnic heritage learners. Because these learners bring different needs and expectations to the classroom and have more opportunities to use the language out of class, teachers require different forms of training and administrative support.

How is Heritage Language Maintained? Language Use in a Chinese Language School

Min-hsun Chiang, St. Edward's University, Austin, TX
E-mail: Min-hsun@mail.utexas.edu

Community language schools often shoulder the burden of developing the language skills and cultural knowledge of the speakers of non-English-speaking children in the community. However, using a community-based resource to preserve heritage languages against the pressures of the mainstream culture can be extremely difficult. This presentation is based on a year-long ethnographic study of a seventh-grade class in a Chinese language school in central Texas. Semistructured ethnographic interviews and participant observations are the two primary data collection methods.

The results of the study indicate that in its attempt to maintain Chinese language and culture in the American context, the Chinese school is often caught in the middle. Despite the fact that the school administrators, the parents, and the teachers invested a tremendous amount of effort to construct an environment to facilitate the teaching of the Chinese language, their choices in language use for both formal and informal occasions unwittingly defeated the language maintenance efforts by allowing English to encroach upon the domain designated for Chinese. Besides the Chinese language class, this community provided little or no social incentive for using Chinese in the community context. The analyses of the classroom interactions revealed that in day-to-day instruction, the Chinese teacher struggled with the dilemma of establishing rapport with the students by using the language with which they felt most comfortable (English), while at the same time reinforcing their Chinese language and cultural knowledge.

An Inquiry-Based Learner-Mentor Network: Toward a Collaborative Educational Culture for Chinese Heritage Language Development

Yuanzhong Zhang, University of Arizona, Tucson
E-mail: yz1208@hotmail.com

There has been a long-standing concern over the trend of language shift toward English monolingualism among U.S.-born Chinese Americans (Chao, 1968). Drawing from Vygotsky's (1978) work on the social perspective on learning and on the master-apprentice language learning program successfully implemented to revive endangered languages in California (Hinton, 1997), this inquiry-based learner-mentor partnership program was developed to foster Chinese language proficiency among U.S.-born Chinese Americans. Of the 24 learners and mentors who took part in the program, 10 were in a related study regarding language attitudes and ethnolinguistic vitality (Zhang, in press).

The partnership program brought together heritage language learners and mentors, who were native or fluent speakers of Chinese willing to work with the learners to provide authentic, comprehensible input in Chinese. Capitalizing on learners' engagement with the language through dynamic sociocultural interaction, the program incorporates elements from the authoring cycle model used in inquiry-based learning (Short & Harste with Burke, 1996).

According to the learners' and mentors' evaluations, the inquiry-based partnership program supported collaborative inquiry in heritage language learning. By reconnecting learners with their ethnic communities, it helped bridge the gap between their perceptions of cultural identity and actual heritage language competency, and brought them a heightened awareness of the role of heritage language and culture in self-enrichment.

Linking Hispanics to Higher Education Through High-School-to-College Programs

Leslie Lobos and Ana Maria Schwartz, University of Maryland, Baltimore County
E-mail: aschwart@umbc.edu

As the U.S. Hispanic population continues to grow, enrollment rates in colleges and universities have not kept pace. An Educational Testing Service study (1999) indicates that Hispanics who are qualified for college never attend and thus face limited job prospects. U.S. Census statistics (1998) show that 71.2% of Hispanics over the age of 25 have never attended college, and that only 7.4% have bachelor's degrees. High-school-to-college transition programs focus on increasing high school graduation rates and enrollment in 4-year colleges.

The purpose of this research was to survey existing high-school-to-college transition programs for Hispanic youth and to identify the characteristics common to successful programs. Three essential program components were identified: a supportive community, access to mentors and role models, and leadership development. Use and knowledge of Spanish was found to be a key element. Many programs include in their goals the ability to communicate fluently in Spanish and strive to achieve this goal through encouraging participants to enroll in Spanish for Native Speaker courses in high school and college. Language also figures prominently in outreach and mentoring activities, in how issues of identity are addressed, and in the effort to help develop leaders that will serve as models for the community

A Model for the Continued Acquisition and Stabilization of Heritage Languages in the United States

Florencia Riegelhaupt and Roberto Luis Carrasco, Northern Arizona University, Flagstaff
E-mail: Roberto.Carrasco@nau.edu

This presentation is an outgrowth of previous META work done in Spanish heritage language classes in the United States, Mexico, and Spain during immersion experiences (Carrasco & Riegelhaupt, 1992; Riegelhaupt & Carrasco, 1999). META refers to the acquisition of metalinguistic, metacultural, metapsychological, and metacognitive knowledge and strategies necessary to develop increased proficiency in the heritage language and to succeed in heritage language classes. The META Approach proposed for this session provides heritage language learners, researchers, and their teachers with a way of using and interpreting natural communications with community and family members that occur outside of the classroom as an object and theme for study and discussion in the classroom. This presentation displays materials necessary to implement the META Approach for heritage language research and instruction in all languages in which students possess a basic knowledge of the spoken and written language.

META activities displayed in the presentation include the following:

- Student transcriptions (and their corrections) of conversations recorded between heritage learners and other native speakers, often members of their own family
- Interview data including information about heritage language learners and their families' experiences and attitudes about the heritage language and its further acquisition
- Journals kept throughout heritage learners' experiences as they continue to acquire their heritage language

This presentation also demonstrates how heritage learners can continue to implement the META Approach beyond the limits of the classroom during and following their academic experience.

Polish Saturday Schools and Spanish Bilingual Programs: Two Perspectives on Supports and Barriers to Developing Bilingualism in the United States
Margy McClain, University of Wisconsin—Whitewater

This presentation compares the impact of two educational contexts in Chicago, Illinois, on the development of bilingualism among immigrant children.

In 1982, the author conducted an ethnographic study of Polish Saturday schools in Chicago as part of a national project on ethnic heritage and language schools sponsored by the American Folklife Center at the Library of Congress. The study explored the structure of the schools, subjects, instruction, teachers and administrators, parents, and students. The schools offered 12 years of instruction; graduates could function on a college level in Polish. Yet in spite of efforts over a number of years on the part of ethnic schools, the Illinois State Board of Education could not find a way to provide mainstream education credit or recognition for these students' achievements. In Spanish-speaking communities in Chicago, no such schools emerged.

In the mid-1990s the author conducted ethnographic re-search on a Mexican-American family's efforts to help their son become fluently bilingual. In third grade, they transferred him from a public school bilingual program to an English language parochial school. The study reconstructed the family's experiences and decision-making process in this move. It then followed the child through third grade, documenting ways in which a young teacher with no ESL preparation taught a class of Spanish-dominant children of Mexican descent and the barriers to learning that the children encountered in the instruction and curricular materials. This family's experiences illustrate the ways in which current schooling practices, policies, and options inhibit the development of immigrant children as fluent bilinguals.

Silicon Valley Korean School: Teaching a Heritage Language through a Community-Based Institution

Mohan Kim, San Jose State University, San Jose
Hyekyung Sung, Stanford University, Palo Alto
E-mail: sung@stanford.edu

This presentation describes a heritage language community-based school. Silicon Valley Korean School is one of the largest Korean community-based schools in the United States. The school is housed at Cupertino High School in San Jose, California, with more than 500 students enrolled in 23 classes, divided into 7 different proficiency levels. The mission of the school is to raise future generations of Korean Americans with cultural pride, dignity, and a command of Korean. To accomplish the mission, the goals are to have an enriched and well-designed curriculum for Korean language education, to staff the school with well-qualified bilingual teachers, to have adequately equipped facilities, to offer special activities for Korean cultural enrichment, to run a model community institution for language education, and to develop responsible and well-behaved students who are respectful of property and the rights of others.

Teaching Literature to Heritage Language Students
Ruth Mabanglo, University of Hawai'i
E-mail: mabanglo@hawaii.edu

This presentation discusses how the teaching of heritage folk literature (e.g., myths, legends, epics, folk songs, and proverbs) can empower Filipino American students to discover their roots, appreciate and emulate their culture, and establish their identity. The presentation illustrates how heritage literature should be taught by teachers using schema theory. This approach uses a five-part process: a prereading activity, in which relevant historical, cultural, political, social, and linguistic items are used as a springboard; skimming, in which students get the gist of main ideas; scanning, in which specific items and details related to a main idea are discussed or specific questions are answered; a linguistic activity, in which problems related to structure, vocabulary, idiomatic expressions, and cultural meanings are discussed; and a postreading activity, in which students develop other skills from ideas and concepts learned in the reading (e.g., discussing political and social issues related to the reading, having a debate, writing an essay, and doing role plays).

Teaching Written Spanish to Heritage Spanish Speakers: A Symbiotic Case
Luis Silva-Villar, Mesa State College, Grand Junction, CO
E-mail: lsilvav@mesastate.edu

The presenter reported qualitative and quantitative data from the experience of teaching written Spanish (using a Freirean approach) to heritage Spanish students and second language students in the same classroom. The course, titled Spanish Composition Through Literature, is a 3-year class in the Spanish language program at UCLA. Although the course is not designed specifically for heritage students, an average of 30% to 40% of the students enrolled in this class are heritage speakers who are either unable or unwilling to enroll in the bilingual track.

After teaching this class for 4 years, the presenter concluded that heritage language instruction needs to be considered an instructional specialization; heritage language instruction need not focus on the specific inherited culture of students; heritage language learners have no trouble distinguishing narrative styles and can do so systematically and consistently in their writing; the use of literary (close to prestige) varieties of Spanish can lead to a range of similar problems for both heritage and nonheritage learners; heritage learners with no formal schooling in Spanish show knowledge of Spanish language varieties learned through their regular exposure to the Spanish media (films, TV, radio, and newspapers).

The presenter analyzes successful and unsuccessful instructional strategies. Helping students develop awareness of language variation is an example of a successful strategy, while focusing on correctness is an example of an unsuccessful strategy. The presenter also discusses the contributions of both groups of learners to the task of developing writing skills in Spanish and proposes a theoretical framework within which to evaluate the findings.

A Thematic Approach to Chinese Heritage Language Pedagogy
Kylie Hsu, California State University, Los Angeles
E-mail: kyliehsu@email.msn.com

This presentation discusses a study of a third-grade Chinese heritage language class that used a thematic approach. The class, made up of Chinese American students, met for two hours each week. Class sessions were videotaped for analysis.

In addition to teaching lessons in the textbooks, the teacher often chose a related topic as a theme. This presentation focuses on a thematic unit on the moon, taught around the time of the Moon Festival or Mid-Autumn Festival that takes place during the eighth month of the lunar calendar. Students learned language related to the moon through the following activities: learning vocabulary related to the moon; practicing the writing of Chinese characters with the moon radical; guessing riddles about the moon and about Chinese characters related to the moon; illustrating natural phenomena related to the moon, such as a solar eclipse; describing festivals related to the lunar calendar; listening to stories about the moon and the Moon Festival; and learning scientific facts about the moon through games.

The thematic unit provided a holistic, natural approach to teaching language through literature, culture, art, and science. It maximized language acquisition by providing students with comprehensible input in meaningful contexts.

Teacher Professional Development

Educating University Foreign Language Teachers to Work with Heritage Spanish Speakers

Kim Potowski, University of Illinois at Chicago
E-mail: kpotow1@uic.edu

Heritage Spanish-speaking university students often take courses designed for foreign language learners of Spanish (Gonzalez Pino & Pino, 2000), sometimes despite the existence of heritage Spanish courses. This creates a difficult pedagogical challenge for teachers, particularly since heritage speakers exhibit a wide range of language abilities (Valdés, 1997). A pilot study (Potowski, 1999) elicited the experiences of 25 heritage Spanish speakers who took introductory level and advanced content courses in Spanish at the University of Illinois at Urbana-Champaign. Students' poignant oral narratives about their experiences in these courses, combined with follow-up interviews with seven instructors, suggested that Spanish instructors often lacked knowledge of bilingual students' sociolinguistic realities and as a result provided students with insensitive feedback on their Spanish production.

In response, a 90-minute teacher preservice session on sociolinguistic aspects of Spanish in the United States (particularly the Chicago area) was carried out with new instructors. The principal idea was that while it is a valid goal to expose bilingual students to a more formal variety of Spanish and expect it to be used in academic work, correction should not be the framework. Instead, on responding to heritage students' language, instructors need guidelines, as called for by both Roca (1997) and Gutierrez (1997). Using group work activities, the session elicited instructors' beliefs and knowledge about language variation and presented guidelines for providing sensitive, useful feedback. The final report (Potowski, 2001) includes details about the session as well as suggestions for improvement, including pre- and postsession activities.

Retaining and Regaining Bilingualism for California's School Children

Nena Torrez, California State University, San Bernadino
E-mail: ntorrez@mail.csusb.edu

Responsiveness to the surrounding communities has always been a hallmark of programs and course work in the California State University (CSU) system. Nowhere is this more evident than in the area of teacher training. Over the years the various campuses have adjusted and modified their course offerings and teacher credentialing programs not only to reflect the mandates of the California Commission on Teacher Credentialing but also to meet the specific needs of their surrounding communities. Because of the wide variation among areas in California, some campuses have no bilingual programs while other campuses offer programs for multiple languages.

The most readily available and critical bilingual teacher training program in California is the Spanish BCLAD (Bilingual Cross-Cultural Academic Development Credential) program, which is offered at every CSU campus with a bilingual teacher training program. Because Spanish is the most prevalent non-

English first language of school-age children in California, this presentation deals exclusively with the Spanish BCLAD programs, with a primary focus on the issues surrounding the training of teachers and bilingual individuals to be bilingual teachers. Special attention is given to the Bilingual Paraprofessional Career Ladder program. Data from students and teachers currently or formerly involved with high school future bilingual teachers are also provided.

In addition to these two ways to preserve and maximize the heritage language skills in the CSUSB service area, there is a middle school outreach program. In addition, the Inland Empire Future Leaders Institute takes Latino eighth- and ninth-grade students to an intensive camp and training program that focuses on culture, education, and leadership. This institute has been helping Latino youth for the past 15 years. The statistics from both of these youth programs are impressive in terms of the number of college and graduate students who have participated.

Language Policies

Aquí No Se Habla Español: Stories of Linguistic Repression in Southwest Schools
Patricia MacGregor-Mendoza, New Mexico State University, Las Cruces

In the United States, the debate over the language to be used in schools by teachers and students has a long history. Proponents of English-only legislation and detractors of bilingual education programs argue that the earlier children speak English, the better their chances for academic success. While the validity of this argument remains suspect, such opinions nonetheless have given rise to school policies that discourage the use of Spanish among students in the classroom, in the cafeteria, and on the playground.

A 1989 survey of university students in Texas showed that such policies were still common 17 years after the 1972 report of the U.S. Commission on Civil Rights documenting language-based discrimination. In the survey, 40% of the students surveyed reported that schools had disapproved of Spanish use in school and employed various forms of threats and verbal and physical punishments in order to enforce their institution's "no Spanish" rule. Recent events, such as the rise in official English bills being placed before Congress, as well as California's newly passed Proposition 227, popularly promoted as "English for the Children," points to a climate of increasing linguistic intolerance.

While historical evidence of the repression of Spanish in Southwest schools exists, not enough has been done to record the actual experiences of the students subjected to such policies and to document the long-term impact that these policies have had on individuals later in life. In order to bridge this gap in the literature, this presentation documents the childhood experiences of several adult Spanish speakers who attended school in southern New Mexico and El Paso, Texas, and reports the effects of language policy on their self-esteem as children and adults and on their current use of and attitudes toward Spanish and English.

Heritage Language Resources

Japanese as a Heritage/International Language
Nariyo Kono, The University of Arizona, Tucson
E-mail: nariyo@U.Arizona.edu
Web site: http://www.u.arizona.edu/~nariyo/Homepage.htm]

This presentation describes the design for a homepage on Japanese as a heritage/international language, with the goal of sparking ideas for research and teaching. The homepage includes research references, material and textbook information, teachers associations and organizations, and lesson plans. The homepage is organized as follows:

What is a Heritage Language?
Language and Identity
Identity and Ethnic Identity
Language Loss and Language Maintenance
Home Language and School Language
Japanese Language Education and Foreign Language Policy
Heritage/International Language—Canada
Languages Other Than English—Australia
  (cf. Bilingual Education—USA)
Research References
Publications
Web Sites
Teachers Guide
Materials and Textbooks
Teachers, Organizations, and Workshops
Lesson Plans

Private German Language Schools Network: German Language Schools Conference
Renate Ludanyi, Western Connecticut State University, Danbury
Web site: http://www.germanschools.org

To link the private German language schools within a central organization for information and support, the German Consulate General in New York, along with some German language schools in Connecticut, New Jersey, New York, and Pennsylvania, founded the German Language School Conference (GLSC) in 1977. Most private German language schools are members, and the network of GLSC has grown from 5 founding German language schools to more than 40 members. Today, GLSC is the national organization for private German language schools.

GLSC has the following goals:

• To help individuals and groups interested in German language education establish private German language schools

- To help member schools teach German language and culture at all proficiency levels
- To help member schools promote goodwill and respect for the heritage of German-speaking peoples
- To help member schools select and produce teaching materials and official testing instruments for articulation with further language study in the United States and Germany
- To provide a forum for the discussion of topics concerning German language, literature, and culture
- To enhance the professional development of its members through close cooperation, academic collegiality, and fellowship

References

Amastae, J. 1989. Contact and bilingualism in the Hispanic World: Reflections on the state of the art. *Hispania, 72*(4): 810-820.

Baars, B. J. (1992). The many uses of error. In B. J. Baars (Ed.), Experimental slips and human error (pp. 3-34). New York: Plenum Press.

Carrasco, R.L., & Riegelhaupt, F. (1992). META: Un modelo holístico de la adquisición del español. In P. Barros (Ed.), *Aspectos de la enseñanza del español como lengua extranjera* (pp. 81-90). Granada, Spain: University of Granada Press, Facultad de Ciencias y Letras.

Chao, Y. (1968). *Aspects of Chinese sociolinguistics.* Stanford: Stanford University Press.

Cummins, J. (1981). The role of primary language development in promoting educational success for language minority students. In California State Department of Education (Ed.), *Schooling and language minority students: A theoretical framework* (pp. 9-43). Los Angeles: California State University, Evaluation, Dissemination and Assessment Center.

Dechert, H.W., & Lennon, P. (1989). Collocational blends of advanced second language learners: A preliminary analysis. In W. Oleksy (Ed.), *Contrastive pragmatics* (pp. 131-68). Amsterdam and Philadelphia: John Benjamins.

Dumitrescu, D. (1993). A preliminary approach to the contact phenomena found in Romanian spoken by Romanian Americans of the first generation. *Journal of the Romanian American Academy of Arts and Sciences, 18,* 161-186.

Dumitrescu, D. (1998). Fenómenos paralelos de contacto con el inglés entre el español y el rumano hablados en los Estados Unidos. In G. Ruffino (Ed.), *Atti del XXI Congresso Internazionale di Linguistica e Filologia Romanza, Centro di studi filologici e linguistici siciliani, Università di Palermo, 18-24 settembre 1995: Vol. V. Dialettologia, geolinguistica, sociolinguistica* (pp. 275-83). Tübingen, Germany: Max Niemeyer.

Educational Testing Service. (1999, September 29). *ETS/HACU study: Bridging the Hispanic education/employment gap.* Princeton, NJ: Author. Retrieved June 8, 2001, from http://www.ets.org/aboutets/ news/ 99092901.html

Gardner, R.C., & Lambert, W.E. (1972). *Attitudes and motivation in second-language learning.* Rowley, MA: Newbury House.

Gonzalez Pino, B., & Pino, F. (2000). Serving the heritage speaker across a five-year program. *ADFL Bulletin, 32*(1), 27-35.

Gutierrez, J. (1997). Teaching Spanish as a heritage language: A case for language awareness. *ADFL Bulletin, 29*(1), 33-36.

Hartular, A. (1996). *Merem la America: Incepturile comunitatii romanesti in America.* Bucuresti [Bucarest], Romania: Editura Fundatiei Culturale Romane.

Hinton, L. (1997). Survival of endangered languages: The California master–apprentice program. *International Journal of the Sociology of Language, 123,* 177-191.

James, C. (1998). *Errors in language learning and use.* New York: Addison Wesley Longman.

Muñoz-Sandoval, A.F., Cummins, J., Alvarado, C.G., & Ruef, M.L. (1998). *Bilingual verbal ability tests: Comprehensive manual.* Itasca, IL: Riverside.

Pak, C.-S. (1996). *Newspaper editorials from* The New York Times, El País, *and El Universal: A comparative applied genre analysis.* Unpublished doctoral dissertation, University of Michigan, Ann Arbor.

Potowski, K. (1999). *Experiences of Spanish heritage speakers in university foreign language courses and suggestions for teacher training.* Unpublished manuscript.

Potowski, K. (2001). Educating foreign language teachers to work with heritage Spanish speakers. In B. Johnston & S. Irujo (Eds.), *Research and practice in language teacher education: Voices from the field* (CARLA Working Paper No. 19, pp. 99-113). Minneapolis/St. Paul, MN: University of Minnesota.

Riegelhaupt, F., & Carrasco, R.L. (1999, March). *Heritage Spanish speakers in university second language courses: Some implications for teacher training.* Paper presented at the XVII Congreso sobre el Español de los Estados Unidos/XVII National Conference on Spanish in the United States, Miami, FL.

Roca, A. (1997). Retrospectives, advances, and current needs in the teaching of Spanish to United States Hispanic bilingual students. *ADFL Bulletin, 29*(1), 37-43.

Roceric, A. (1982). *Language maintenance within an American ethnic community: The case of Romanian.* Grass Lake–Jackson, MI: The Romanian-American Heritage Center.

Short, K.G., & Harste, J., with Burke, C. (1996). *Creating classrooms for authors and inquirers.* Portsmouth, NH: Heinemann.

U.S. Census Bureau. (1998, August 7). *March 1997 CPS: College educational attainment level by race-ethnicity, age 25 and over: both sexes-values/percents.* Washington, DC: Author. Retrieved June 8, 2001, from http://www.census.gov/population/socdemo/hispanic/ cps97/tab03-2.txt

Valdés, G. (1997). The teaching of Spanish to heritage Spanish-speaking students: Outstanding issues and unanswered questions. In M.C. Colombi & F.X. Alarcón (Eds.), *La enseñanza del español a hispanohablantes: Praxis y teoría* (pp. 8-44). Boston: Houghton Mifflin.

Vygotsky, L.S. (1978). *Mind in society: The development of higher psychological processes.* Cambridge, MA: Harvard University Press.

Zhang, Y. (in press). *Language attitudes and vitality perceptions: How US-born Chinese value their heritage language* (Kansas Working Papers in Linguistics). Lawrence, KS: University of Kansas Press.

A Call to Action

14
Heritage Language Maintenance and Development: An Agenda for Action

Ana Roca
Florida International University

The presentations and discussions that took place at the historic first National Conference on Heritage Languages in America in October 1999 and the resulting papers that make up this volume offer a wealth of information, resources, questions, and recommendations from language scholars and practitioners. The conference has fostered among these educators a sense of community and shared goals and a renewed commitment to work together to develop a country that is richly multilingual. Through collaboration, we can learn from each others' successes and challenges, and can work together to develop educational philosophies and approaches that are effective regardless of the specific language taught.

What We Need to Do

As important as it is to develop heritage language education in its own right, it is just as important to keep our efforts connected to foreign and second language education. To do this, we need to work with the existing structures (associations, centers, and departments) in foreign language and bilingual education. While our efforts might eventually lead to new publications and even new organizations, we do not need to create another separate field. Rather, we need to integrate the knowledge we have accumulated and better coordinate our educational, planning, and policy efforts in the fields of foreign, bilingual, and heritage language education and research.

We have started to accomplish that here. The chapters in this book spell out well-considered recommendations for action in many areas. Topics include national, state, and local policy formation; program articulation, administration, and funding; curricular and pedagogical approaches; teacher recruitment and training; and student and teacher attitudes toward different languages and groups of language speakers and the impact of these attitudes on learning and teaching.

These are critical areas, but if we are to become the multilingual nation that we envision, two larger issues must be addressed through an organized and proactive agenda:

- The formation of sound language policies for education (from prekindergarten through college and adult education), government (including the work of government agencies that require proficiency in different languages, and services such as translation and interpreting), and the private sector (including businesses, corporations, chambers of commerce, and foundations)
- The promotion of positive attitudes toward language diversity and bilingualism, foreign and heritage language speakers, and foreign and heritage language instruction

The entire language profession must work together, not to make more conference resolutions, but rather to make a real investment in promoting positive and informed views on foreign language, heritage language, and bilingual proficiency in the United States. This effort will entail using resources that we already have at our disposal as well as raising additional funds. The academic organizations that must work together include both the professional language associations, such as the American Council on the Teaching of Foreign Languages (ACTFL), the Modern Language Association (MLA), the National Association for Bilingual Education (NABE), and Teachers of English to

Speakers of Other Languages (TESOL), and the language-specific associations, such as the American Association of Teachers of Spanish and Portuguese (AATSP), the American Council of Teachers of Russian (ACTR), the Association of Teachers of Japanese, and the Chinese Language Teachers Association (CLTA). These national associations might begin by adding a line to their membership forms seeking an extra few dollars for projects that support the goal of multilingualism in America.

National centers that focus on language issues, such as the Center for Applied Linguistics (CAL), the National Foreign Language Center (NFLC), and the National Foreign Language Resource Centers (NFLRCs), also need to be involved by seeking federal and foundation grants and contracts to carry out teacher professional development projects (similar to the one organized by CAL with NEH support at UCLA in the summer of 2000), and to support research fellows working on heritage language issues. Other important collaborators include faculty in foreign language departments in public and private schools and universities; staff of community centers interested in language; and professionals in related fields such as immigration law, translation and interpretation, international relations, and area studies. One such collaboration is a 3-year project, carried out by ACTFL, Hunter College, and Hunter College High School, to implement new teacher certification requirements for heritage language teaching. With support from the Fund for the Improvement of Postsecondary Education (FIPSE), this project has also created a model heritage language curriculum (Roca, 2000; Webb & Miller, 2000).

One project that all of us involved in language education might undertake together is the establishment of a national campaign fund that would promote positive attitudes toward foreign and heritage language learning and toward bilingualism in general. In the same way that children are urged to "Say no to drugs," we should urge them to "Say yes to languages," and "Say yes to bilingualism." We should call on our celebrities—Ricky, Jimmy, Gloria, and Andy, to give four Hispanic examples*—to help us with this cause. We need to take advantage of what I call the "Ricky Martin effect" to create a continuous, strong, and well-informed educational and political campaign promoting linguistic and cultural diversity. If we can use the pop culture embrace of ethnic talent to sell the benefits of heritage and foreign language study and the value of bilingualism, we will have truly seized the moment for the benefit of multilingualism in the United States.

Serious and professional public relations media campaigns take sizeable resources. Given the language and cultural realities of this country today, however, investment in this effort should be a priority of language professionals committed to creating a multilingual America. We must raise money from private foundations and from interested businesses and corporations.

Now is the time. We are at a turning point in our history when the foreign-born population, particularly Spanish speakers, has reached critical mass. According to the 2000 census, nearly 18% of U.S. residents age 5 and older speak a language other than English at home (U.S. Census Bureau, 2001). In the last decade non-English populations have grown more than 40%, and the 2000 Census informs us that the U.S. Hispanic population increased by more than 50% from 1990 to 2000, reaching 35.3 million or 12.5% of the total U.S. population (Guzmán, 2001). We also see Spanish speakers settling in parts of the country, such as in Georgia and North Carolina, where they have not traditionally been found in sizeable numbers (Sack, 2001).

In this time of high prosperity, the Spanish-speaking population in particular has caught the media's attention as a source

---

*These four stars, well known to many in the United States by first name only, are Ricky Martin, Jimmy Smits, Gloria Esteban, and Andy Garcia.

of stories about positive social change in America. From series in *The New York Times* and National Public Radio to coverage by NBC's *Nightly News*, a day does not go by that the growing Latino presence is not commented on in the mass media, often positively. We should not let this moment pass without having our voices heard regarding the value of multilingualism in our nation.

Although Spanish speakers are clearly the largest linguistic minority population in the United States, and therefore receive the bulk of media attention, we should not ignore the many other languages struggling for survival in heritage communities around the nation. Our efforts to preserve and develop this country's rich linguistic resources must include Arabic, Chinese, Haitian Creole, Korean, and Yiddish, to name just a few of the more than 150 languages that exist in the United States today (Brecht & Rivers, 2000). (See, for example, the list of languages represented at the conference, on page vii of this volume.)

How We Can Accomplish Our Goals

How do we further the goal of developing a society that is productively multilingual? How can we promote positive attitudes toward bilingualism and foreign and heritage language study? We need to reach beyond the readers of this book and share our ideas with our congressional representatives, our local school board members, our city commissioners, and members of our local communities. We need to move beyond simply relying on the efforts of advocacy groups such as the Joint Committee for Languages (JNCL) and the National Council for Languages and International Studies (NCLIS).

We need to communicate better with businesses and corporations that are desperately seeking qualified bilingual professionals and that may be willing to provide funding to promote educational goals that would advance their causes. We need to work with government agencies concerned with foreign language training, such as the Foreign Service Institute and the Defense Language Institute. We need to help government agencies and business organizations understand that they do not have to start from scratch when they develop new language programs. They can use the recently developed national foreign language standards as general guidelines (National Standards in Foreign Language Education Project, 1996). They can also collaborate with academic institutions that already have established heritage language courses. These courses can be supplemented with more advanced language study exploring areas of specialized interest.

Working in cooperation with JNCL-NCLIS and other language organizations, we should also create an activist organization or committee that will lobby at the national level and assist those who at regional and local levels are organizing for change in their schools, towns, and cities. The new organization would launch a full-blown media campaign with assistance from professional associations and centers that could provide entrée to schools and workplaces. Do we hear public service announcements on the radio or television about the positive aspects of bilingualism and foreign language study? How about signs on bus benches, billboards, and metro trains? We need to "step out" and let our voices be heard. We should ask ourselves if we are hiding behind terms like *heritage language education* because we are afraid to use expressions like *bilingual education* or *bilingualism*. We need not be afraid, and we should say what we mean, even if it seems that we are raising issues that the profession has been raising for decades.

It is time to take a stand. Speakers of languages other than English need to recognize and value the language resources that they possess. We need to tap the forces of community and ethnic pride that Fishman (this volume) tells us preserved German in late 19th and early 20th century America. We need to point out that bilingualism need not be a case of dueling languages but rather of *dual* languages. We need to accentuate the positive side of knowing more than one language.

We need to stamp out the perception of bilingual education as a favor that the government and schools do for linguistic minorities while they are learning English. In its place, we must help the general public as well as elected officials to become better informed and to better understand the more positive idea of language riches for all. In the United States, multilingualism needs to acquire the same cachet that coffee did with the advent of Starbucks. It is all a question of marketing. Not so very long ago, people were content to buy coffee for fifty cents a cup. Now, through the genius of marketing, many are even happier to pay upwards of three dollars—and no free refills! Multilingualism, like coffee, needs an image adjustment. It needs to be seen in the United States, as it is seen in most other countries, as an asset with clear social and financial benefits.

Efforts to change language attitudes are underway around the country. Soon we should have a better idea of what is being done. For example, California Tomorrow (in Oakland, CA) is conducting a national project to document and highlight the efforts of schools and communities that support young people in developing and maintaining their heritage languages. Part of this project involves compiling examples of local, state, and national policies that support the reclamation, maintenance, and development of heritage languages, as well as policies that promote bilingualism for all children (Ann Jaramillo, personal communication, June 18, 2001; see www.californiatomorrow .org/projects/cts.pl?project_id=9).

Specific Actions We Can Take Now

Marcos and Peyton (1998) have mapped out a plan of action for parents, teachers, school administrators, policymakers, and business and community members, with specific actions that these groups can take to promote language proficiency in this country. Possible actions include the following:

Parents who know languages other than English can speak those languages with their children, expose their children to individuals from other language and cultural backgrounds, and speak positively to their children about the value of learning languages in addition to English.

Teachers can find out which languages are spoken locally (by school staff, students, and members of the community) and use those resources to promote language and cultural awareness among students; set up class lending libraries with books, magazines, and videotapes in other languages and about other cultures for students and parents to use; and give students opportunities to use other languages in and outside their classrooms.

School administrators can establish language programs, if they are not in place, by learning about excellent language programs across the country that might be replicated or adapted in their area. If a program is in place, administrators can ensure that all students have opportunities to participate, that excellent teachers are hired, and that materials are available.

Policymakers can budget adequate financial resources to establish and improve language programs in their school, district, or state; support and fund professional development programs for teachers; and establish policies that promote the study of second languages at all levels by all students.

Business leaders can make policymakers aware of the need for workers who are proficient in more than one language; send company representatives to school career days to talk with students about the importance of proficiency in different languages in their companies; and work with schools to help prepare students to work in an increasingly global economy.

Conclusion

Helping Americans to value linguistic and cultural diversity need not result in the separation of the country into different battling ethnic groups. Quite the contrary, the economic and practical advantages of knowing more than one language can strengthen and unite us. When bilingualism is no longer perceived as a detriment and is looked upon as an asset, whether developed at home as a heritage language, learned in school as a foreign language, or acquired through some other experience, we will have made progress. While university scholars and teachers continue to make advances in the areas of research and practice that have been so eloquently described in this volume, our profession must also place its energies into efforts that will raise public awareness and lead to positive political and public policy change.

References

Brecht, R.D., & Rivers, W.P. (2000). *Language and national security in the 21st century: The role of Title VI/Fulbright-Hays in supporting national language capacity.* Dubuque, IA: Kendall/Hunt.

Guzmán, B. (2001, May). *The Hispanic population* (Census 2000 Brief No. C2KBR/ 01-3). Washington, DC: U.S. Census Bureau. Retrieved from http://www.census.gov/prod/2001pubs/c2kbr01-3.pdf

Marcos, K.M., & Peyton, J.K. (1998, Fall). Putting it all together: Fostering a language-proficient society. *K–12 foreign language education. The ERIC Review, 6*(1), 70-72. Retrieved from http://www.accesseric.org/resources/ericreview/vol6no1/splash.html

National Standards in Foreign Language Education Project. (1996). *Standards for foreign language learning: Preparing for the 21st century.* Lawrence, KS: Author.

Roca, A. (Ed.). (2000). *Research on Spanish in the United States: Linguistic issues and challenges.* Somerville, MA: Cascadilla Press.

Sack, Kevin. (2001, July 30). Far from Mexico, making a place like home. *The New York Times*, pp. A1, A14.

U.S. Census Bureau. (2001). *Census 2000 supplementary survey: Profile of selected social characteristics.* Retrieved from http://factfinder .census.gov/home/en/c2ss.html

Webb, J.B., & Miller, B.L. (2000). *Teaching heritage language learners: Voices from the classroom.* Yonkers, NY: American Council on the Teaching of Foreign Languages.

15
The Genealogy of Language Organizations and the Heritage Languages Initiative

James E. Alatis
Georgetown University

During the discussions that took place at the1999 National Heritage Languages Conference in Long Beach, California, I came to the realization that I might be participating in the formation of yet another professional organization. That possibility brought to mind two words not normally associated with the language profession: fissiparity and omphaloskepsis. Fissiparity is a term taken from biology that refers to "a form of . . . reproduction . . . in which the parent organism divides into two or more parts, each becoming an independent individual" (Webster's Third New International Dictionary). Omphaloskepsis refers to the "contemplation of one's navel as a part of mystical experiences" (Webster's Third New International Dictionary).

I use these terms playfully to describe two countervailing tendencies in a professional organization: on the one hand, the tendency of the organization to maintain its own identity, unity, and status quo, and, on the other hand, the tendency of groups within that organization to break off and form their own organizations when it appears that their goals and needs will best be met through this action. Notwithstanding the playfulness of these terms, they address a serious point I would like to make about our profession: At a time of great challenge and opportunity in language education, we must control both separatist and navel-gazing tendencies in order to work together to accomplish common goals.

Fissiparity and Omphaloskepsis in Language Education

Americans are a nation of joiners; we belong to countless organizations, which proliferate over time into more organizations. The historical development of the language profession in the United States can be likened to Biblical genealogies. Early in this century, linguists established the American Philological Society (APS), which dealt primarily with the classical languages. Later, scholars interested in modern languages separated and created the Modern Language Association of America (MLA). Thus, APS "begat" MLA. Because MLA dealt primarily with English and foreign *literatures* at the *university* level, the National Council of Teachers of English (NCTE), which dealt with the teaching of English *language* in the *schools,* was created. Thus, MLA begat NCTE. The American Council on the Teaching of Foreign Languages (ACTFL), in turn, was formed to deal with foreign language (rather than literature) teaching at all levels of education. Thus, MLA also begat ACTFL. Teachers of English to Speakers of Other Languages (TESOL) had multiple parents: MLA, the Center for Applied Linguistics (CAL), the American Speech Association (ASA, later the American Speech and Hearing Association), NCTE, and the National Association for Foreign Student Affairs (NAFSA).

When some members of TESOL felt that bilingual education should have its own focus, activities, and organization, the National Association for Bilingual Education (NABE) was created. When some members of the Linguistics Society of America (LSA) felt that there should be a professional organization in the United States for applied linguistics (the application of the insights, methods, and findings of linguistic science to practical language problems, including the teaching and learning of languages), the American Association for Applied Linguistics (AAAL) was created. (For years, applied linguists in the United States had been members of the Association Internationale de Linguistique Appliqué [AILA] and had traveled overseas to attend AILA conventions). Members of TESOL also became involved in the formation and support of AAAL, feeling that TESOL did not have a strong enough research focus. More recently, scholars working in the field of World English formed a separate organization, the International Association for World Englishes (IAWE), when they felt that TESOL had failed to respond to their needs.

A Need for Unity

There are those among us who would argue that the creation of new organizations is a natural and even healthy development. To a certain extent it is. New organizations beget new energy and new ideas. Unchecked proliferation, however, can be harmful. It can divide us against ourselves, consume energy, lead to needless duplication of effort, and displace constructive programs needed to develop an effective profession. Now more than ever, we need less division and more cooperation. Our common goals and purposes, after all, are more apparent and much more important than our differences. Whatever our particular areas of interest—teaching English in English-speaking countries (TESL), teaching English in non-English-speaking countries (TEFL), foreign language education, bilingual education, cross-cultural communication, or heritage language education—most of us share core values and goals. We want language and education policies that will ensure access to good language instruction for individuals in this country and around the world; promote a "language-competent society" at home, as Richard Tucker (1989) advocates; improve cross-cultural understanding both within our increasingly diverse country and between the United States and other nations; help to preserve the linguistic and cultural birthright of all Americans; and contribute to the solution of our most pressing national problems—our poverty-stricken ethnic barrios, alienated immigrant communities, and isolated Indian reservations.

To do this, we need to be unified as a profession. The linguistics, TESOL, bilingual education, foreign languages, international studies, and, now, heritage language education segments of our profession must learn to live together in a new symbiotic relationship. If our profession is to acquire and maintain the intellectual strength and political power needed in these troubled times, we must rebuild our profession, based on a concept of a unified professional entity. We must recognize that jurisdictional battles waste energy and frustrate the realization of our common goals. Through them, we only weaken ourselves and our mission. We must learn to govern our own profession and to better educate the general public about our goals.

Happily, there are centripetal as well as centrifugal forces at work in our profession today. At the same time that new organizations form, old ones coalesce, creating coalitions to better accomplish their goals. The collaborative work of CAL, the National Foreign Language Center (NFLC), and the National Council of Organizations of Less Commonly Taught Languages (NCOLCTL) on the heritage languages initiative is one example. As another example, the American Council on the Teaching of Foreign Languages (ACTFL) has joined with its parent organization, the MLA, to form the advocacy group, the Joint National Committee for Languages and the National Council for Languages and International Studies (JNCL-NCLIS), which consists of 60 member associations. This advocacy group includes CAL and other non-association organizations, such as the Northeast Conference, the Central States Conference, and the Georgetown University Roundtable (GURT), as well as regional associations and coalitions, such as the Coalition of the Foreign Language Associations of Arkansas, North Dakota, and Iowa (ANDI). The JNCL-NCLIS goals, as stated in their brochure (JNCL-NCLIS, n.d.), are to unify the language profession, promote policies that respect and develop the language abilities of Americans, and increase language awareness by the public. These coalitions and consortia form associational fellowships, cooperating with each other and coordinating their activities toward a common purpose.

An Opportune Time

It is especially important that we work together at this juncture because we may be living in a time of unprecedented opportunity for our profession. We need to form new coalitions so that we can come together—as English and foreign language educators, linguists, and specialists in heritage language and bilingual education. We need planned integration of interrelated language and area study groups—ACTFL, CAL, JNCL-NCLIS, LSA, MLA, NABE, NAFSA, NCTE, TESOL, and the language-specific professional associations—each with specialized functions, all directed toward common purposes. To make the best use of our time and energies and to ensure that we speak with one voice on the issues that matter most to us, we should support only the most effective and honest professional organizations.

Most pertinent to the Long Beach conference and this publication, we must help policymakers at all levels of government understand the links between international education and heritage language education. We must work to identify, value, and develop our rich national resource of heritage languages to better preserve the diversity that is our country's heritage and to better meet our foreign language needs. As Fishman (this volume, pp. 93–94) states, "This will not be easy to do because we have shamelessly neglected our heritage languages for far too long. However, we are beginning the intellectual, tactical, pedagogical, and *organizational* [emphasis added] struggle to do so, and we may well be remembered by posterity for having done so."

Conclusion

We end where we began, at the Heritage Languages Conference in Long Beach, California, where we spoke of launching another professional organization. Certainly the time for attention to the heritage languages spoken in this country has come. Historically, heritage languages have been neglected in the United States, and it is time that we recognize the important resource that these languages and their speakers represent for developing a language-competent American society, cross-cultural communication, educational exchange among nations, social justice, and world peace. These are all good reasons to support the heritage languages initiative. A final reason may be less obvious but is directly relevant to the point of my chapter: Since heritage language education cuts across many fields and disciplines, perhaps it might turn out to be not just another separate field with its separate agenda but instead a reunifying force for the language profession as a whole.

References

JNCL-NCLIS. (n.d.) JNCL-NCLIS: *Your voice in Washington* [Brochure]. Washington, DC: Author. (Available from JNCL-NCLIS, 4646 40th Street NW, Washington DC 20016-1859; see also http://www.languagepolicy.org)

Tucker, G.R. (1989). *Developing a language competent American society: The role of language planning* (Paper presented at the McGill University Conference on Bilingualism, Montreal, Canada, May, 1989). Washington, DC: Center for Applied Linguistics. (ERIC Document Reproduction Service No. ED 312 896)

Webster's Third New International Dictionary Unabridged. (1961). Springfield, MA: G&C Merriam.

About the Contributors

James E. Alatis (alatisj@georgetown.edu) is Dean Emeritus of the School of Languages and Linguistics at Georgetown University in Washington, DC, Distinguished Professor of Linguistics and Modern Greek, and Senior Advisor to the Dean of Georgetown College for International Language Programs and Research. He also serves as the President of the TESOL International Research Foundation (TIRF) Board. His interests include English as a world language, bilingual education, international education, and Greek and other heritage languages.

Regla Armengol is founder and director of the Heritage Language Literacy Club at Bailey's Elementary School for the Arts and Sciences in Falls Church, Virginia. She is interested in creating programs at the elementary school level that promote the positive aspects of bilingualism and in mentoring heritage speakers toward becoming multilingual professionals.

Russell N. Campbell (campruss@humnet.ucla.edu) is a Professor Emeritus in the Applied Linguistics/TESL Department at the University of California, Los Angeles (UCLA). He is especially interested in the linguistic, sociolinguistic, and cultural factors that distinguish first, second, and heritage language acquisition theories and how these factors might define and govern educational programs.

María Carreira (carreira@csulb.edu) is Associate Professor of Spanish Linguistics at California State University, Long Beach, where she teaches courses on Spanish linguistics and Spanish for native speakers. Her research interests include Spanish in the United States, dialectology, historical linguistics, and phonological theory. She was co-organizer of the first national Heritage Languages in America conference.

Donna Christian (donna@cal.org) is President of the Center for Applied Linguistics in Washington, DC. She is an advisor on the Heritage Languages Initiative and is particularly interested in the contributions of school-based program approaches, such as two-way immersion, to the maintenance and development of heritage languages.

Carol J. Compton (parishcompton@hotmail.com) is Immediate Past President of the Council of Teachers of Southeast Asian Languages (COTSEAL). She is a linguist who has served as Coordinator of the Hmong Lao Khmer Heritage Language Project and as Language Director of the Southeast Asian Studies Summer Institute (SEASSI) at the University of Wisconsin—Madison. She is interested in the articulation between community language programs and institutions of higher education and the development of curriculum and materials to support heritage language teaching in America.

Joshua A. Fishman is Distinguished University Research Professor of Social Sciences, Emeritus, at Yeshiva University and Visiting Professor at Stanford University and New York University. He is co-director of a research project at Stanford University on community opinions and views regarding Spanish for Native Speakers courses at high schools and colleges in California. His major interest for nearly 50 years has been in maximizing the language resources of the United States.

Surendra Gambhir (sgambhir@sas.upenn.edu) teaches Indic languages and linguistics at the University of Pennsylvania. He is the current Language Committee Chair of the American Institute of Indian Studies and has directed many study abroad programs over the years. His research interests include the effects of diaspora on language use, second language acquisition, multilingualism, and the processes of koinization. He has been actively involved with several national initiatives on South Asian languages.

Nancy Green, a former teacher of advanced placement Spanish language and literature and Spanish for Spanish speakers, is currently the Foreign Language Curriculum Leader for Long Beach Unified School District, Long Beach, California.

Nariyo Kono (nariyo@u.arizona.edu) is a member of the Department of East Asian Studies at the University of Arizona. Her research interests include theories in language planning and language policy, classroom cultures, language pedagogy, and Japanese linguistics. Her current research focuses on heritage language learners in a Japanese program in Tucson, Arizona, and on language revitalization efforts on the Warm Springs reservation in Oregon.

Scott McGinnis (smcginnis@nflc.org) is Executive Director of the National Council of Organizations of Less Commonly Taught Languages (NCOLCTL) and Associate for Less Commonly Taught Languages at the National Foreign Language Center (NFLC) in Washington, DC. Prior to working at the NFLC, he taught Chinese at the college level for over fifteen years and served two terms as President of the Chinese Language Teachers Association. Dr. McGinnis has worked to bring about greater interaction and cooperation among the various settings in which Chinese is taught—K–12, college and universities, and heritage schools—and is regularly invited to participate in major projects on standards, articulation, and teacher training and materials development for the less commonly taught languages, Chinese in particular.

Joy Kreeft Peyton (joy@cal.org) is Vice President of the Center for Applied Linguistics in Washington, DC, and director of the ERIC Clearinghouse on Languages and Linguistics. She is a member of the CAL/NFLC working group on the Heritage Languages Initiative and is particularly interested in ways that schools and community-based language programs can work effectively to promote proficiency in more than one language.

Donald A. Ranard (daranard@cal.org) is a consulting editor for the Center for Applied Linguistics in Washington, DC. He has worked in language education in the United States and Asia since 1970. He is interested in international education, refugee and immigrant education, and Chinese language teaching.

Ana Roca (rocaa@fiu.edu) is Professor of Spanish and Linguistics in the Department of Modern Languages at Florida International University in Miami, Florida, where she directed the Spanish language program for over 10 years. She is interested in English–Spanish bilingualism, language policy, and the teaching of Spanish as a heritage language in the United States. She was a faculty member in the 2000 NEH Summer Institute on Teaching Spanish to Native Speakers held at UCLA and serves on the National Foreign Language Center's LangNet Spanish Advisory Board.

Ana María Schwartz (aschwart@umbc.edu) is Assistant Professor of Spanish and Second Language Pedagogy at the University of Maryland Baltimore County (UMBC), where she teaches undergraduate Spanish courses and graduate-level methods and second language acquisition and learning courses. She is interested in teacher development and is conducting research on heritage Spanish speakers' writing strategies.

Guadalupe Valdés (gvaldes@stanford.edu) is Professor of Spanish and Portuguese and Professor of Education at Stanford University. Her work has focused on the English–Spanish bilingualism of Latinos in the United States and on discovering and describing how two languages are developed, used, and maintained by individuals who become bilingual in immigrant communities.

Shuhan C. Wang (swang@state.de.us) is Education Associate for World Languages at the Department of Education in the State of Delaware. She is a member of the National Council of State Supervisors of Foreign Languages (NCSSFL) and the National Council of the Associations of Chinese Language Schools (NCACLS). Her research interests include preparing heritage/native language teachers for the heritage and formal educational systems and searching for ways that individuals, families, ethnic communities, and educational systems can work together to help heritage language students integrate into the mainstream society while maintaining their own culture, identity, and language.

Terrence G. Wiley (twiley@asu.edu) is Professor of Language and Literacy Policy Studies and Social and Philosophical Foundations of Education, and Director of the Division of Educational Leadership and Policy Studies at Arizona State University, Tempe. His research interests include educational language policies, politics, and history; literacy and biliteracy theory and policies; and the history of education of diverse groups. He is co-editor of the *Journal of Language, Identity and Education.*

Other CAL Publications Available From Delta Systems

www.delta-systems.com • toll-free phone 800-323-8270

Immigrant and Refugee Populations and Education

Access and Engagement: Program Design and Instructional Approaches for Immigrant Students in Secondary School
Aída Walqui

The American Bilingual Tradition (1998, second edition)
Heinz Kloss

From the Classroom to the Community: A Fifteen-Year Experiment in Refugee Education
Donald A. Ranard & Margo Pfleger, Editors

Into, Through, and Beyond Secondary School: Critical Transitions for Immigrant Youths
Tamara Lucas

Literacy and Language Diversity in the United States
Terrence G. Wiley

New Concepts for New Challenges: Professional Development for Teachers of Immigrant Youth
Josué M. González & Linda Darling-Hammond

Through the Golden Door: Educational Approaches for Immigrant Adolescents With Limited Schooling
Betty Mace-Matluck, Rosalind Alexander-Kasparik, & Robin M. Queen

English Language Education

Cooperative Learning: A Response to Linguistic and Cultural Diversity
Daniel D. Holt, Editor

English Language Learners With Special Needs: Identification, Placement, and Instruction (Upcoming: Spring, 2002)
Alfredo J. Artiles & Alba A. Ortiz, Editors

Making the Connection: Language and Academic Achievement Among African American Students
Carolyn Temple Adger, Donna Christian, & Orlando Taylor, Editors

Foreign Language Education

Foreign Language Assessment in Grades K–8: An Annotated Bibliography of Assessment Instruments
Lynn Thompson

Foreign Language Instruction in the United States: A National Survey of Elementary and Secondary Schools
Nancy C. Rhodes & Lucinda E. Branaman

Lessons Learned: Model Early Foreign Language Programs
Douglas F. Gilzow & Lucinda E. Branaman

Profiles in Two-Way Immersion Education
Donna Christian, Christopher L. Montone, Kathryn J. Lindholm, & Isolda Carranza

Adult ESL Education

Adult Biliteracy in the United States
David Spener, Editor

Approaches to Adult ESL Literacy Instruction
JoAnn Crandall & Joy Kreeft Peyton, Editors

Assessing Success in Family Literacy and Adult ESL (2000, second edition)
Daniel D. Holt & Carol H. Van Duzer, Eds.

Immigrant Learners and Their Families: Literacy to Connect the Generations
Gail Weinstein-Shr & Elizabeth Quintero, Editors

Making Meaning, Making Change: Participatory Curriculum Development for Adult ESL Literacy
Elsa Roberts Auerbach

Writing Our Lives: Reflections on Dialogue Journal Writing with Adults Learning English
Joy Kreeft Peyton & Jana Staton, Editors

ERIC℠
Educational Resources Information Center

The Educational Resources Information Center (ERIC) is a nation-wide information network that aims to improve educational practice by providing ready access to current, high-quality education litera-ture. ERIC maintains the world's largest database of education-related materials. The ERIC database is available worldwide via the Internet, CD-ROM, and monthly printed indexes.

ERIC also provides direct assistance to those seeking informa-tion on education through its network of subject-specific clearing-houses, each of which offers a question-answering service and pro-vides a wide range of free and low-cost publications on current topics in education.

The ERIC Clearinghouse on Languages and Linguistics (ERIC/CLL) collects and disseminates information related to foreign lan-guage education, the teaching and learning of English as a second language, bilingual education, and all aspects of linguistics. In addi-tion to the Language in Education series, ERIC/CLL publishes a semi-annual newsletter, the *ERIC/CLL News Bulletin*; a quarterly electronic newsletter, *ERIC/CLL Language Link*; a series of 1500-word informa-tion digests on current topics in language education; one-sheet minibibliographies; and online resource guides.

ERIC/CLL is operated by the Center for Applied Linguistics, a private nonprofit organization, with funding from the National Li-brary of Education of the U.S. Department of Education's Office of Educational Research and Improvement.

Further information on the publications, services, and other activities of ERIC/CLL can be obtained via mail, telephone, e-mail, or our web site.

ERIC Clearinghouse on Languages and Linguistics
4646 40th Street NW
Washington DC 20016-1859
800-276-9834
202-362-0700 ext 204
eric@cal.org
http://www.cal.org/ericll